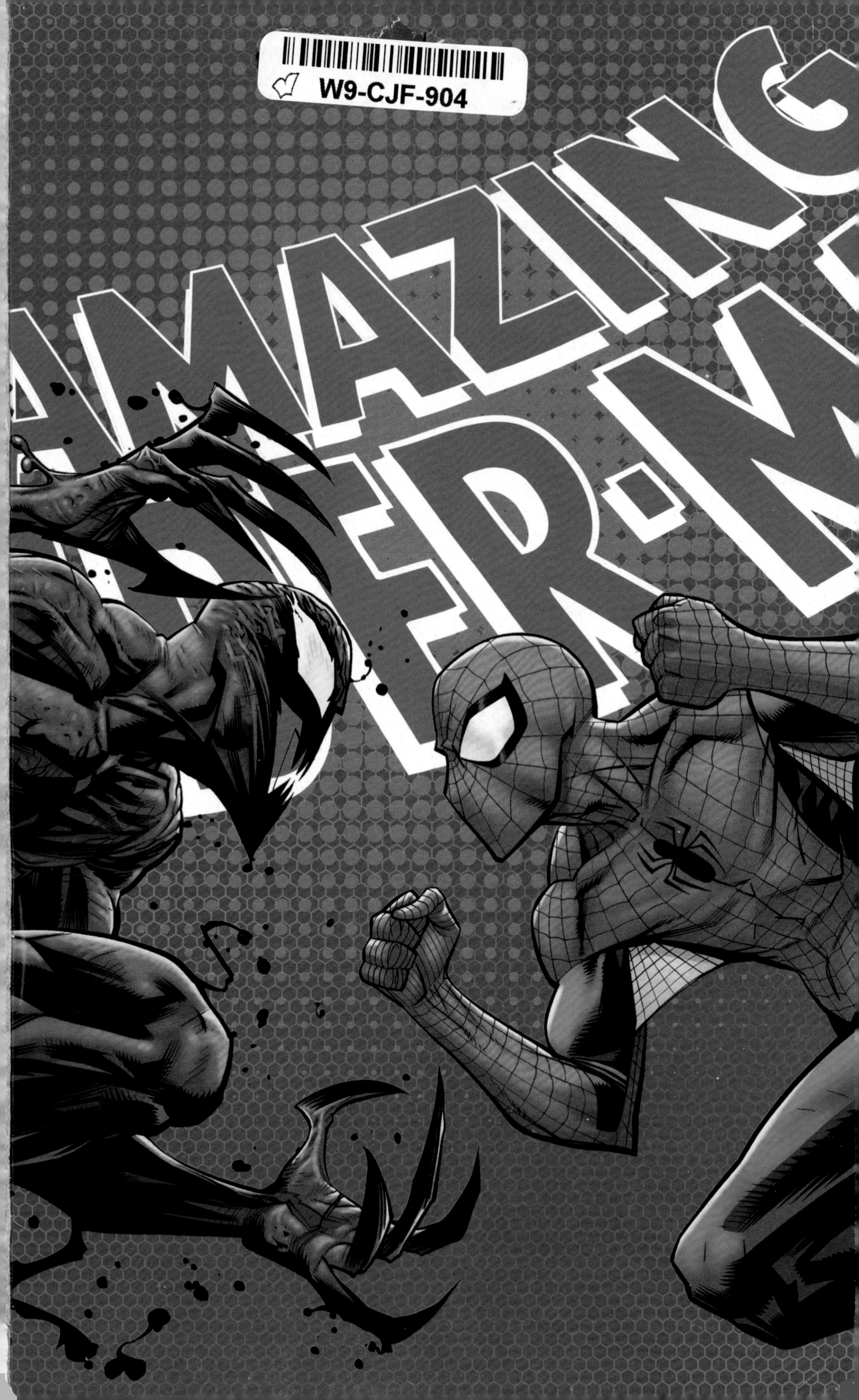
AMAZING

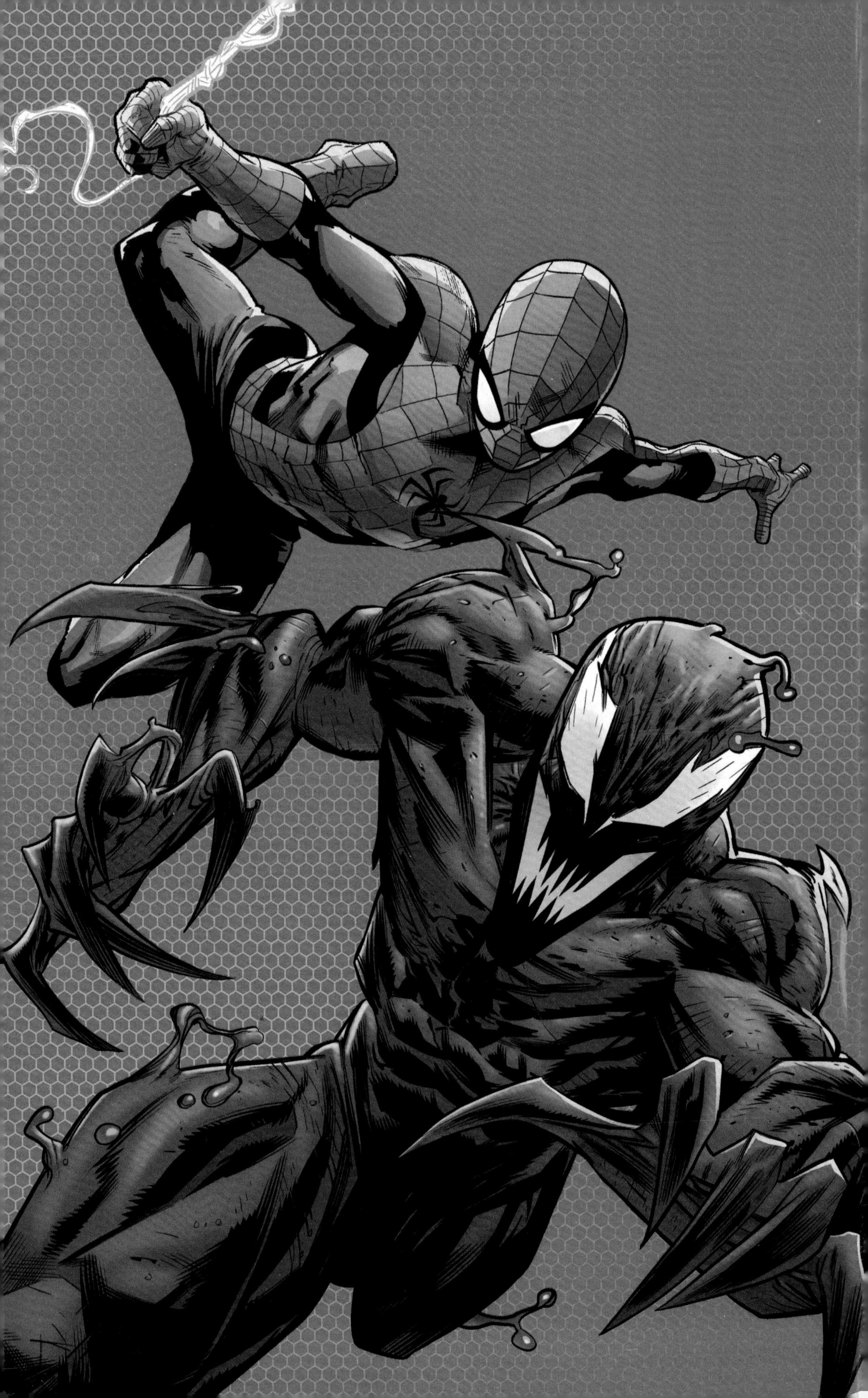

THE AMAZING SPIDER-MAN
ABSOLUTE CARNAGE

WRITER NICK SPENCER

AMAZING SPIDER-MAN #29

ARTIST FRANCESCO MANNA

COLOR ARTIST CARLOS LOPEZ

AMAZING SPIDER-MAN #30-31

PENCILER RYAN OTTLEY

INKER CLIFF RATHBURN

COLORIST NATHAN FAIRBAIRN

VC's JOE CARAMAGNA
LETTERER

**RYAN OTTLEY &
NATHAN FAIRBAIRN**
COVER ART

KATHLEEN WISNESKI
ASSISTANT EDITOR

NICK LOWE
EDITOR

RED GOBLIN: RED DEATH

WRITERS ROB FEE, SEAN RYAN & PATRICK GLEASON

ARTISTS PETE WOODS, RAY-ANTHONY HEIGHT & MARC DEERING

COLOR ARTISTS PETE WOODS, DONO SÁNCHEZ-ALMARA & PROTOBUNKER

VC's JOE SABINO
LETTERER

**PHILIP TAN &
JAY DAVID RAMOS**
COVER ART

LINDSEY COHICK
ASSISTANT EDITOR

JAKE THOMAS
EDITOR

SPIDER-MAN CREATED BY STAN LEE & STEVE DITKO

COLLECTION EDITOR JENNIFER GRÜNWALD
ASSISTANT EDITOR CAITLIN O'CONNELL ✦ ASSOCIATE MANAGING EDITOR KATERI WOODY
EDITOR, SPECIAL PROJECTS MARK D. BEAZLEY ✦ VP PRODUCTION & SPECIAL PROJECTS JEFF YOUNGQUIST
BOOK DESIGNERS STACIE ZUCKER with JAY BOWEN

SVP PRINT, SALES & MARKETING DAVID GABRIEL ✦ DIRECTOR, LICENSED PUBLISHING SVEN LARSEN
EDITOR IN CHIEF C.B. CEBULSKI ✦ CHIEF CREATIVE OFFICER JOE QUESADA
PRESIDENT DAN BUCKLEY ✦ EXECUTIVE PRODUCER ALAN FINE

AMAZING SPIDER-MAN BY NICK SPENCER VOL. 6: ABSOLUTE CARNAGE. Contains material originally published in magazine form as AMAZING SPIDER-MAN (2018) #29-31 and RED GOBLIN: READ DEATH (2019) #1. First printing 2019. ISBN 978-1-302-91727-2. Published by MARVEL WORLDWIDE, INC., a subsidiary of MARVEL ENTERTAINMENT, LLC. OFFICE OF PUBLICATION: 135 West 50th Street, New York, NY 10020. © 2019 MARVEL No similarity between any of the names, characters, persons, and/or institutions in this magazine with those of any living or dead person or institution is intended, and any such similarity which may exist is purely coincidental. **Printed in Canada.** DAN BUCKLEY, President, Marvel Entertainment; JOHN NEE, Publisher; JOE QUESADA, Chief Creative Officer; TOM BREVOORT, SVP of Publishing; DAVID BOGART, Associate Publisher & SVP of Talent Affairs; DAVID GABRIEL, VP of Print & Digital Publishing; JEFF YOUNGQUIST, VP of Production & Special Projects; DAN CARR, Executive Director of Publishing Technology; ALEX MORALES, Director of Publishing Operations; DAN EDINGTON, Managing Editor; SUSAN CRESPI, Production Manager; STAN LEE, Chairman Emeritus. For information regarding advertising in Marvel Comics or on Marvel.com, please contact Vit DeBellis, Custom Solutions & Integrated Advertising Manager, at vdebellis@marvel.com. For Marvel subscription inquiries, please call 888-511-5480. **Manufactured between 11/8/2019 and 12/10/2019 by SOLISCO PRINTERS, SCOTT, QC, CANADA.**

10 9 8 7 6 5 4 3 2 1

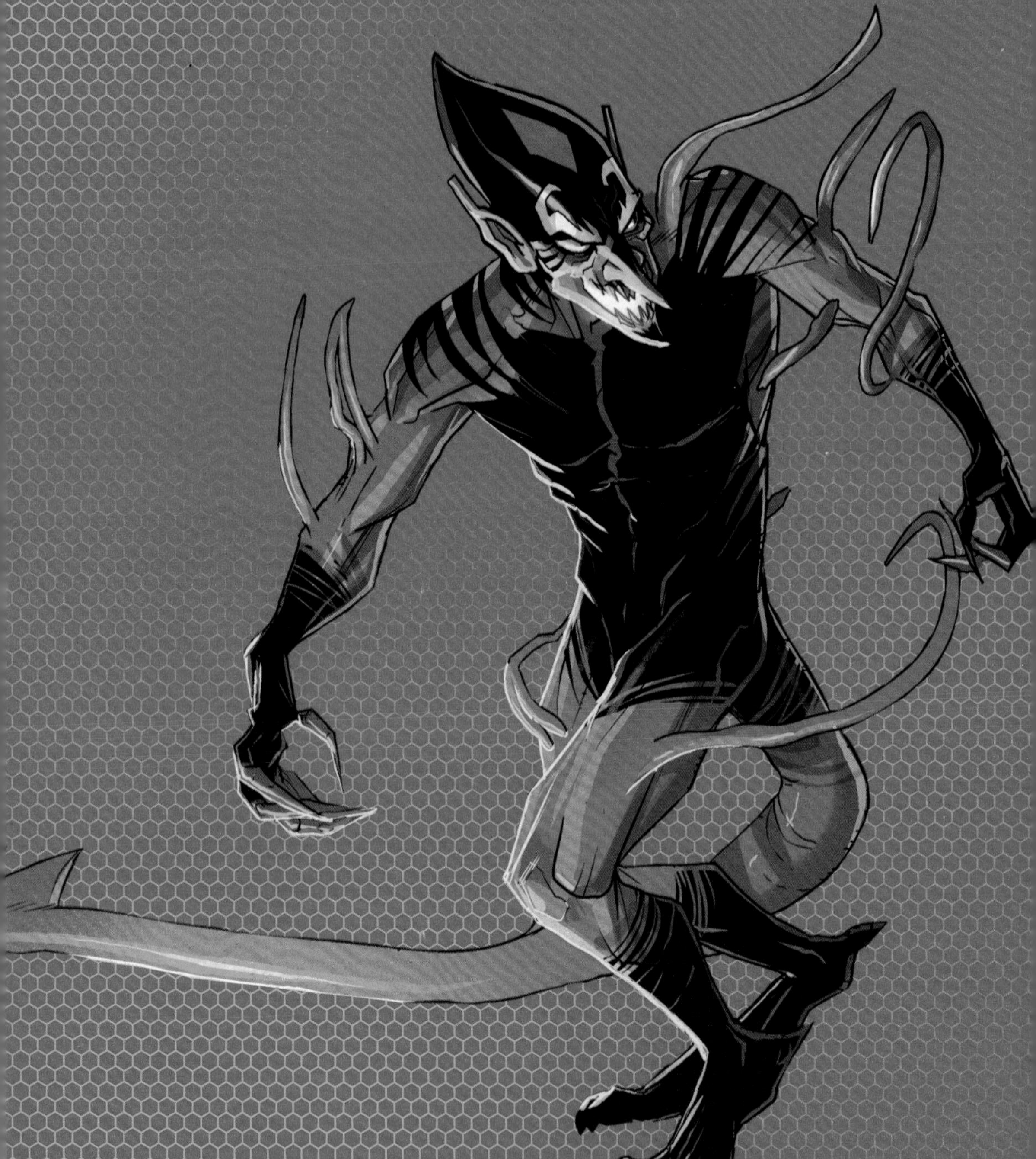

Even though the F.E.A.S.T. community center was wrecked twice before Aunt May could officially open it, it's now under the pro bono protection of fancy-pants lawyer Janice Lincoln! (Never mind that Janice wrecked it one of those times as the Beetle while leading the Syndicate criminal organization. She's trying to make it up to her boyfriend, F.E.A.S.T. employee and Parker family friend Randy Robertson.) And after Mary Jane saved a theater of innocents from Electro by impersonating the villain's real target, she got an incredible job offer. Dare we say things are looking up for Spider-Man and his amazing friends?

29

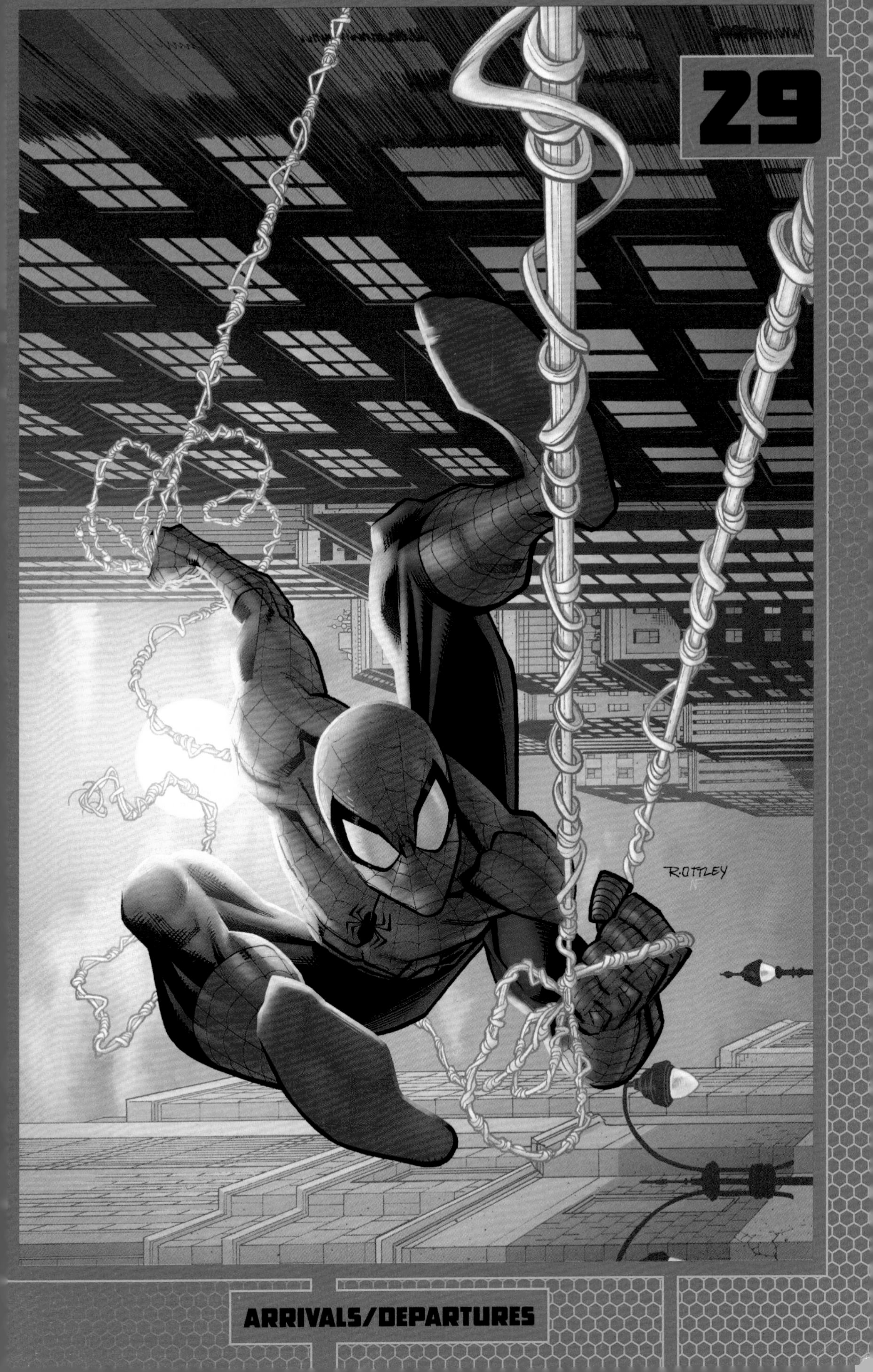
R.OTTLEY

ARRIVALS/DEPARTURES

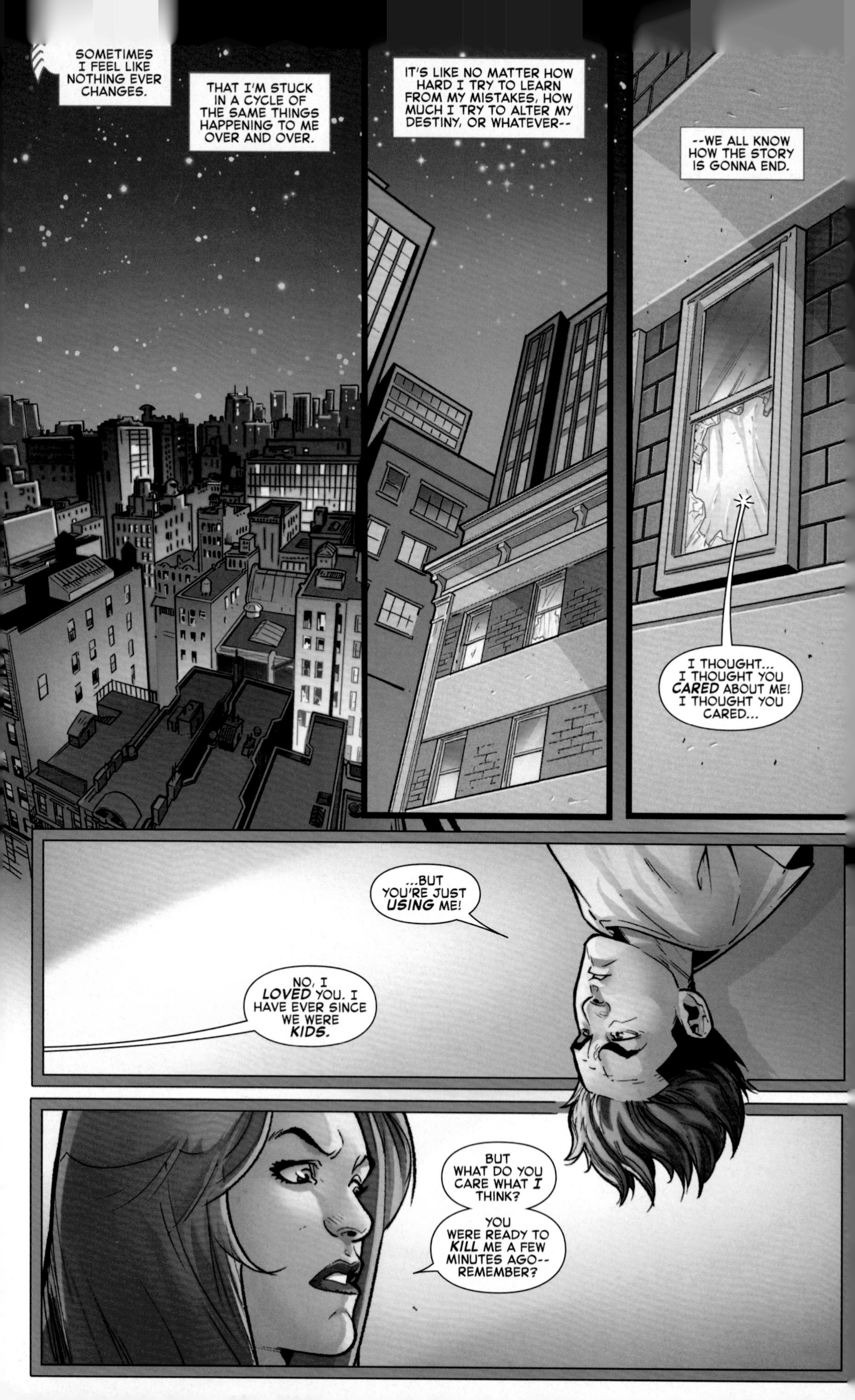
SOMETIMES I FEEL LIKE NOTHING EVER CHANGES.
THAT I'M STUCK IN A CYCLE OF THE SAME THINGS HAPPENING TO ME OVER AND OVER.
IT'S LIKE NO MATTER HOW HARD I TRY TO LEARN FROM MY MISTAKES, HOW MUCH I TRY TO ALTER MY DESTINY, OR WHATEVER--
--WE ALL KNOW HOW THE STORY IS GONNA END.
I THOUGHT... I THOUGHT YOU CARED ABOUT ME! I THOUGHT YOU CARED...
...BUT YOU'RE JUST USING ME!
NO, I LOVED YOU. I HAVE EVER SINCE WE WERE KIDS.
BUT WHAT DO YOU CARE WHAT I THINK?
YOU WERE READY TO KILL ME A FEW MINUTES AGO--REMEMBER?

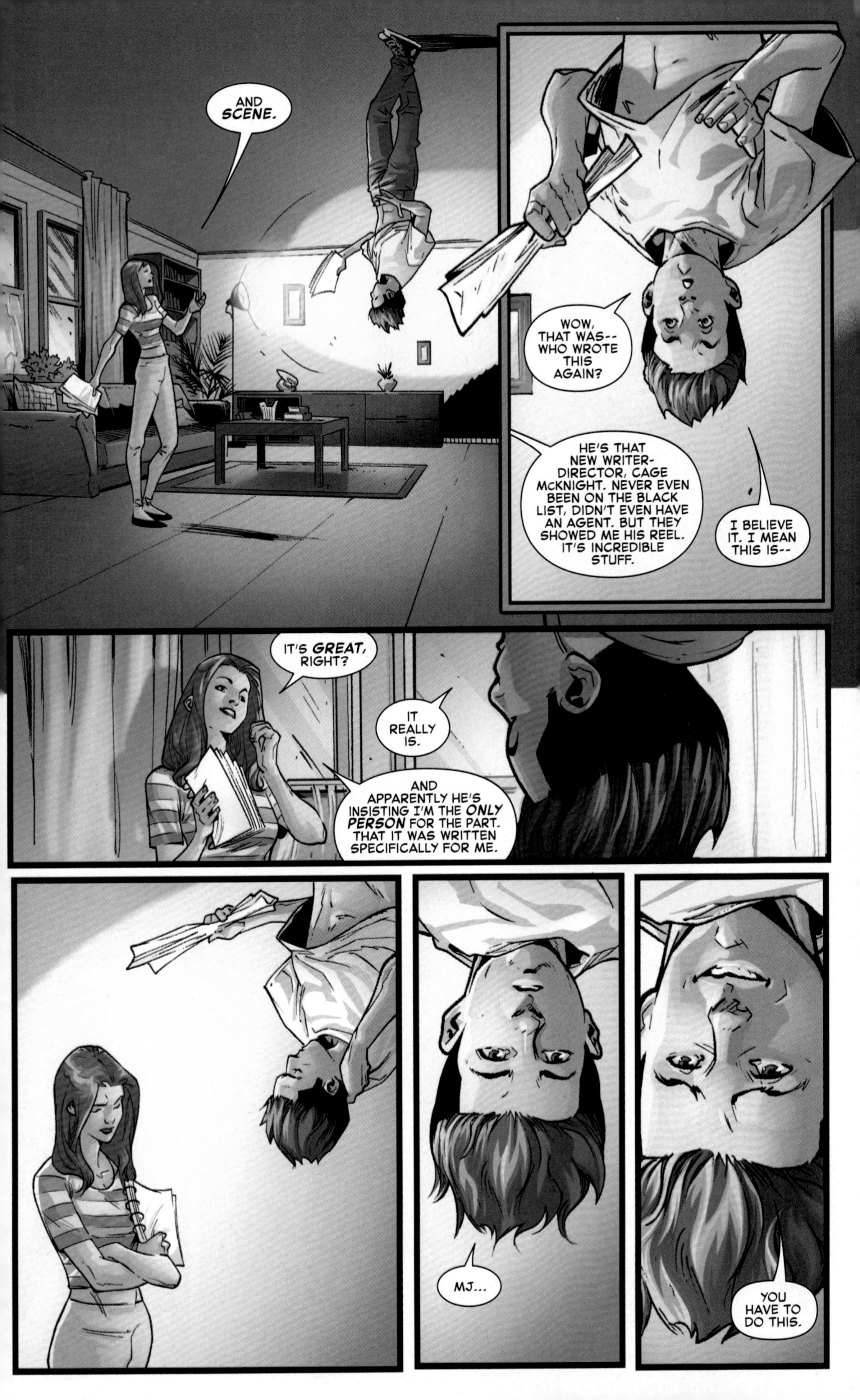
AND SCENE.
WOW, THAT WAS-- WHO WROTE THIS AGAIN?
HE'S THAT NEW WRITER-DIRECTOR, CAGE McKNIGHT. NEVER EVEN BEEN ON THE BLACK LIST, DIDN'T EVEN HAVE AN AGENT. BUT THEY SHOWED ME HIS REEL. IT'S INCREDIBLE STUFF.
I BELIEVE IT. I MEAN THIS IS--
IT'S GREAT, RIGHT?
IT REALLY IS.
AND APPARENTLY HE'S INSISTING I'M THE ONLY PERSON FOR THE PART. THAT IT WAS WRITTEN SPECIFICALLY FOR ME.
MJ...
YOU HAVE TO DO THIS.

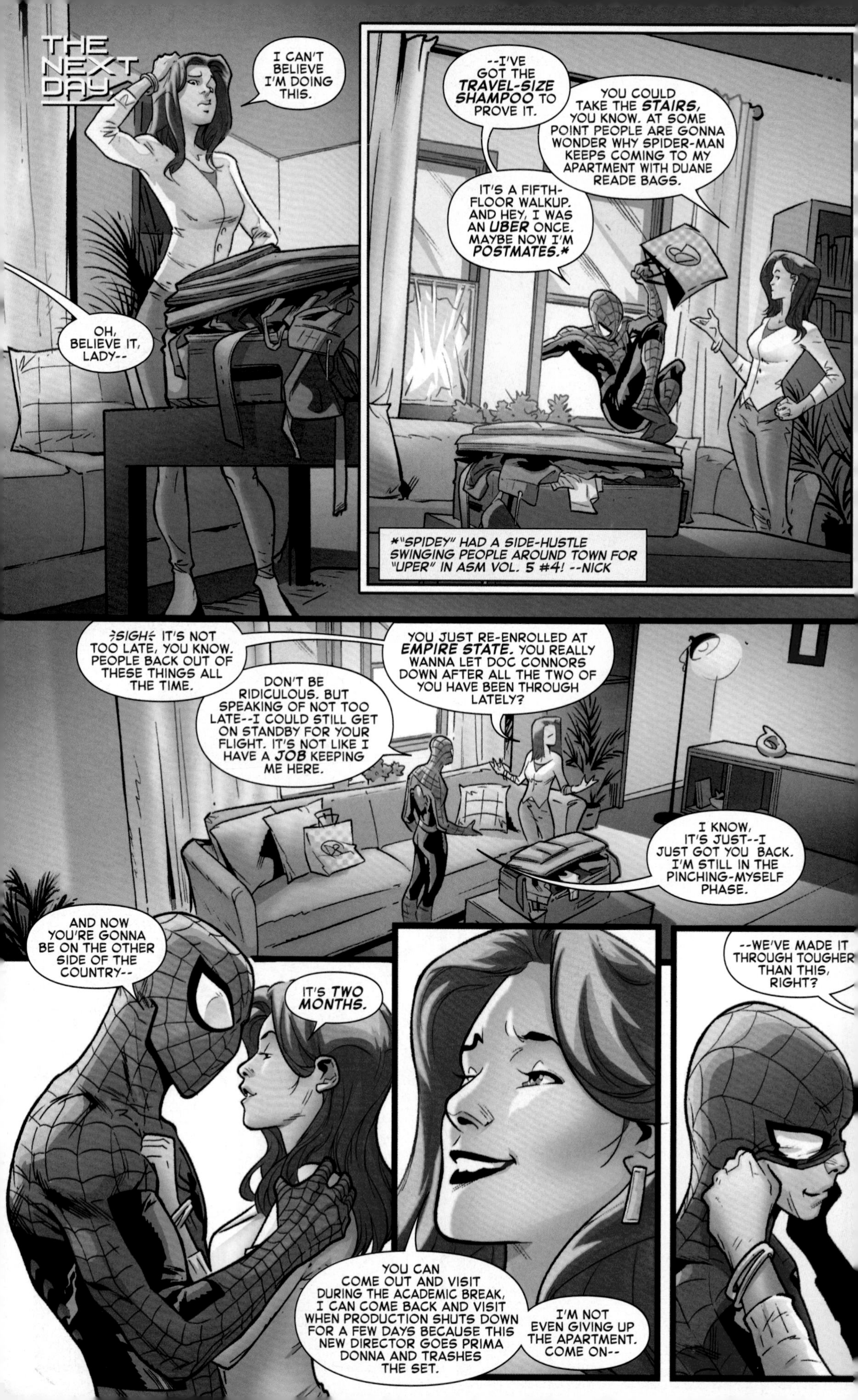
THE NEXT DAY.
I CAN'T BELIEVE I'M DOING THIS.
OH, BELIEVE IT, LADY--
--I'VE GOT THE TRAVEL-SIZE SHAMPOO TO PROVE IT.
YOU COULD TAKE THE STAIRS, YOU KNOW. AT SOME POINT PEOPLE ARE GONNA WONDER WHY SPIDER-MAN KEEPS COMING TO MY APARTMENT WITH DUANE READE BAGS.
IT'S A FIFTH-FLOOR WALKUP. AND HEY, I WAS AN UBER ONCE. MAYBE NOW I'M POSTMATES.*
*"SPIDEY" HAD A SIDE-HUSTLE SWINGING PEOPLE AROUND TOWN FOR "UPER" IN ASM VOL. 5 #4! --NICK
SIGH IT'S NOT TOO LATE, YOU KNOW. PEOPLE BACK OUT OF THESE THINGS ALL THE TIME.
YOU JUST RE-ENROLLED AT EMPIRE STATE. YOU REALLY WANNA LET DOC CONNORS DOWN AFTER ALL THE TWO OF YOU HAVE BEEN THROUGH LATELY?
DON'T BE RIDICULOUS. BUT SPEAKING OF NOT TOO LATE--I COULD STILL GET ON STANDBY FOR YOUR FLIGHT. IT'S NOT LIKE I HAVE A JOB KEEPING ME HERE.
I KNOW, IT'S JUST--I JUST GOT YOU BACK. I'M STILL IN THE PINCHING-MYSELF PHASE.
AND NOW YOU'RE GONNA BE ON THE OTHER SIDE OF THE COUNTRY--
IT'S TWO MONTHS.
YOU CAN COME OUT AND VISIT DURING THE ACADEMIC BREAK, I CAN COME BACK AND VISIT WHEN PRODUCTION SHUTS DOWN FOR A FEW DAYS BECAUSE THIS NEW DIRECTOR GOES PRIMA DONNA AND TRASHES THE SET.
I'M NOT EVEN GIVING UP THE APARTMENT. COME ON--
--WE'VE MADE IT THROUGH TOUGHER THAN THIS, RIGHT?

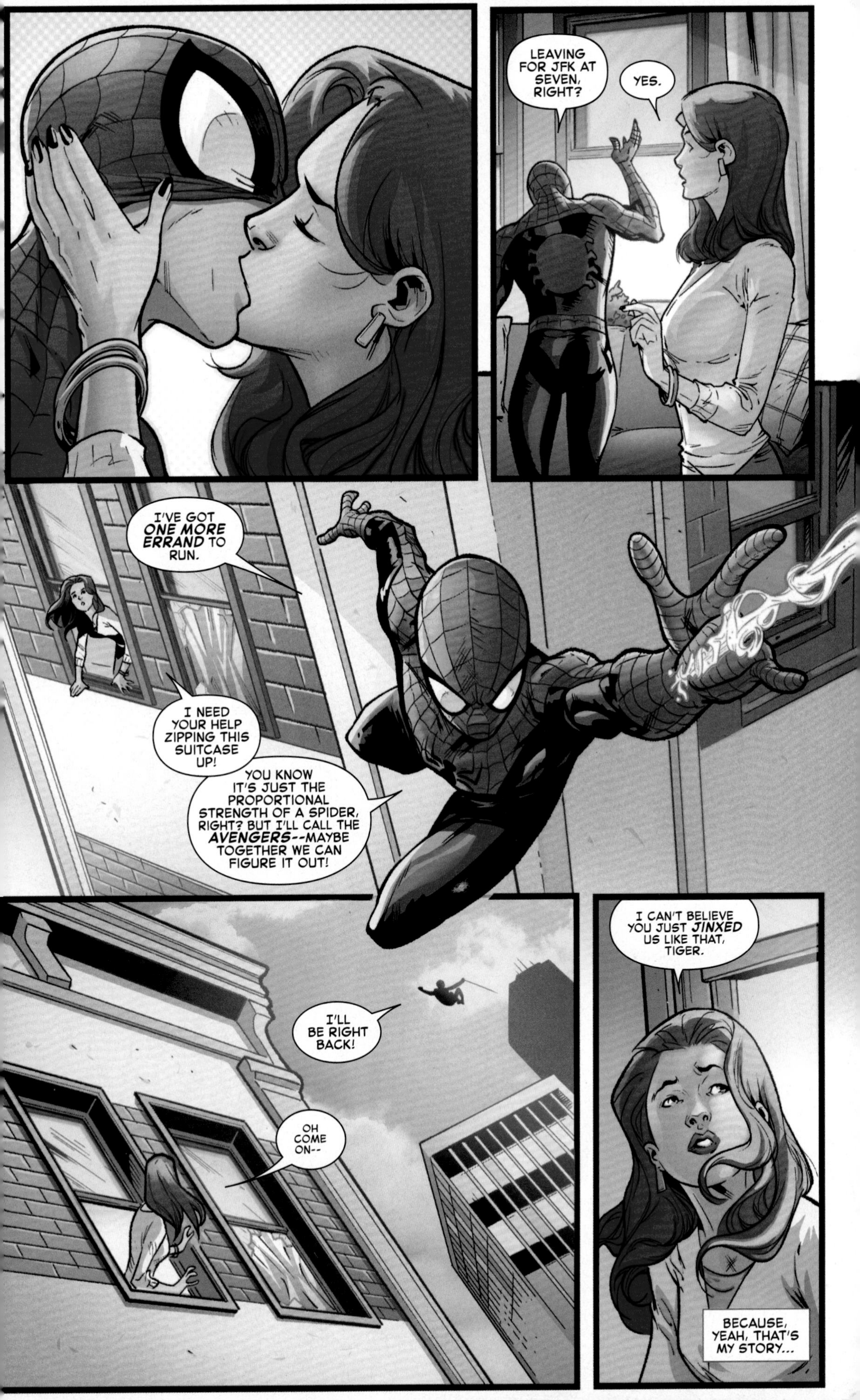
LEAVING FOR JFK AT SEVEN, RIGHT?
YES.
I'VE GOT ONE MORE ERRAND TO RUN.
I NEED YOUR HELP ZIPPING THIS SUITCASE UP!
YOU KNOW IT'S JUST THE PROPORTIONAL STRENGTH OF A SPIDER, RIGHT? BUT I'LL CALL THE AVENGERS--MAYBE TOGETHER WE CAN FIGURE IT OUT!
I'LL BE RIGHT BACK!
OH COME ON--
I CAN'T BELIEVE YOU JUST JINXED US LIKE THAT, TIGER.
BECAUSE, YEAH, THAT'S MY STORY...

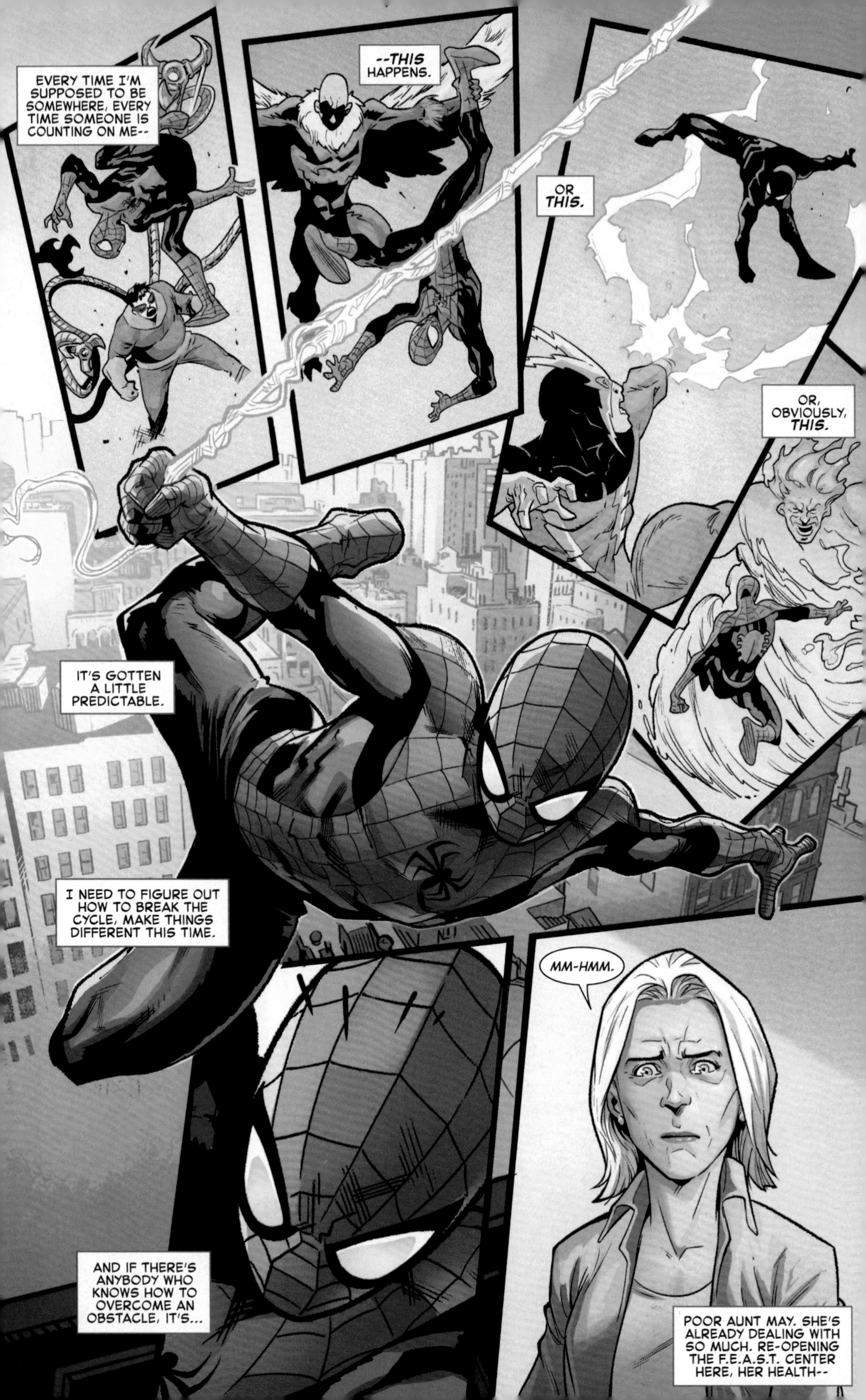
EVERY TIME I'M SUPPOSED TO BE SOMEWHERE, EVERY TIME SOMEONE IS COUNTING ON ME--
--THIS HAPPENS.
OR THIS.
OR, OBVIOUSLY, THIS.
IT'S GOTTEN A LITTLE PREDICTABLE.
I NEED TO FIGURE OUT HOW TO BREAK THE CYCLE, MAKE THINGS DIFFERENT THIS TIME.
MM-HMM.
AND IF THERE'S ANYBODY WHO KNOWS HOW TO OVERCOME AN OBSTACLE, IT'S...
POOR AUNT MAY. SHE'S ALREADY DEALING WITH SO MUCH. RE-OPENING THE F.E.A.S.T. CENTER HERE, HER HEALTH--

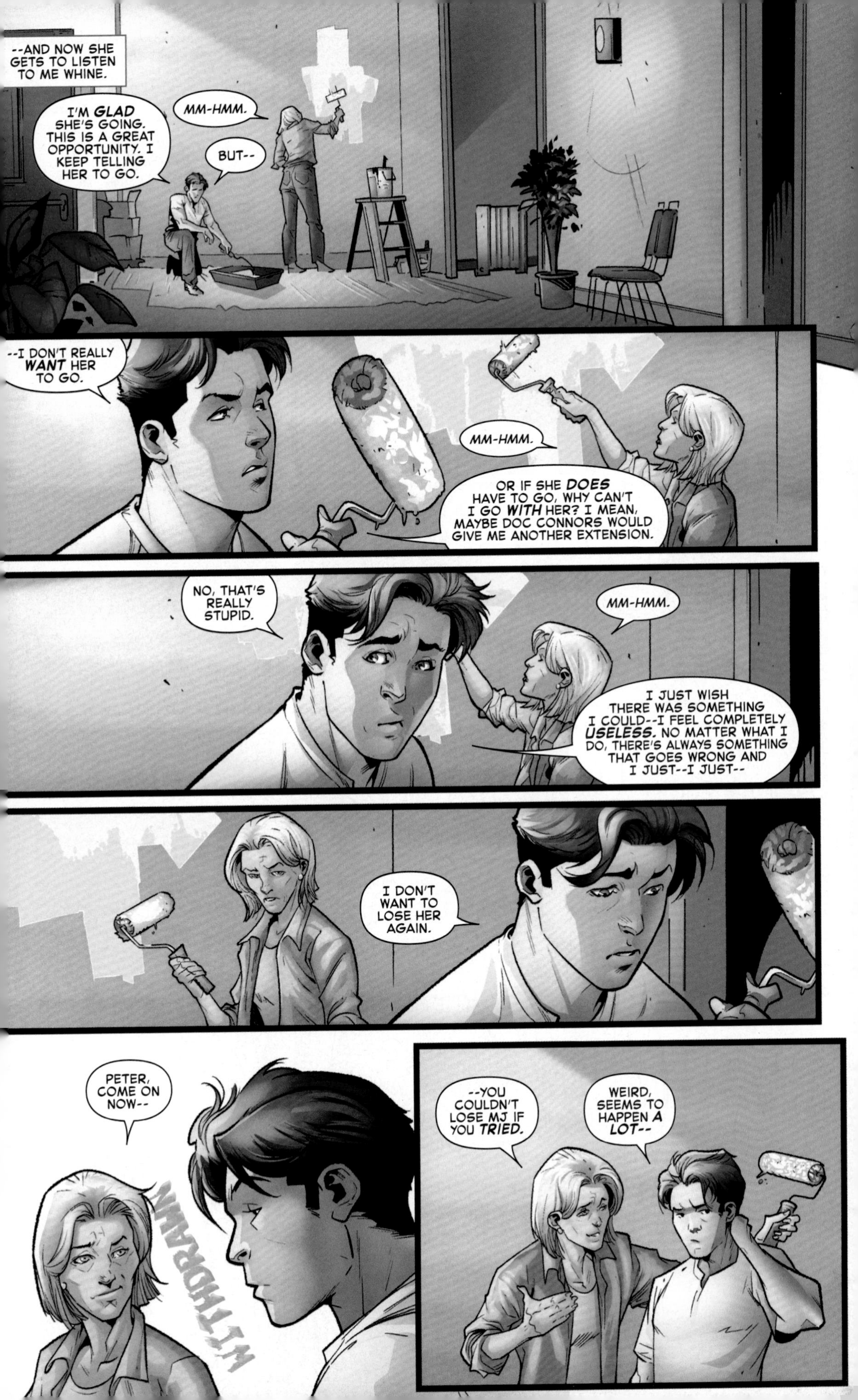
--AND NOW SHE GETS TO LISTEN TO ME WHINE.
I'M GLAD SHE'S GOING. THIS IS A GREAT OPPORTUNITY. I KEEP TELLING HER TO GO.
MM-HMM.
BUT--
--I DON'T REALLY WANT HER TO GO.
MM-HMM.
OR IF SHE DOES HAVE TO GO, WHY CAN'T I GO WITH HER? I MEAN, MAYBE DOC CONNORS WOULD GIVE ME ANOTHER EXTENSION.
NO, THAT'S REALLY STUPID.
MM-HMM.
I JUST WISH THERE WAS SOMETHING I COULD--I FEEL COMPLETELY USELESS. NO MATTER WHAT I DO, THERE'S ALWAYS SOMETHING THAT GOES WRONG AND I JUST--I JUST--
I DON'T WANT TO LOSE HER AGAIN.
PETER, COME ON NOW--
--YOU COULDN'T LOSE MJ IF YOU TRIED.
WEIRD, SEEMS TO HAPPEN A LOT--

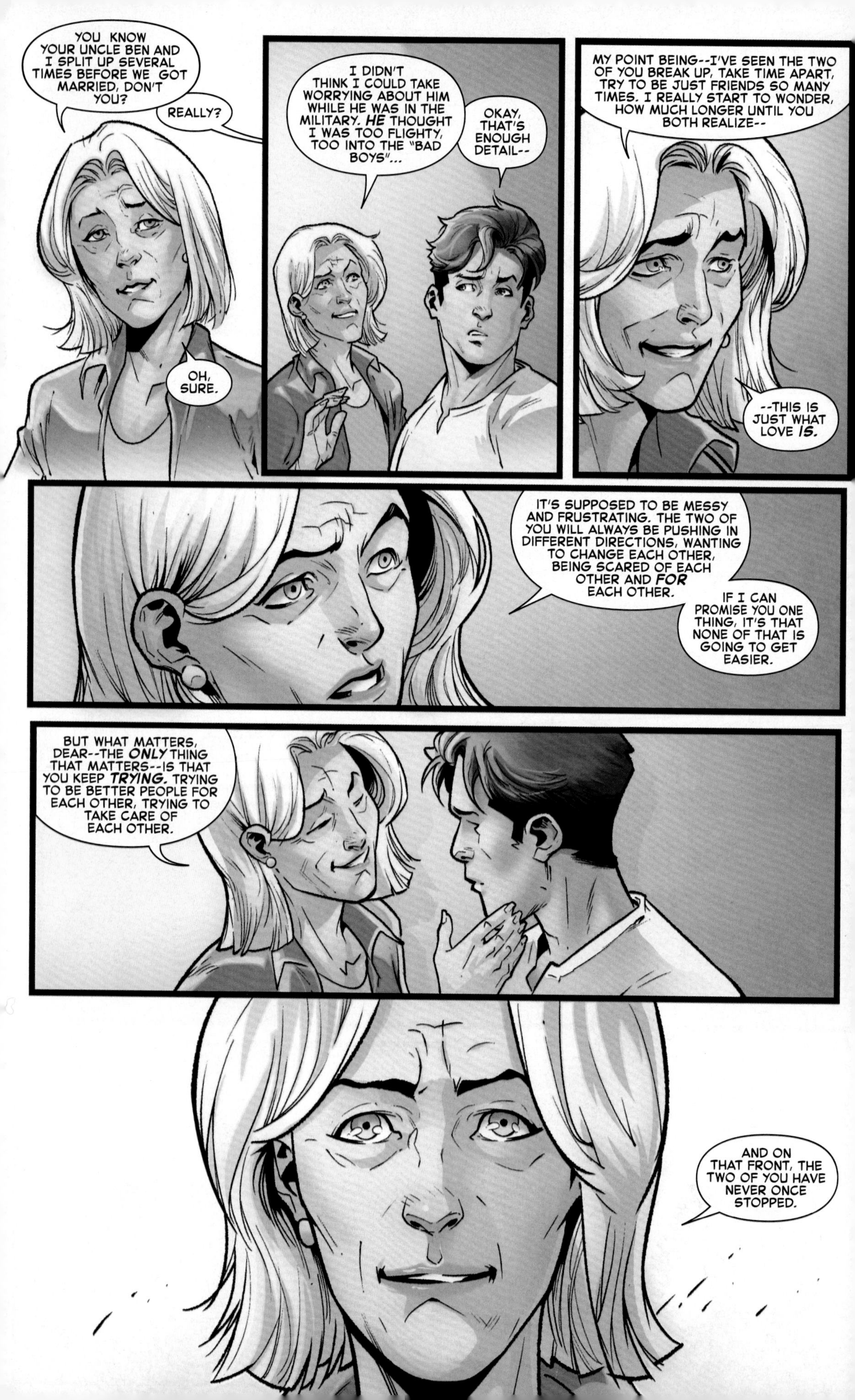
YOU KNOW YOUR UNCLE BEN AND I SPLIT UP SEVERAL TIMES BEFORE WE GOT MARRIED, DON'T YOU?
REALLY?
OH, SURE.
I DIDN'T THINK I COULD TAKE WORRYING ABOUT HIM WHILE HE WAS IN THE MILITARY. *HE* THOUGHT I WAS TOO FLIGHTY, TOO INTO THE "BAD BOYS"...
OKAY, THAT'S ENOUGH DETAIL--
MY POINT BEING--I'VE SEEN THE TWO OF YOU BREAK UP, TAKE TIME APART, TRY TO BE JUST FRIENDS SO MANY TIMES. I REALLY START TO WONDER, HOW MUCH LONGER UNTIL YOU BOTH REALIZE--
--THIS IS JUST WHAT LOVE *IS.*
IT'S SUPPOSED TO BE MESSY AND FRUSTRATING. THE TWO OF YOU WILL ALWAYS BE PUSHING IN DIFFERENT DIRECTIONS, WANTING TO CHANGE EACH OTHER, BEING SCARED OF EACH OTHER AND *FOR* EACH OTHER.
IF I CAN PROMISE YOU ONE THING, IT'S THAT NONE OF THAT IS GOING TO GET EASIER.
BUT WHAT MATTERS, DEAR--THE *ONLY* THING THAT MATTERS--IS THAT YOU KEEP *TRYING.* TRYING TO BE BETTER PEOPLE FOR EACH OTHER, TRYING TO TAKE CARE OF EACH OTHER.
AND ON THAT FRONT, THE TWO OF YOU HAVE NEVER ONCE STOPPED.

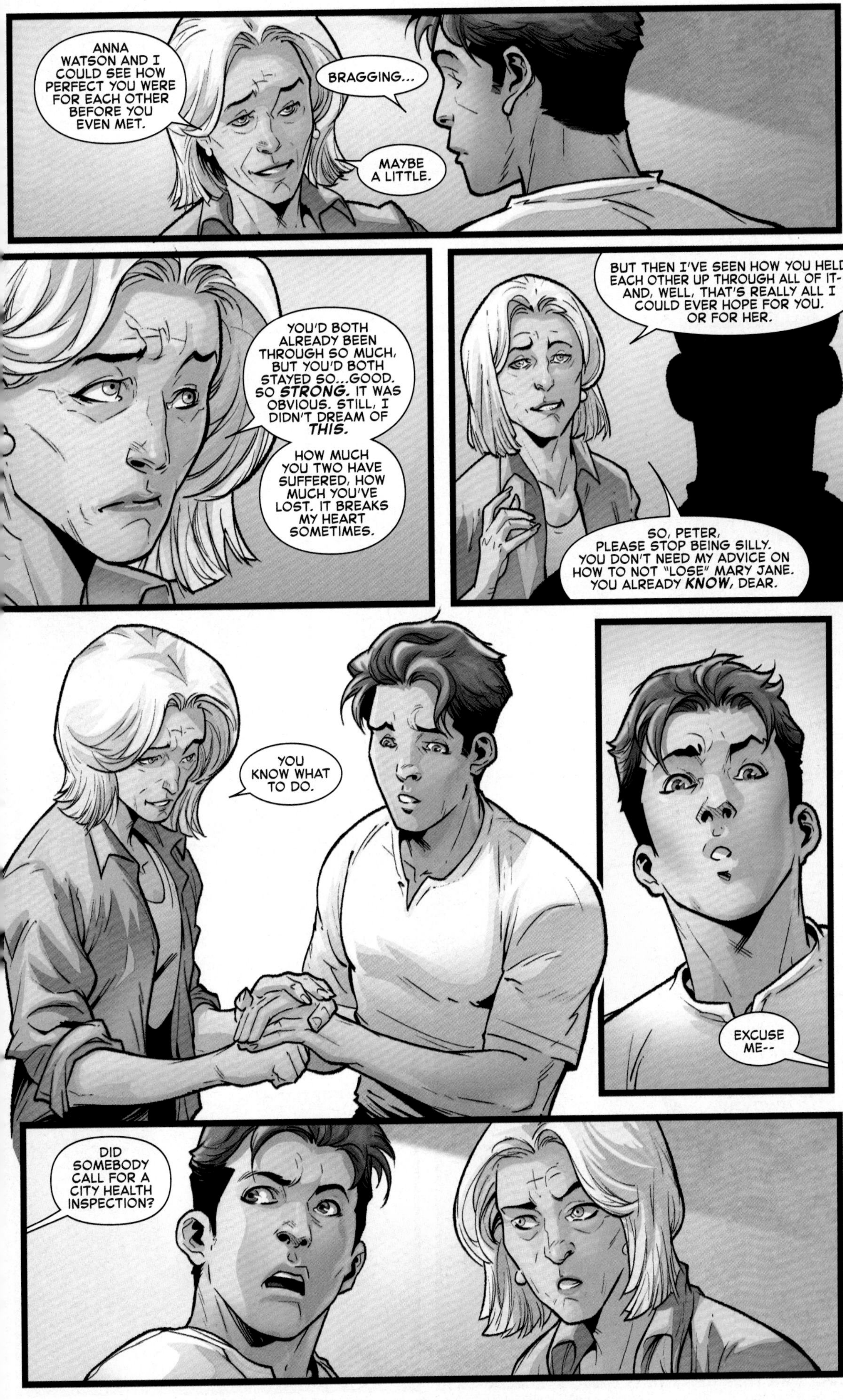
ANNA WATSON AND I COULD SEE HOW PERFECT YOU WERE FOR EACH OTHER BEFORE YOU EVEN MET.
BRAGGING...
MAYBE A LITTLE.
YOU'D BOTH ALREADY BEEN THROUGH SO MUCH, BUT YOU'D BOTH STAYED SO...GOOD. SO STRONG. IT WAS OBVIOUS. STILL, I DIDN'T DREAM OF THIS.
HOW MUCH YOU TWO HAVE SUFFERED, HOW MUCH YOU'VE LOST. IT BREAKS MY HEART SOMETIMES.
BUT THEN I'VE SEEN HOW YOU HELD EACH OTHER UP THROUGH ALL OF IT-- AND, WELL, THAT'S REALLY ALL I COULD EVER HOPE FOR YOU. OR FOR HER.
SO, PETER, PLEASE STOP BEING SILLY. YOU DON'T NEED MY ADVICE ON HOW TO NOT "LOSE" MARY JANE. YOU ALREADY KNOW, DEAR.
YOU KNOW WHAT TO DO.
EXCUSE ME--
DID SOMEBODY CALL FOR A CITY HEALTH INSPECTION?

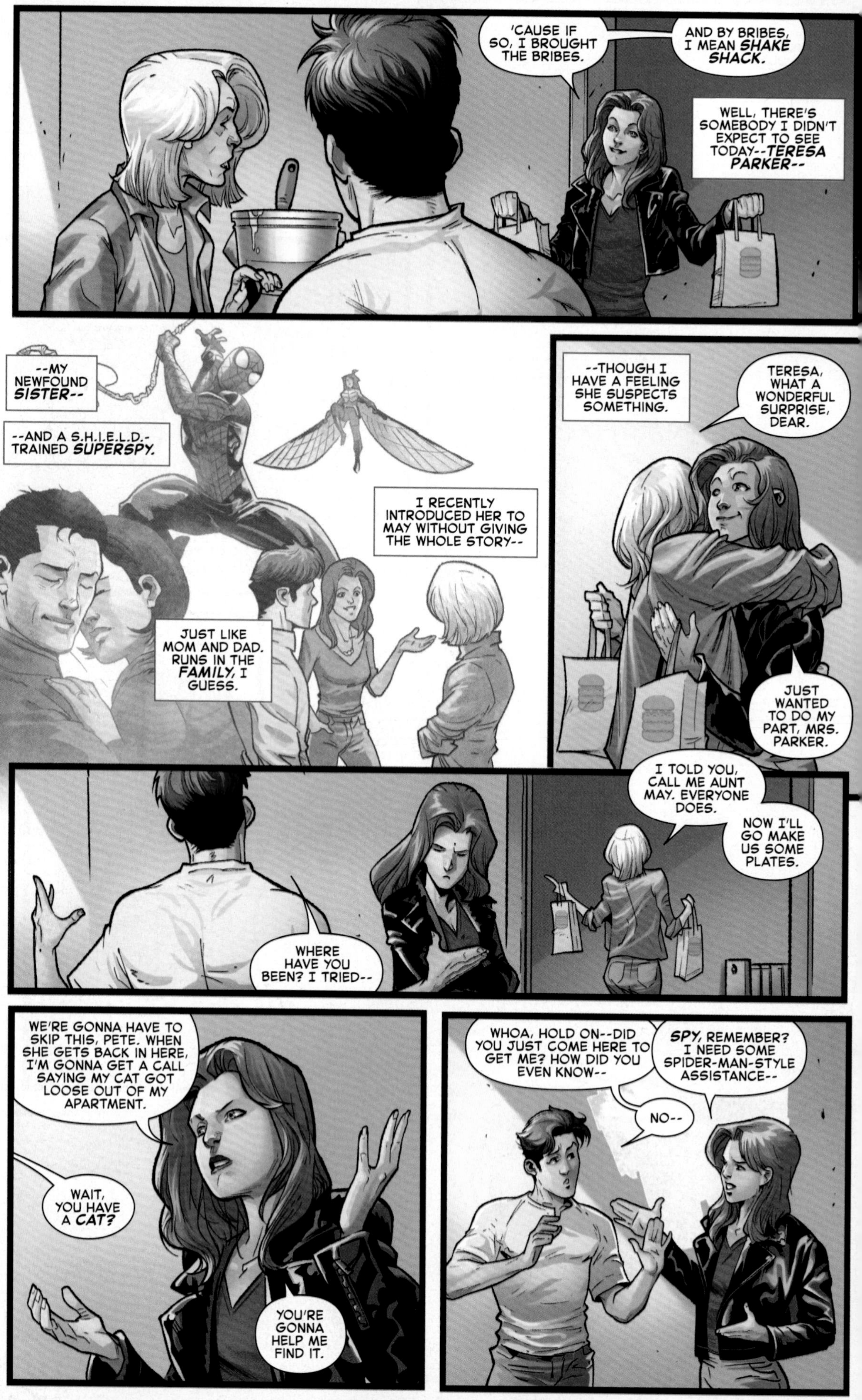

'CAUSE IF SO, I BROUGHT THE BRIBES.
AND BY BRIBES, I MEAN SHAKE SHACK.
WELL, THERE'S SOMEBODY I DIDN'T EXPECT TO SEE TODAY--TERESA PARKER--
--MY NEWFOUND SISTER--
--AND A S.H.I.E.L.D.-TRAINED SUPERSPY.
I RECENTLY INTRODUCED HER TO MAY WITHOUT GIVING THE WHOLE STORY--
JUST LIKE MOM AND DAD. RUNS IN THE FAMILY, I GUESS.
--THOUGH I HAVE A FEELING SHE SUSPECTS SOMETHING.
TERESA, WHAT A WONDERFUL SURPRISE, DEAR.
JUST WANTED TO DO MY PART, MRS. PARKER.
I TOLD YOU, CALL ME AUNT MAY. EVERYONE DOES.
NOW I'LL GO MAKE US SOME PLATES.
WHERE HAVE YOU BEEN? I TRIED--
WE'RE GONNA HAVE TO SKIP THIS, PETE. WHEN SHE GETS BACK IN HERE, I'M GONNA GET A CALL SAYING MY CAT GOT LOOSE OUT OF MY APARTMENT.
WAIT, YOU HAVE A CAT?
YOU'RE GONNA HELP ME FIND IT.
WHOA, HOLD ON--DID YOU JUST COME HERE TO GET ME? HOW DID YOU EVEN KNOW--
SPY, REMEMBER? I NEED SOME SPIDER-MAN-STYLE ASSISTANCE--
NO--

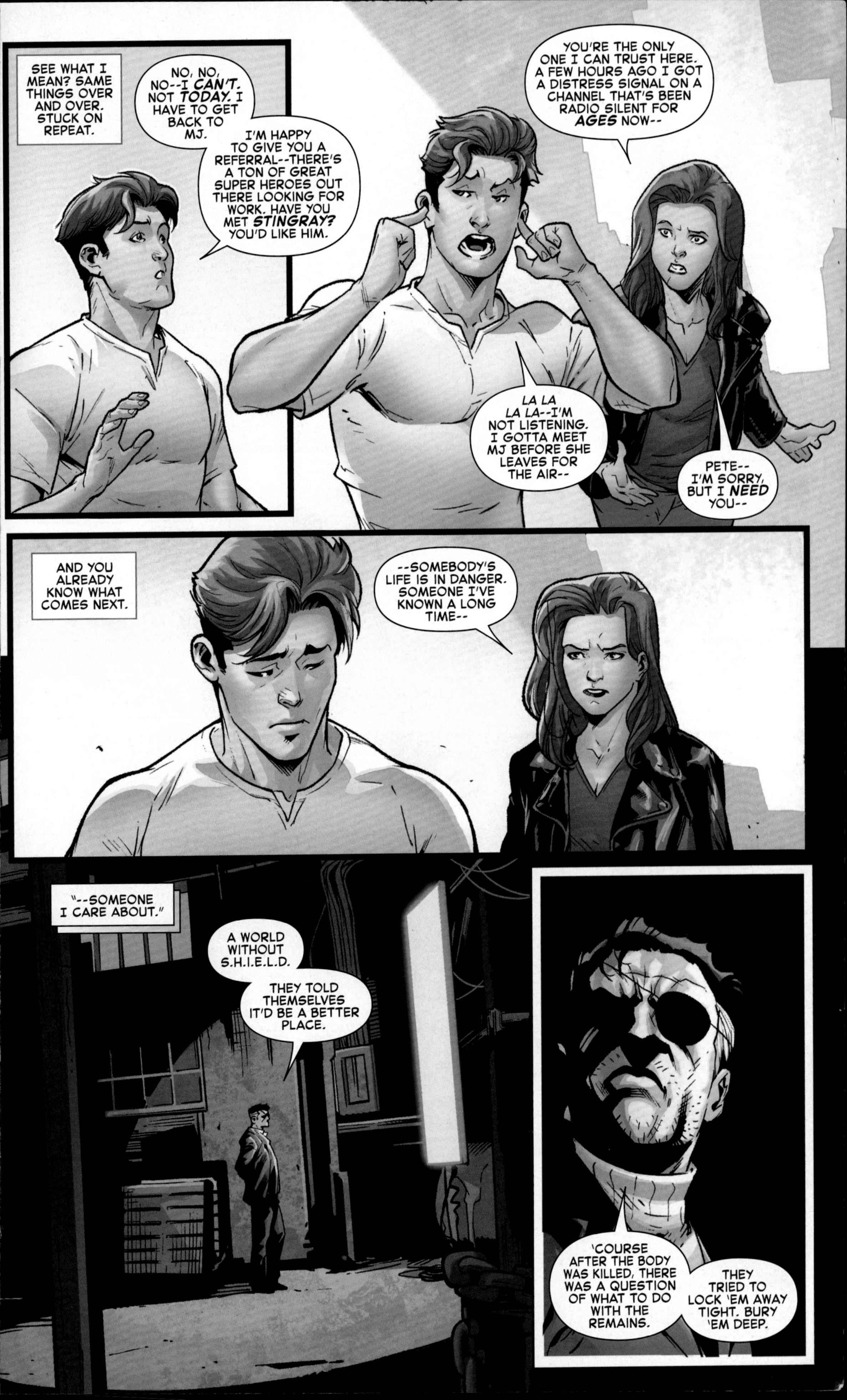
SEE WHAT I MEAN? SAME THINGS OVER AND OVER. STUCK ON REPEAT.
NO, NO, NO--I CAN'T. NOT TODAY. I HAVE TO GET BACK TO MJ.
I'M HAPPY TO GIVE YOU A REFERRAL--THERE'S A TON OF GREAT SUPER HEROES OUT THERE LOOKING FOR WORK. HAVE YOU MET STINGRAY? YOU'D LIKE HIM.
YOU'RE THE ONLY ONE I CAN TRUST HERE. A FEW HOURS AGO I GOT A DISTRESS SIGNAL ON A CHANNEL THAT'S BEEN RADIO SILENT FOR AGES NOW--
LA LA LA LA--I'M NOT LISTENING. I GOTTA MEET MJ BEFORE SHE LEAVES FOR THE AIR--
PETE-- I'M SORRY, BUT I NEED YOU--
AND YOU ALREADY KNOW WHAT COMES NEXT.
--SOMEBODY'S LIFE IS IN DANGER. SOMEONE I'VE KNOWN A LONG TIME--
"--SOMEONE I CARE ABOUT."
A WORLD WITHOUT S.H.I.E.L.D.
THEY TOLD THEMSELVES IT'D BE A BETTER PLACE.
'COURSE AFTER THE BODY WAS KILLED, THERE WAS A QUESTION OF WHAT TO DO WITH THE REMAINS.
THEY TRIED TO LOCK 'EM AWAY TIGHT. BURY 'EM DEEP.

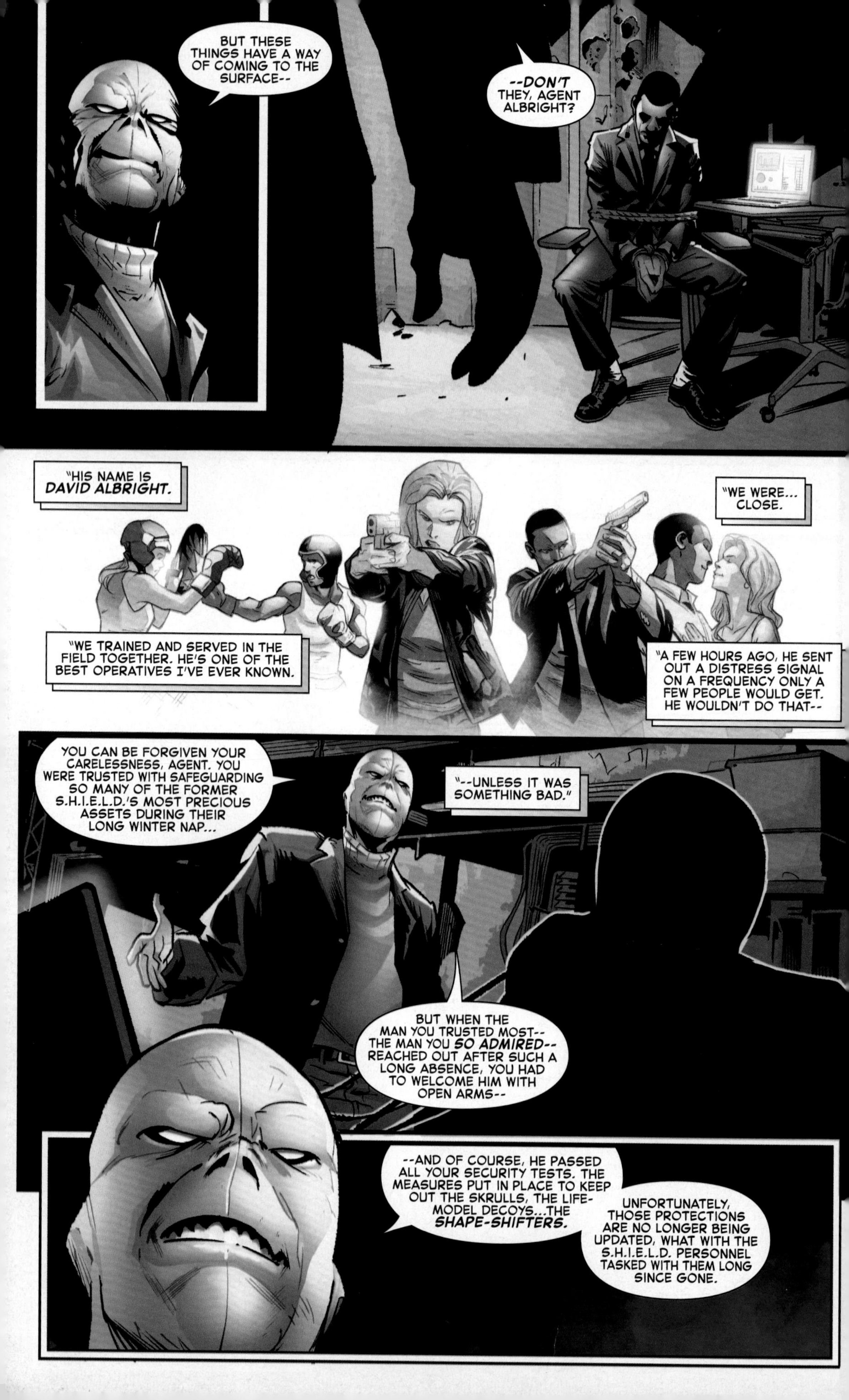
BUT THESE THINGS HAVE A WAY OF COMING TO THE SURFACE--
--DON'T THEY, AGENT ALBRIGHT?
"HIS NAME IS DAVID ALBRIGHT.
"WE TRAINED AND SERVED IN THE FIELD TOGETHER. HE'S ONE OF THE BEST OPERATIVES I'VE EVER KNOWN.
"WE WERE... CLOSE.
"A FEW HOURS AGO, HE SENT OUT A DISTRESS SIGNAL ON A FREQUENCY ONLY A FEW PEOPLE WOULD GET. HE WOULDN'T DO THAT--
YOU CAN BE FORGIVEN YOUR CARELESSNESS, AGENT. YOU WERE TRUSTED WITH SAFEGUARDING SO MANY OF THE FORMER S.H.I.E.L.D.'S MOST PRECIOUS ASSETS DURING THEIR LONG WINTER NAP...
"--UNLESS IT WAS SOMETHING BAD."
BUT WHEN THE MAN YOU TRUSTED MOST-- THE MAN YOU SO ADMIRED-- REACHED OUT AFTER SUCH A LONG ABSENCE, YOU HAD TO WELCOME HIM WITH OPEN ARMS--
--AND OF COURSE, HE PASSED ALL YOUR SECURITY TESTS. THE MEASURES PUT IN PLACE TO KEEP OUT THE SKRULLS, THE LIFE-MODEL DECOYS...THE SHAPE-SHIFTERS.
UNFORTUNATELY, THOSE PROTECTIONS ARE NO LONGER BEING UPDATED, WHAT WITH THE S.H.I.E.L.D. PERSONNEL TASKED WITH THEM LONG SINCE GONE.

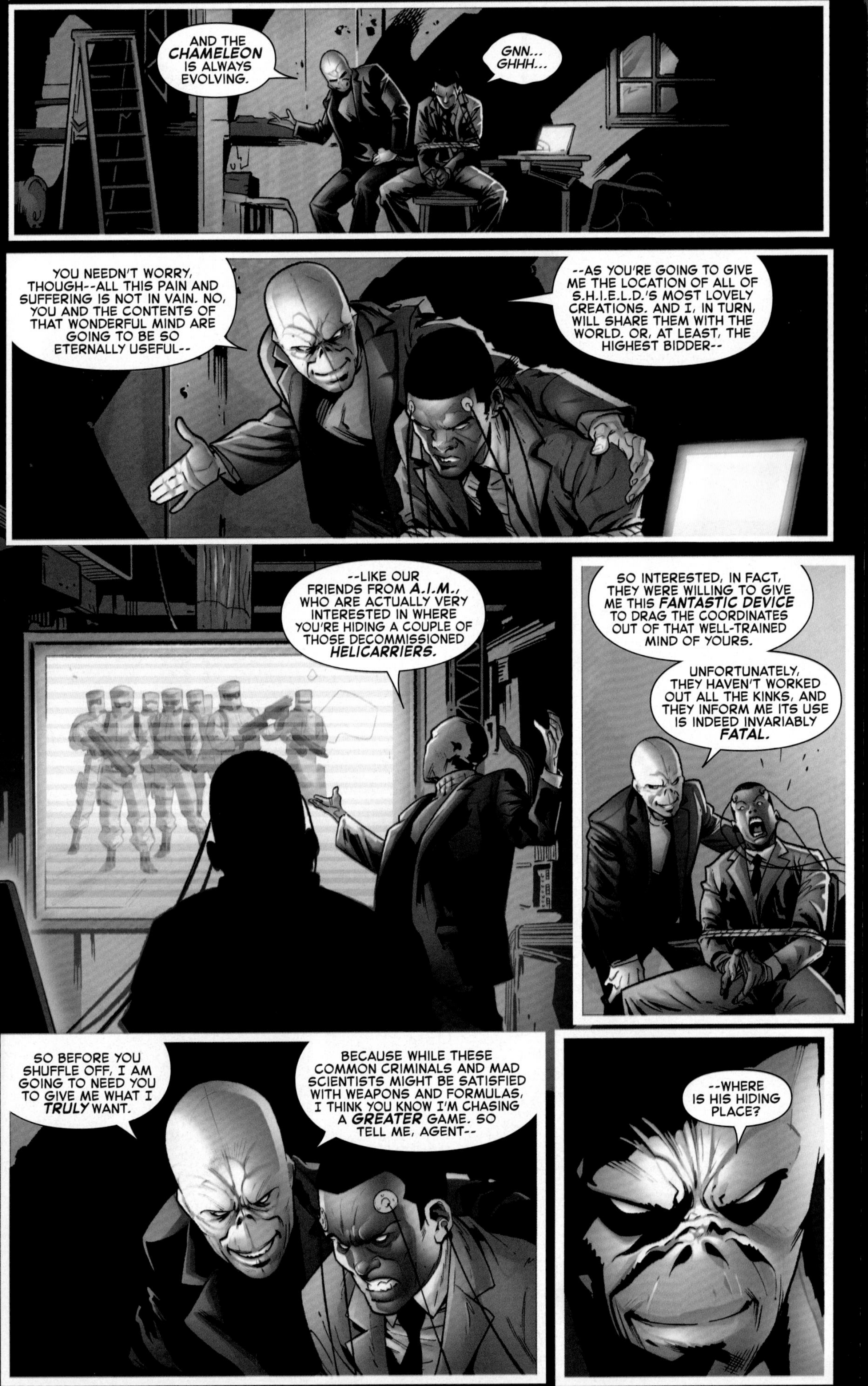
AND THE CHAMELEON IS ALWAYS EVOLVING.
GNN... GHHH...
YOU NEEDN'T WORRY, THOUGH--ALL THIS PAIN AND SUFFERING IS NOT IN VAIN. NO, YOU AND THE CONTENTS OF THAT WONDERFUL MIND ARE GOING TO BE SO ETERNALLY USEFUL--
--AS YOU'RE GOING TO GIVE ME THE LOCATION OF ALL OF S.H.I.E.L.D.'S MOST LOVELY CREATIONS. AND I, IN TURN, WILL SHARE THEM WITH THE WORLD. OR, AT LEAST, THE HIGHEST BIDDER--
--LIKE OUR FRIENDS FROM A.I.M., WHO ARE ACTUALLY VERY INTERESTED IN WHERE YOU'RE HIDING A COUPLE OF THOSE DECOMMISSIONED HELICARRIERS.
SO INTERESTED, IN FACT, THEY WERE WILLING TO GIVE ME THIS FANTASTIC DEVICE TO DRAG THE COORDINATES OUT OF THAT WELL-TRAINED MIND OF YOURS.
UNFORTUNATELY, THEY HAVEN'T WORKED OUT ALL THE KINKS, AND THEY INFORM ME ITS USE IS INDEED INVARIABLY FATAL.
SO BEFORE YOU SHUFFLE OFF, I AM GOING TO NEED YOU TO GIVE ME WHAT I TRULY WANT.
BECAUSE WHILE THESE COMMON CRIMINALS AND MAD SCIENTISTS MIGHT BE SATISFIED WITH WEAPONS AND FORMULAS, I THINK YOU KNOW I'M CHASING A GREATER GAME. SO TELL ME, AGENT--
--WHERE IS HIS HIDING PLACE?

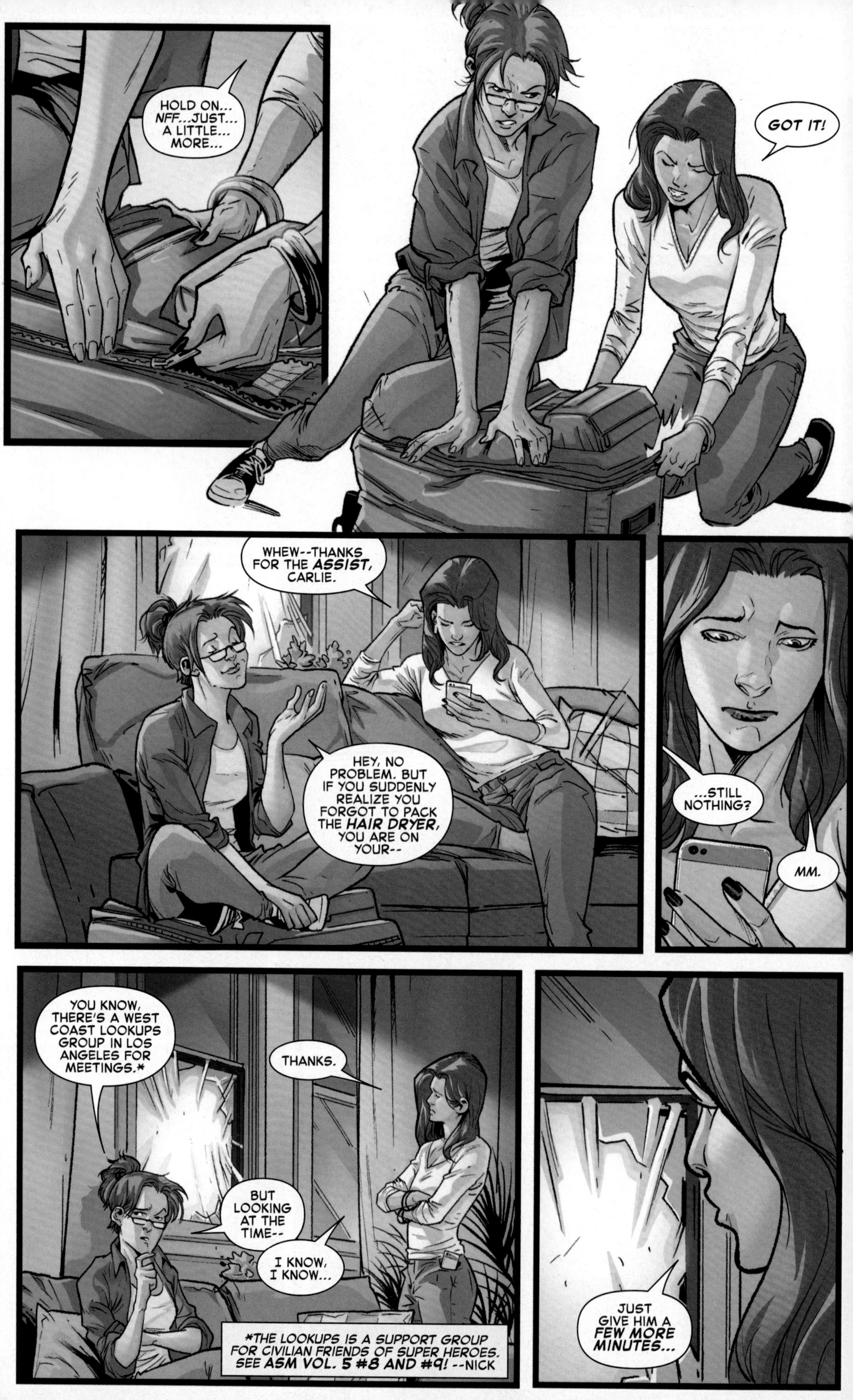

HOLD ON... NFF...JUST... A LITTLE... MORE...
GOT IT!
WHEW--THANKS FOR THE ASSIST, CARLIE.
HEY, NO PROBLEM. BUT IF YOU SUDDENLY REALIZE YOU FORGOT TO PACK THE HAIR DRYER, YOU ARE ON YOUR--
...STILL NOTHING?
MM.
YOU KNOW, THERE'S A WEST COAST LOOKUPS GROUP IN LOS ANGELES FOR MEETINGS.*
THANKS.
BUT LOOKING AT THE TIME--
I KNOW, I KNOW...
*THE LOOKUPS IS A SUPPORT GROUP FOR CIVILIAN FRIENDS OF SUPER HEROES. SEE ASM VOL. 5 #8 AND #9! --NICK
JUST GIVE HIM A FEW MORE MINUTES...

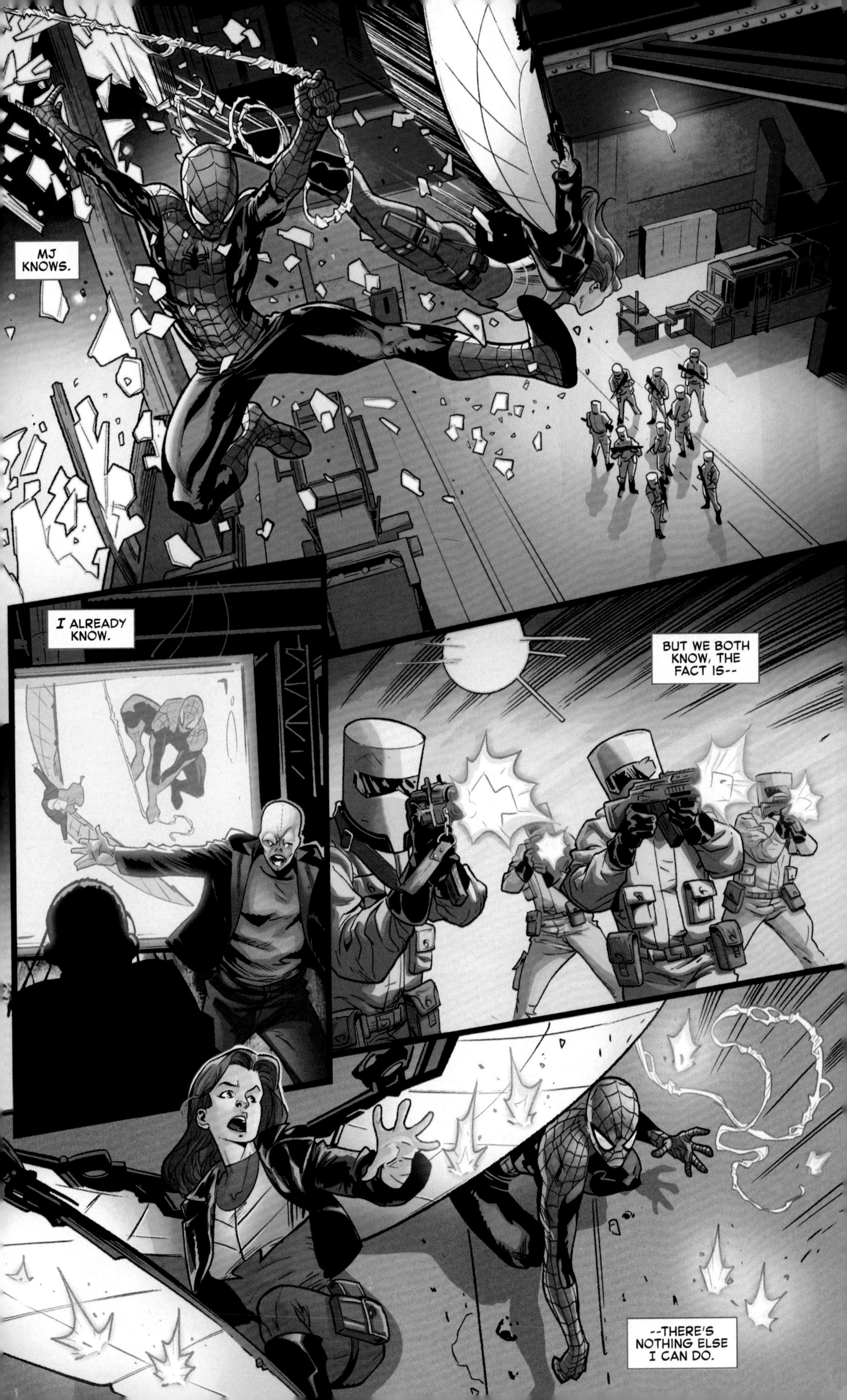
MJ KNOWS.
I ALREADY KNOW.
BUT WE BOTH KNOW, THE FACT IS--
--THERE'S NOTHING ELSE I CAN DO.

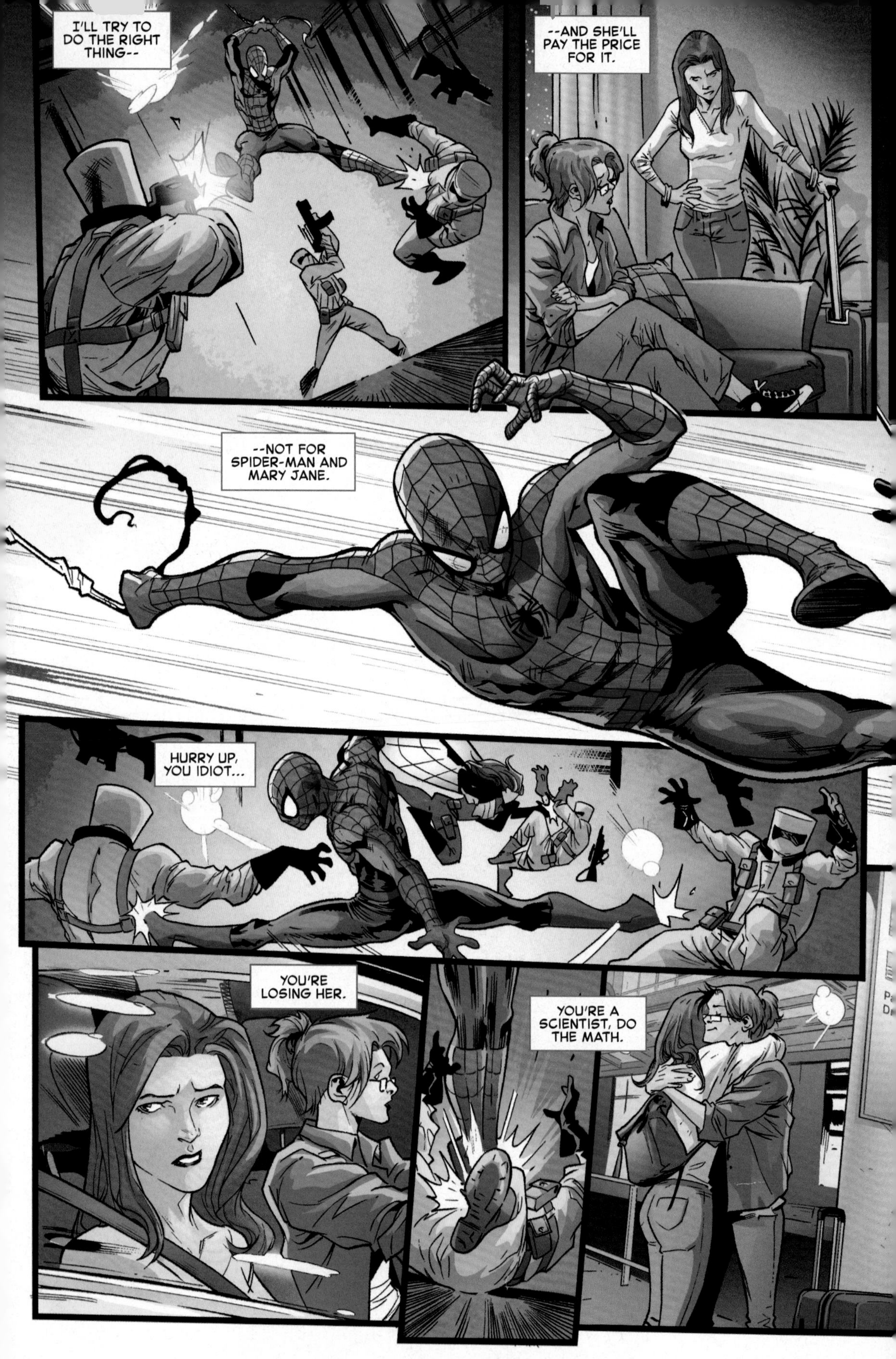
I'LL TRY TO DO THE RIGHT THING--
--AND SHE'LL PAY THE PRICE FOR IT.
--NOT FOR SPIDER-MAN AND MARY JANE.
HURRY UP, YOU IDIOT...
YOU'RE LOSING HER.
YOU'RE A SCIENTIST, DO THE MATH.

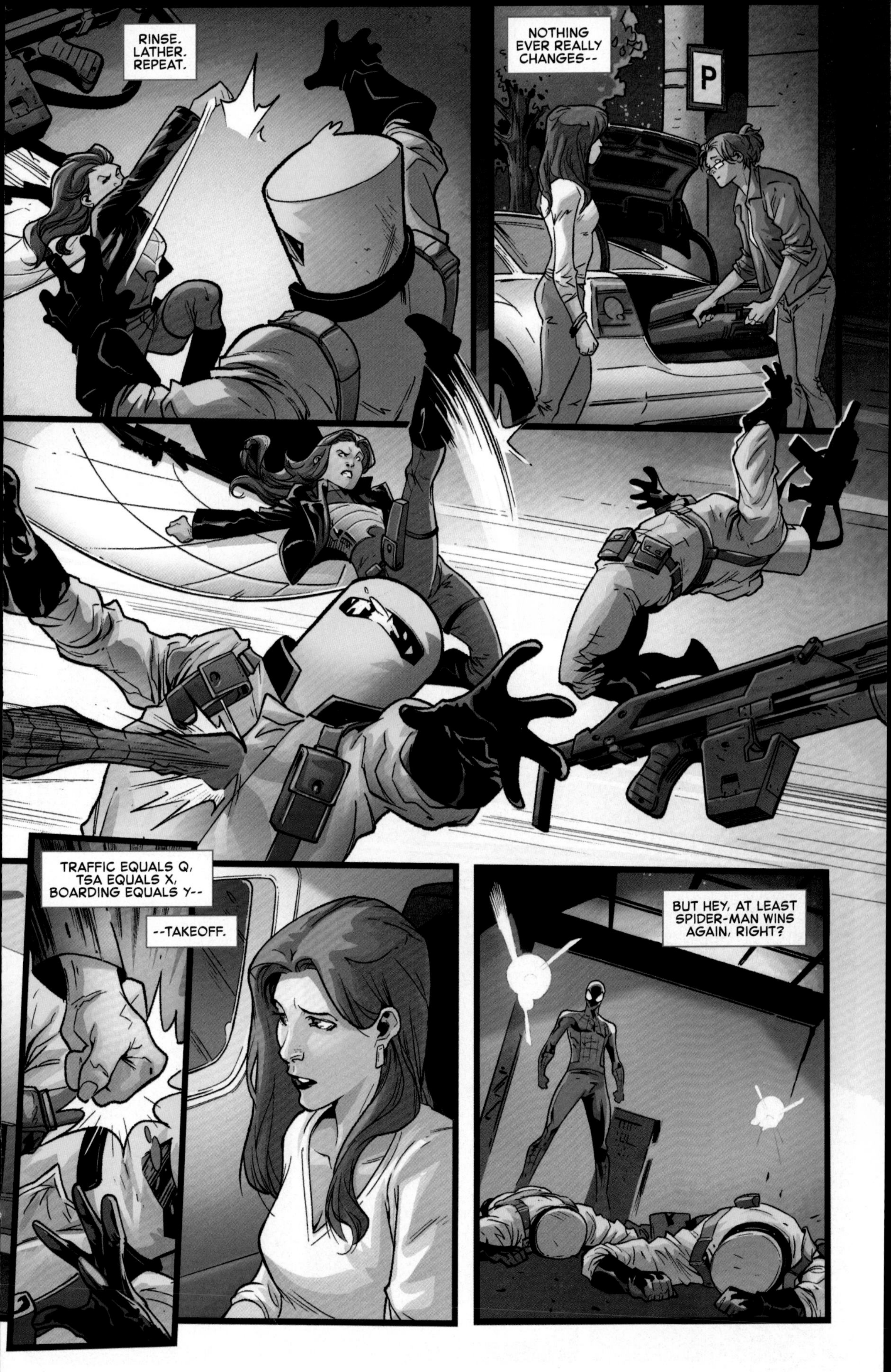
RINSE. LATHER. REPEAT.
NOTHING EVER REALLY CHANGES--
P
TRAFFIC EQUALS Q, TSA EQUALS X, BOARDING EQUALS Y--
--TAKEOFF.
BUT HEY, AT LEAST SPIDER-MAN WINS AGAIN, RIGHT?

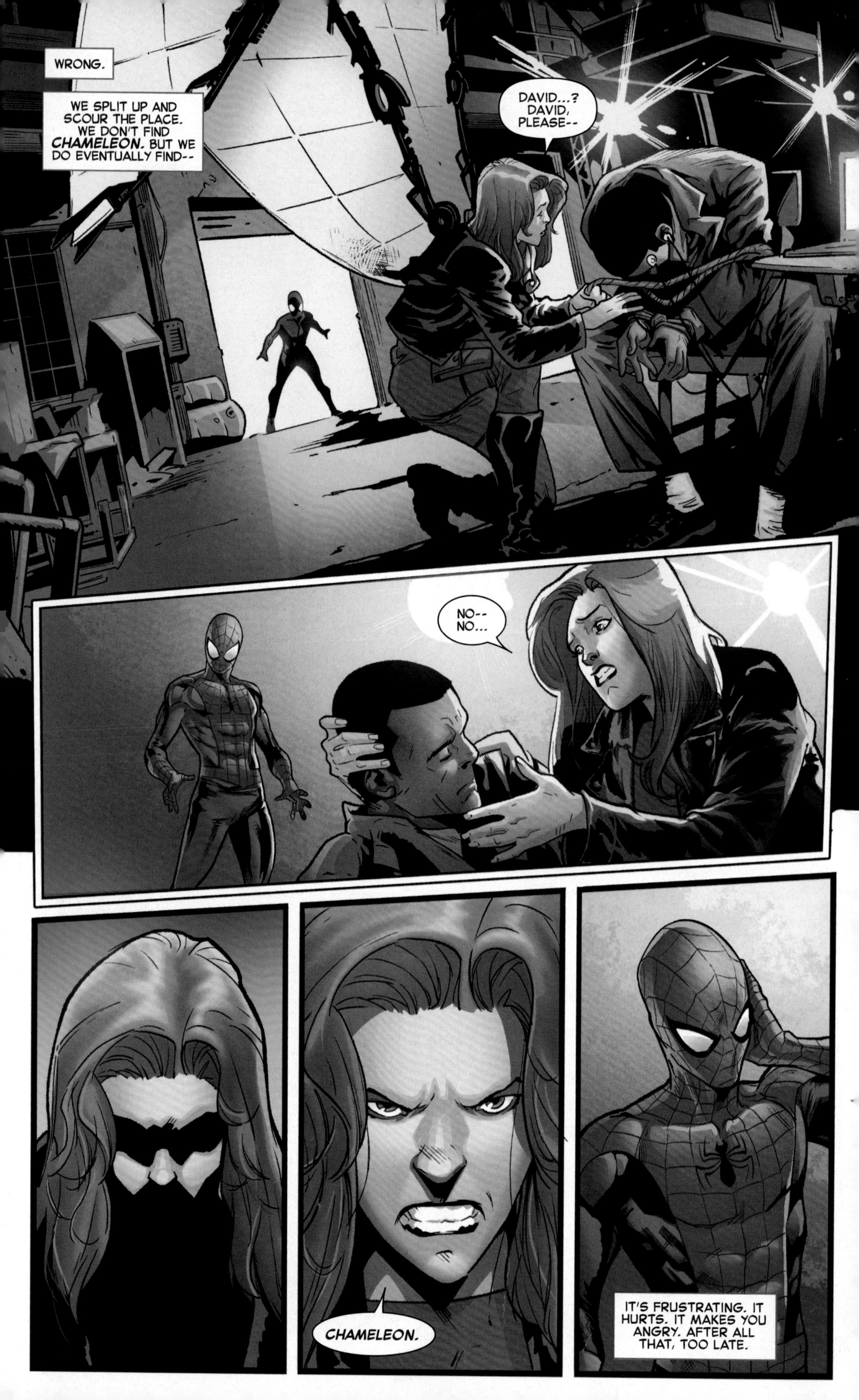
WRONG.
WE SPLIT UP AND SCOUR THE PLACE. WE DON'T FIND CHAMELEON. BUT WE DO EVENTUALLY FIND--
DAVID...? DAVID, PLEASE--
NO-- NO...
CHAMELEON.
IT'S FRUSTRATING. IT HURTS. IT MAKES YOU ANGRY. AFTER ALL THAT, TOO LATE.

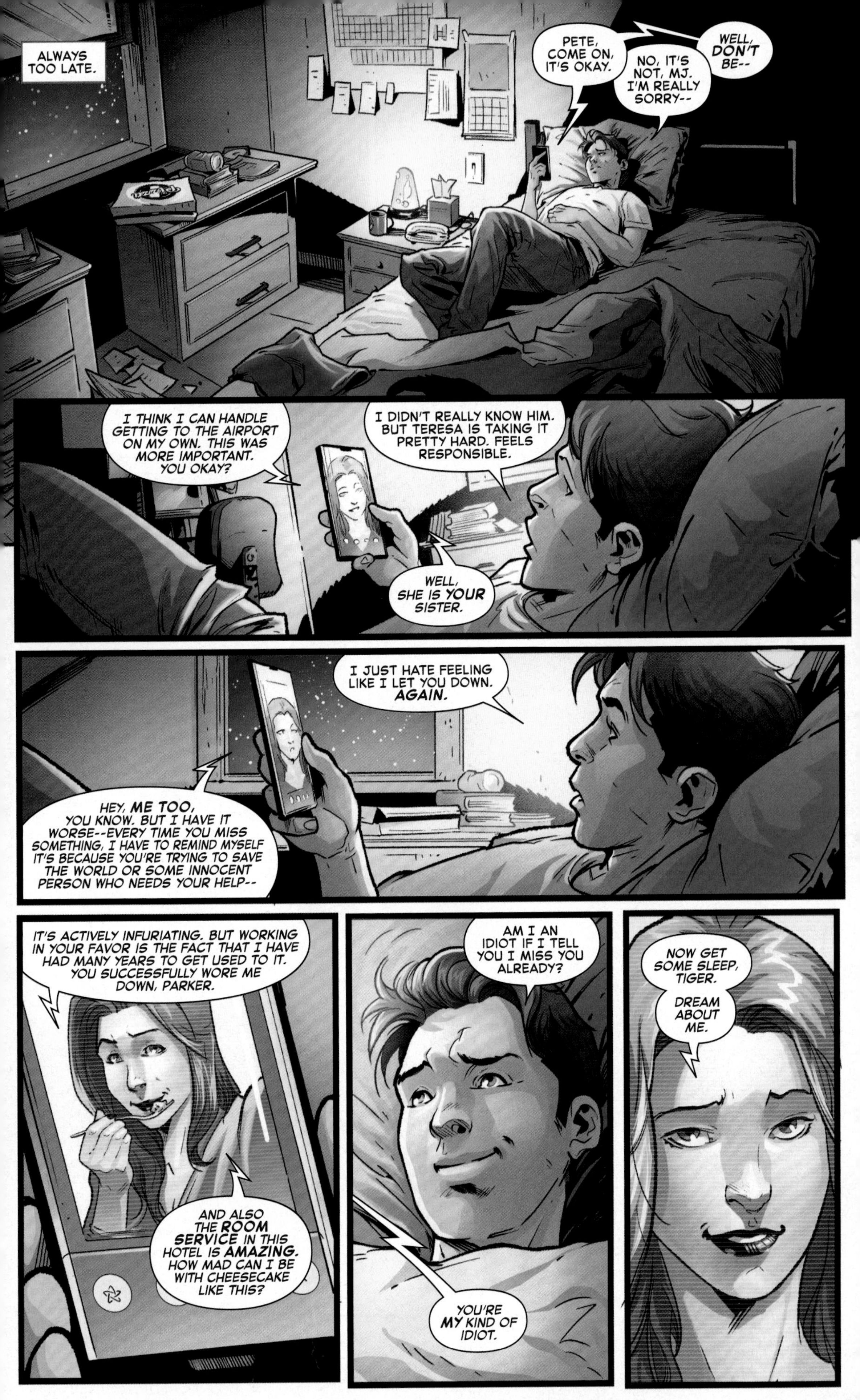
ALWAYS TOO LATE.
PETE, COME ON, IT'S OKAY.
NO, IT'S NOT, MJ. I'M REALLY SORRY--
WELL, DON'T BE--
I THINK I CAN HANDLE GETTING TO THE AIRPORT ON MY OWN. THIS WAS MORE IMPORTANT. YOU OKAY?
I DIDN'T REALLY KNOW HIM. BUT TERESA IS TAKING IT PRETTY HARD. FEELS RESPONSIBLE.
WELL, SHE IS YOUR SISTER.
I JUST HATE FEELING LIKE I LET YOU DOWN. AGAIN.
HEY, ME TOO, YOU KNOW. BUT I HAVE IT WORSE--EVERY TIME YOU MISS SOMETHING, I HAVE TO REMIND MYSELF IT'S BECAUSE YOU'RE TRYING TO SAVE THE WORLD OR SOME INNOCENT PERSON WHO NEEDS YOUR HELP--
IT'S ACTIVELY INFURIATING. BUT WORKING IN YOUR FAVOR IS THE FACT THAT I HAVE HAD MANY YEARS TO GET USED TO IT. YOU SUCCESSFULLY WORE ME DOWN, PARKER.
AND ALSO THE ROOM SERVICE IN THIS HOTEL IS AMAZING. HOW MAD CAN I BE WITH CHEESECAKE LIKE THIS?
AM I AN IDIOT IF I TELL YOU I MISS YOU ALREADY?
YOU'RE MY KIND OF IDIOT.
NOW GET SOME SLEEP, TIGER.
DREAM ABOUT ME.

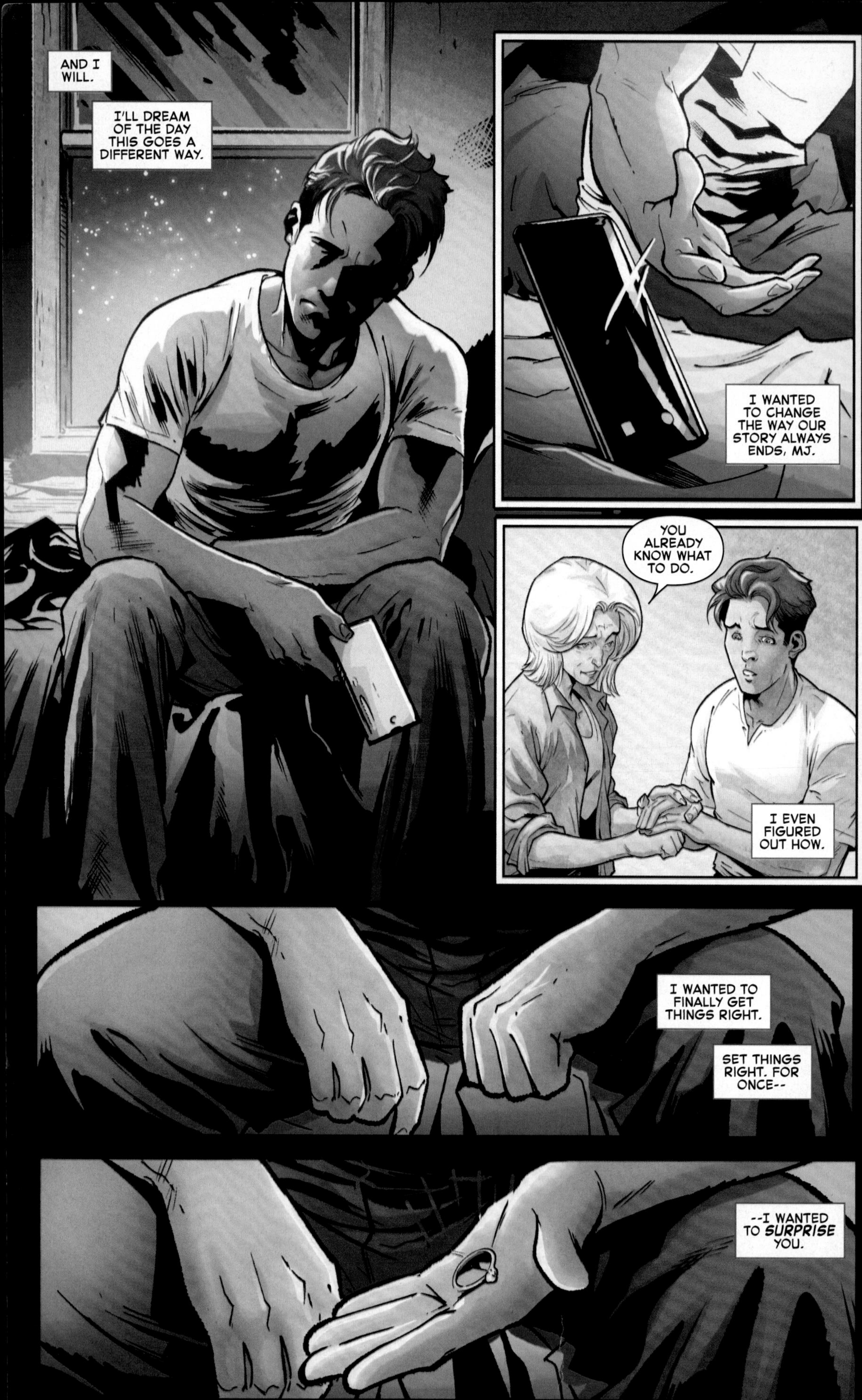
AND I WILL.
I'LL DREAM OF THE DAY THIS GOES A DIFFERENT WAY.
I WANTED TO CHANGE THE WAY OUR STORY ALWAYS ENDS, MJ.
YOU ALREADY KNOW WHAT TO DO.
I EVEN FIGURED OUT HOW.
I WANTED TO FINALLY GET THINGS RIGHT.
SET THINGS RIGHT. FOR ONCE--
--I WANTED TO SURPRISE YOU.

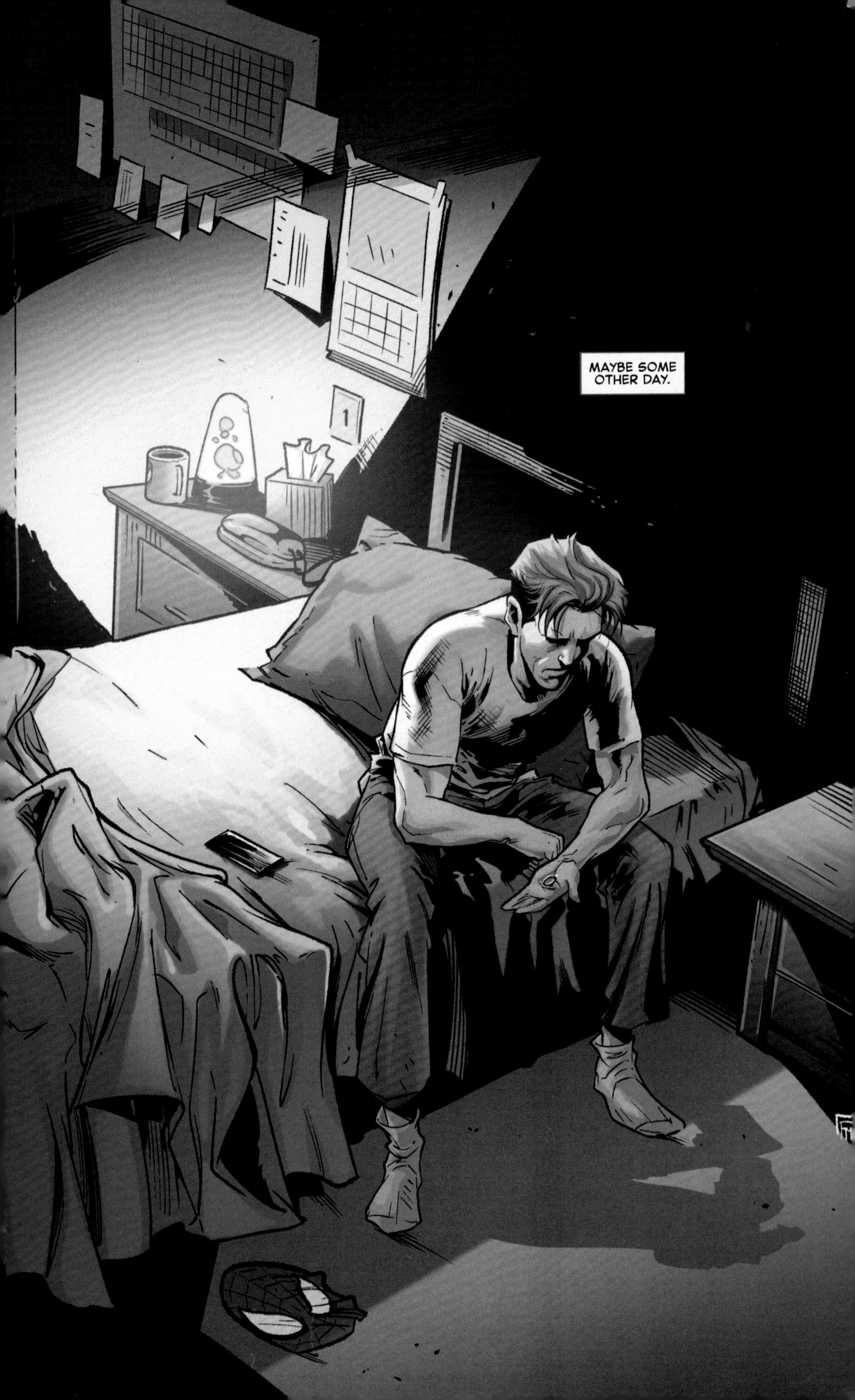
MAYBE SOME OTHER DAY.

30

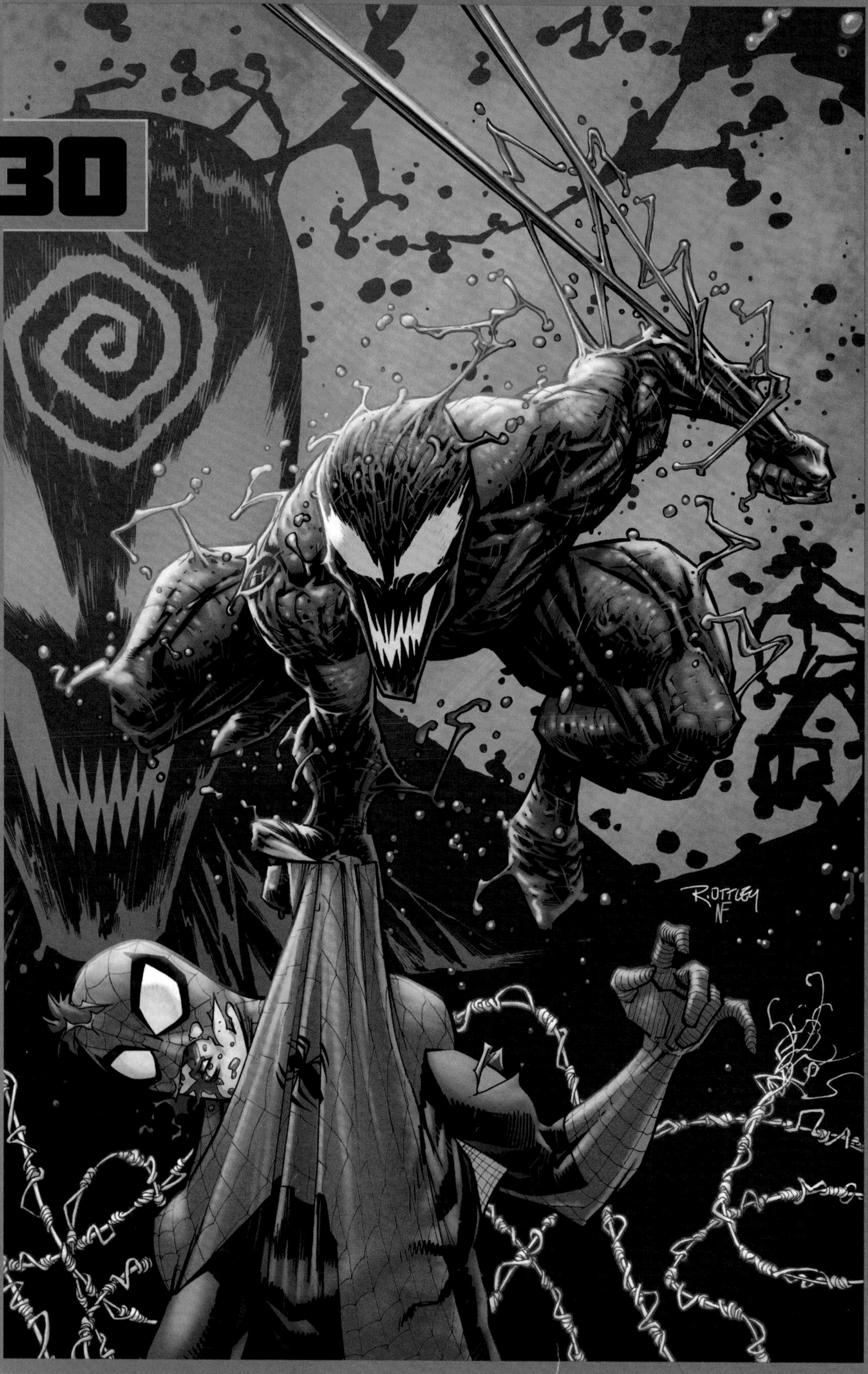
R. OTTLEY
NF

ABSOLUTE CARNAGE PART 1

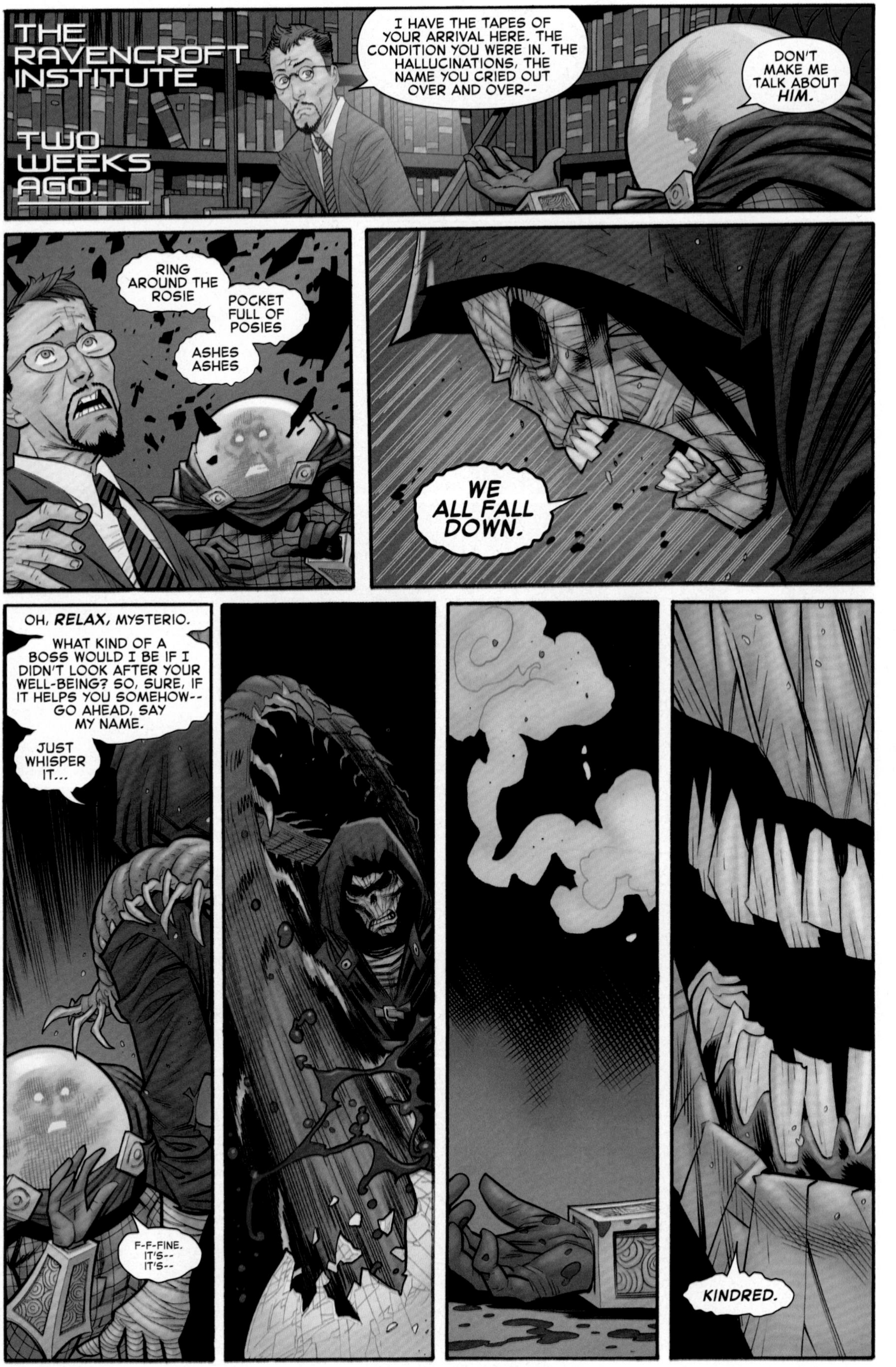
THE RAVENCROFT INSTITUTE
TWO WEEKS AGO.
I HAVE THE TAPES OF YOUR ARRIVAL HERE. THE CONDITION YOU WERE IN. THE HALLUCINATIONS, THE NAME YOU CRIED OUT OVER AND OVER--
DON'T MAKE ME TALK ABOUT HIM.
RING AROUND THE ROSIE
POCKET FULL OF POSIES
ASHES ASHES
WE ALL FALL DOWN.
OH, RELAX, MYSTERIO.
WHAT KIND OF A BOSS WOULD I BE IF I DIDN'T LOOK AFTER YOUR WELL-BEING? SO, SURE, IF IT HELPS YOU SOMEHOW--GO AHEAD, SAY MY NAME.
JUST WHISPER IT...
F-F-FINE. IT'S-- IT'S--
KINDRED.

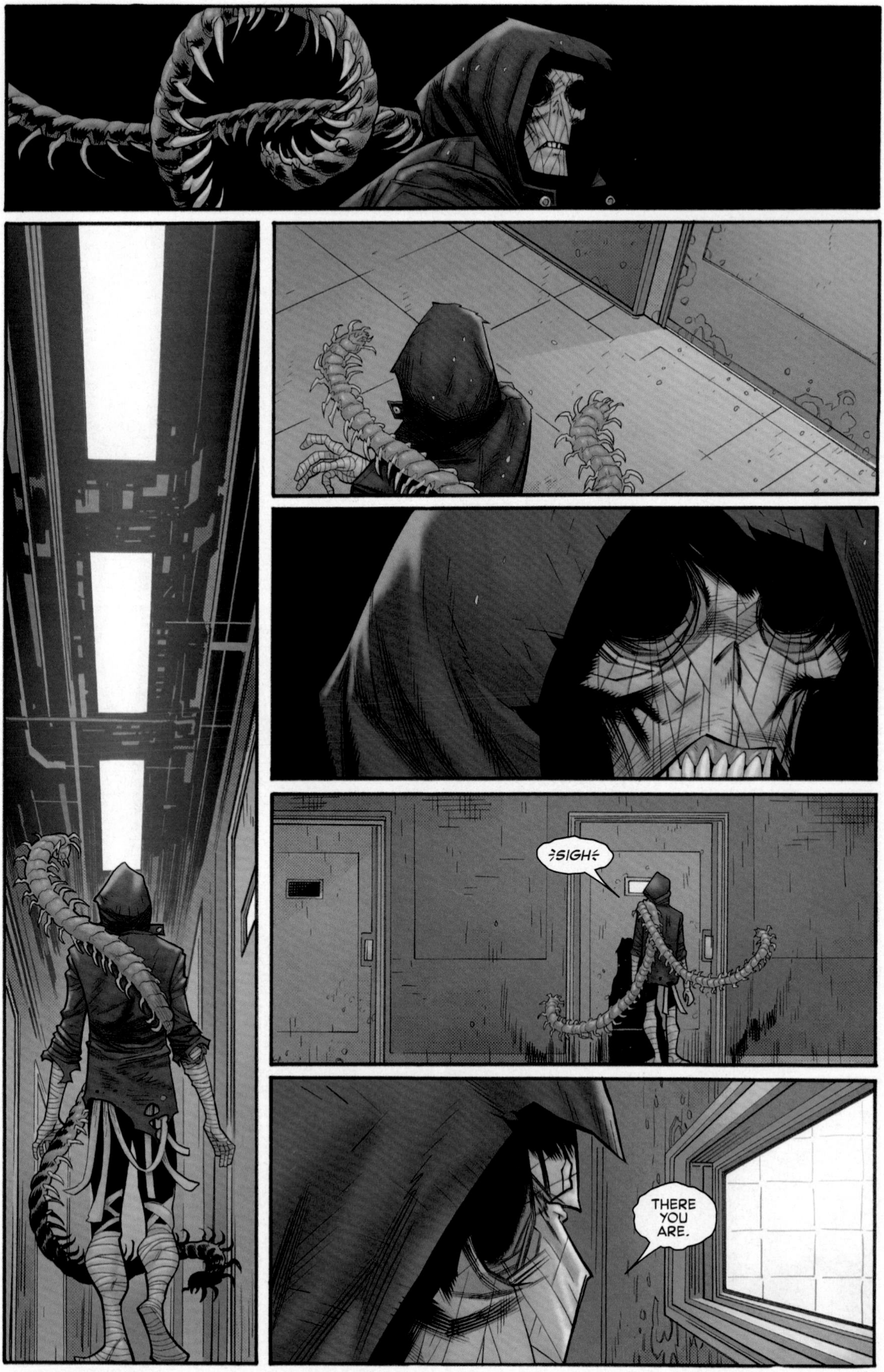
SIGH
THERE YOU ARE.

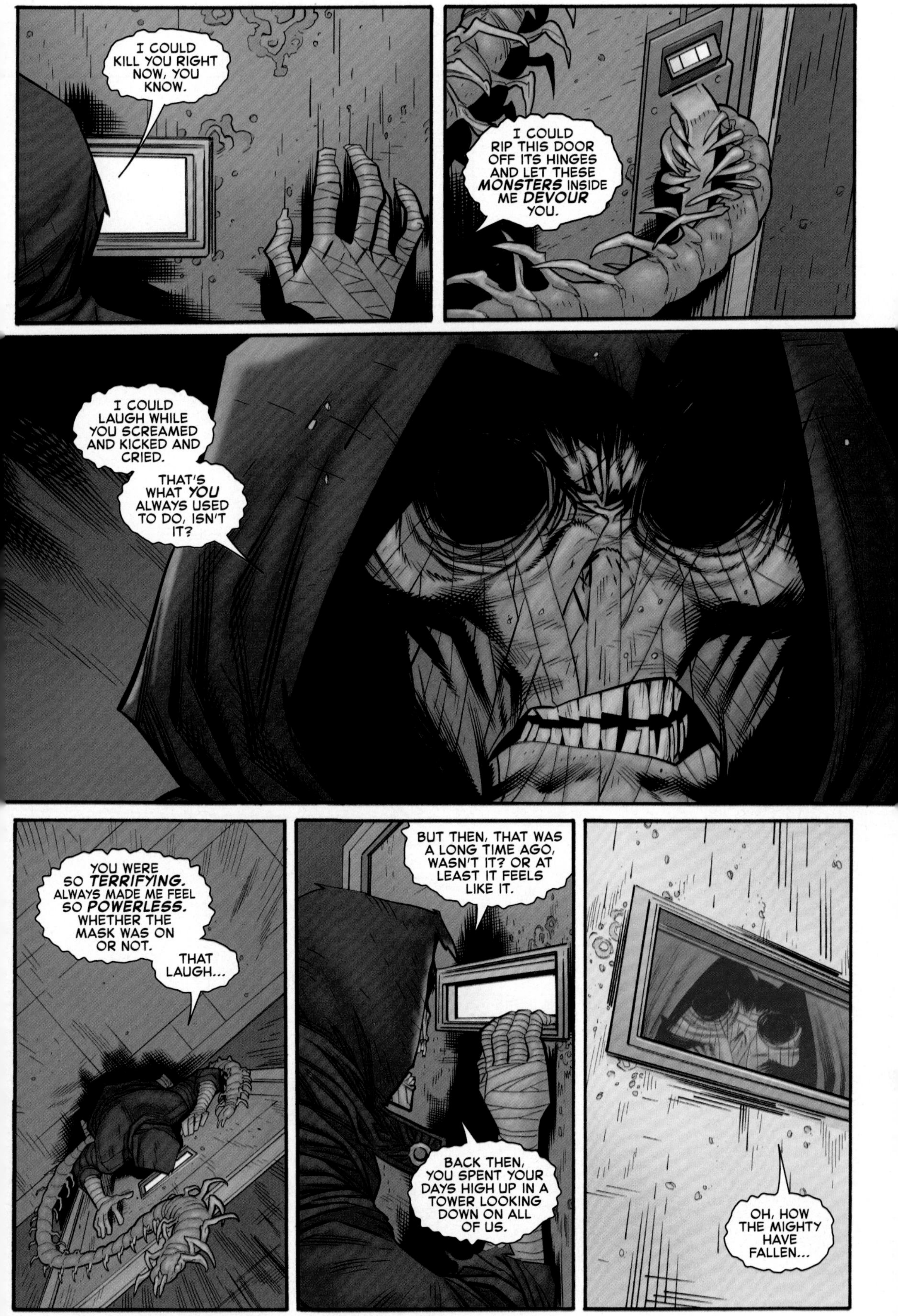
I COULD KILL YOU RIGHT NOW, YOU KNOW.
I COULD RIP THIS DOOR OFF ITS HINGES AND LET THESE *MONSTERS* INSIDE ME *DEVOUR* YOU.
I COULD LAUGH WHILE YOU SCREAMED AND KICKED AND CRIED.
THAT'S WHAT *YOU* ALWAYS USED TO DO, ISN'T IT?
YOU WERE SO *TERRIFYING.* ALWAYS MADE ME FEEL SO *POWERLESS.* WHETHER THE MASK WAS ON OR NOT.
THAT LAUGH...
BUT THEN, THAT WAS A LONG TIME AGO, WASN'T IT? OR AT LEAST IT FEELS LIKE IT.
BACK THEN, YOU SPENT YOUR DAYS HIGH UP IN A TOWER LOOKING DOWN ON ALL OF US.
OH, HOW THE MIGHTY HAVE FALLEN...

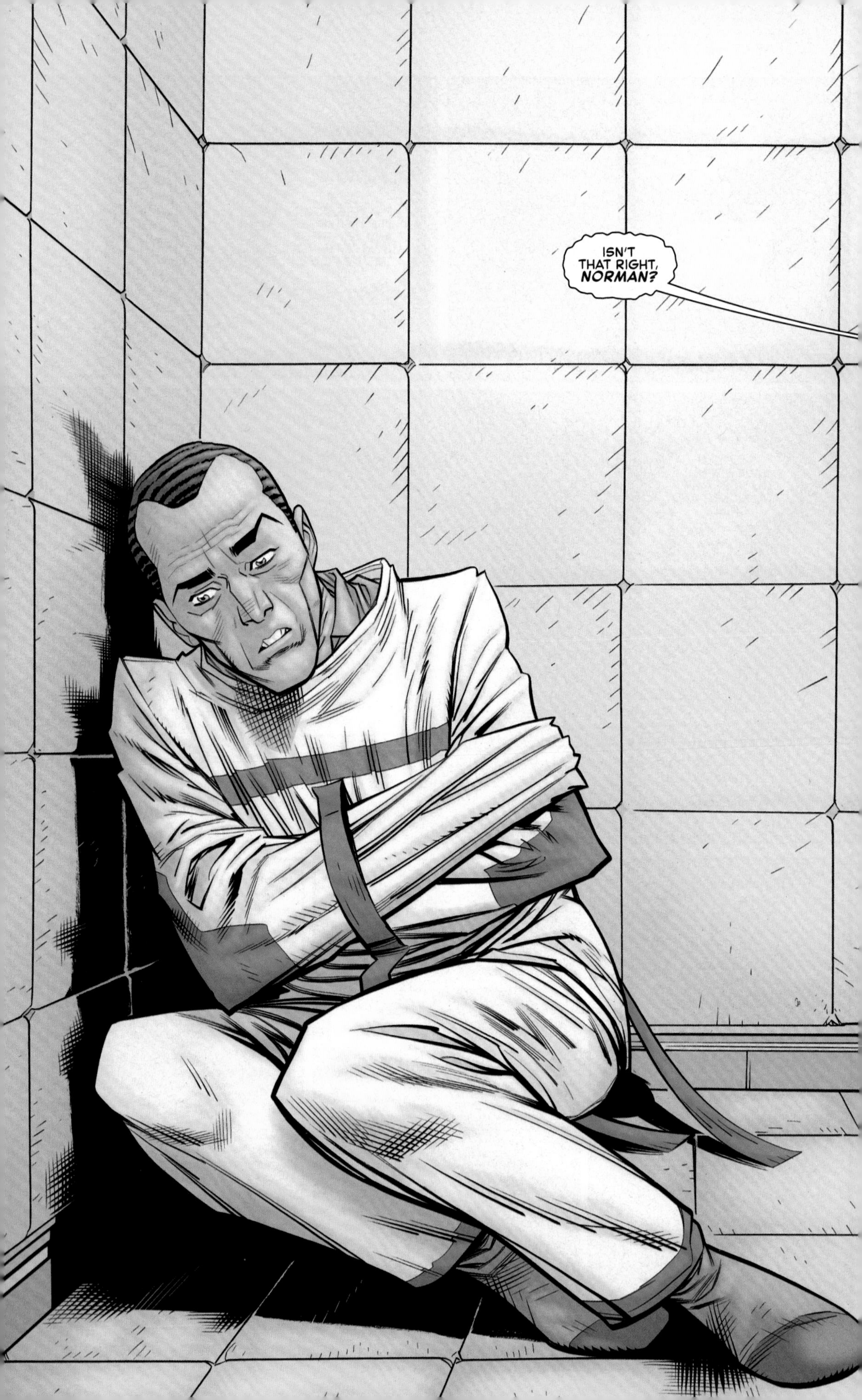
ISN'T THAT RIGHT, NORMAN?

HOW COULD I BE SO STUPID?

STUCK ON SOME OTHER PLANET BY THE BEYONDER, FORCED INTO A WAR, I SAW A BUNCH OF OTHER HEROES GETTING EQUIPMENT UPGRADES--

--AND FOLLOWED THE TRAIL TO THIS MACHINE.

DECIDED TO JUST... GIVE IT A TRY.

I KNOW-- CRAZY, RIGHT?

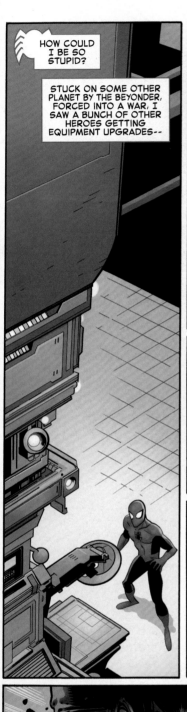

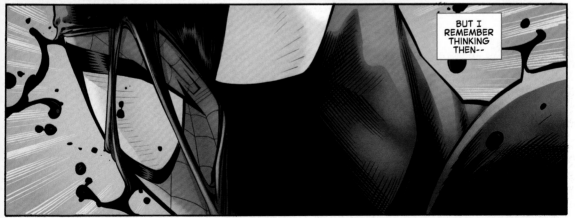

BUT I REMEMBER THINKING THEN--

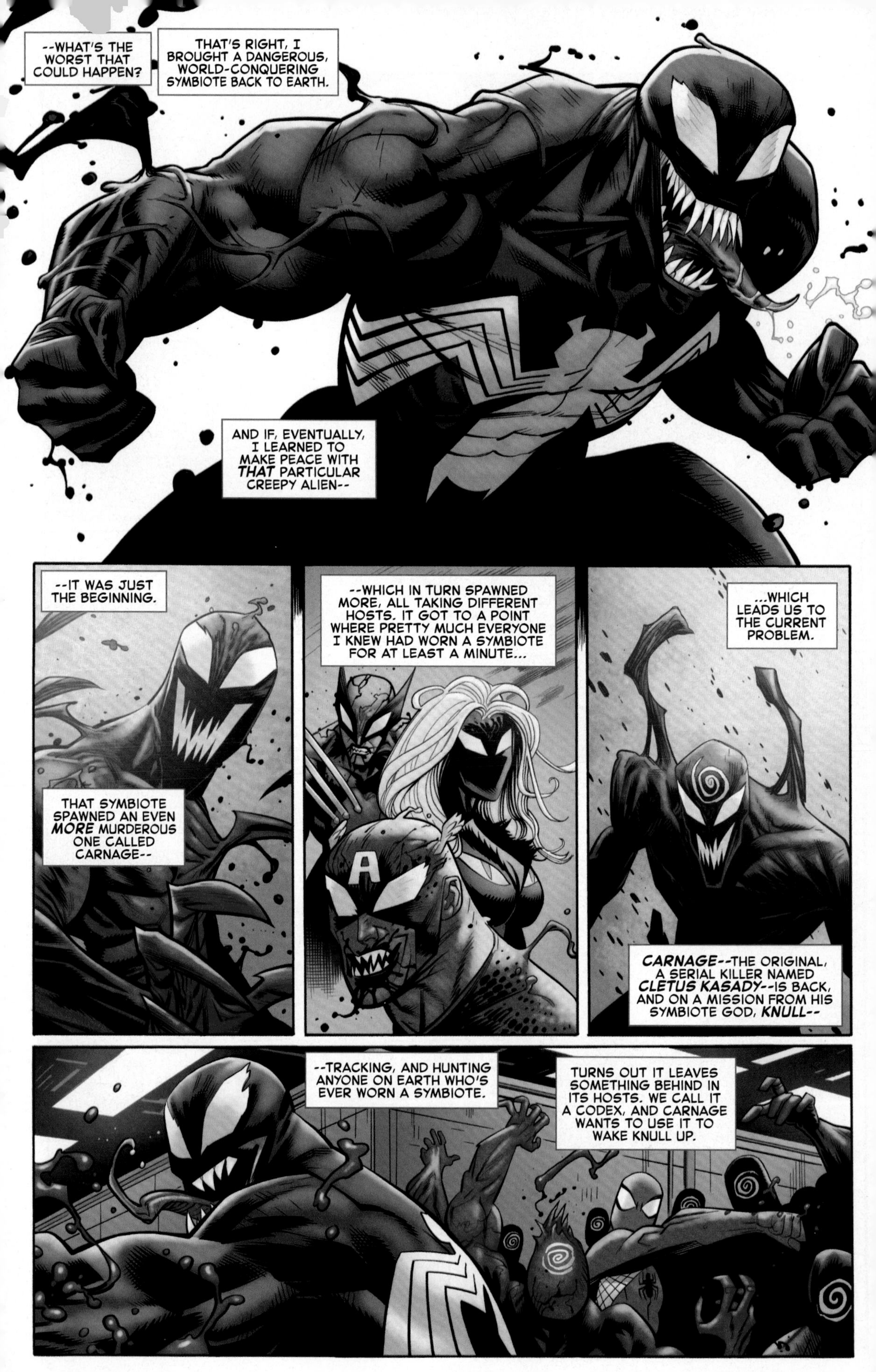
--WHAT'S THE WORST THAT COULD HAPPEN?
THAT'S RIGHT, I BROUGHT A DANGEROUS, WORLD-CONQUERING SYMBIOTE BACK TO EARTH.
AND IF, EVENTUALLY, I LEARNED TO MAKE PEACE WITH *THAT* PARTICULAR CREEPY ALIEN--
--IT WAS JUST THE BEGINNING.
THAT SYMBIOTE SPAWNED AN EVEN *MORE* MURDEROUS ONE CALLED CARNAGE--
--WHICH IN TURN SPAWNED MORE, ALL TAKING DIFFERENT HOSTS. IT GOT TO A POINT WHERE PRETTY MUCH EVERYONE I KNEW HAD WORN A SYMBIOTE FOR AT LEAST A MINUTE...
...WHICH LEADS US TO THE CURRENT PROBLEM.
CARNAGE--THE ORIGINAL, A SERIAL KILLER NAMED *CLETUS KASADY*--IS BACK, AND ON A MISSION FROM HIS SYMBIOTE GOD, *KNULL*--
--TRACKING, AND HUNTING ANYONE ON EARTH WHO'S EVER WORN A SYMBIOTE.
TURNS OUT IT LEAVES SOMETHING BEHIND IN ITS HOSTS. WE CALL IT A CODEX, AND CARNAGE WANTS TO USE IT TO WAKE KNULL UP.

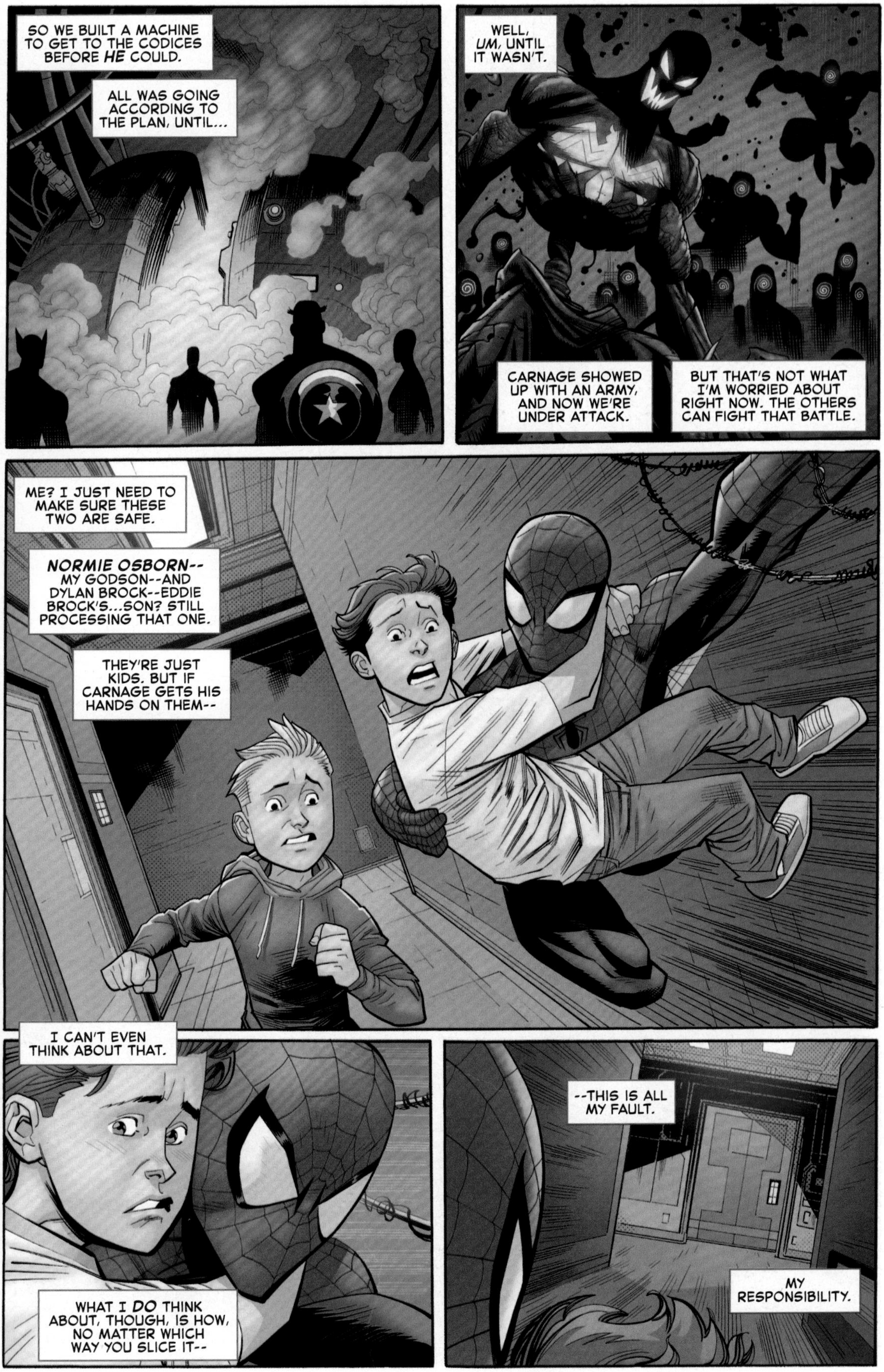
SO WE BUILT A MACHINE TO GET TO THE CODICES BEFORE *HE* COULD.
ALL WAS GOING ACCORDING TO THE PLAN, UNTIL...
WELL, *UM,* UNTIL IT WASN'T.
CARNAGE SHOWED UP WITH AN ARMY, AND NOW WE'RE UNDER ATTACK.
BUT THAT'S NOT WHAT I'M WORRIED ABOUT RIGHT NOW. THE OTHERS CAN FIGHT THAT BATTLE.
ME? I JUST NEED TO MAKE SURE THESE TWO ARE SAFE.
NORMIE OSBORN-- MY GODSON--AND DYLAN BROCK--EDDIE BROCK'S...SON? STILL PROCESSING THAT ONE.
THEY'RE JUST KIDS. BUT IF CARNAGE GETS HIS HANDS ON THEM--
I CAN'T EVEN THINK ABOUT THAT.
WHAT I *DO* THINK ABOUT, THOUGH, IS HOW, NO MATTER WHICH WAY YOU SLICE IT--
--THIS IS ALL MY FAULT.
MY RESPONSIBILITY.

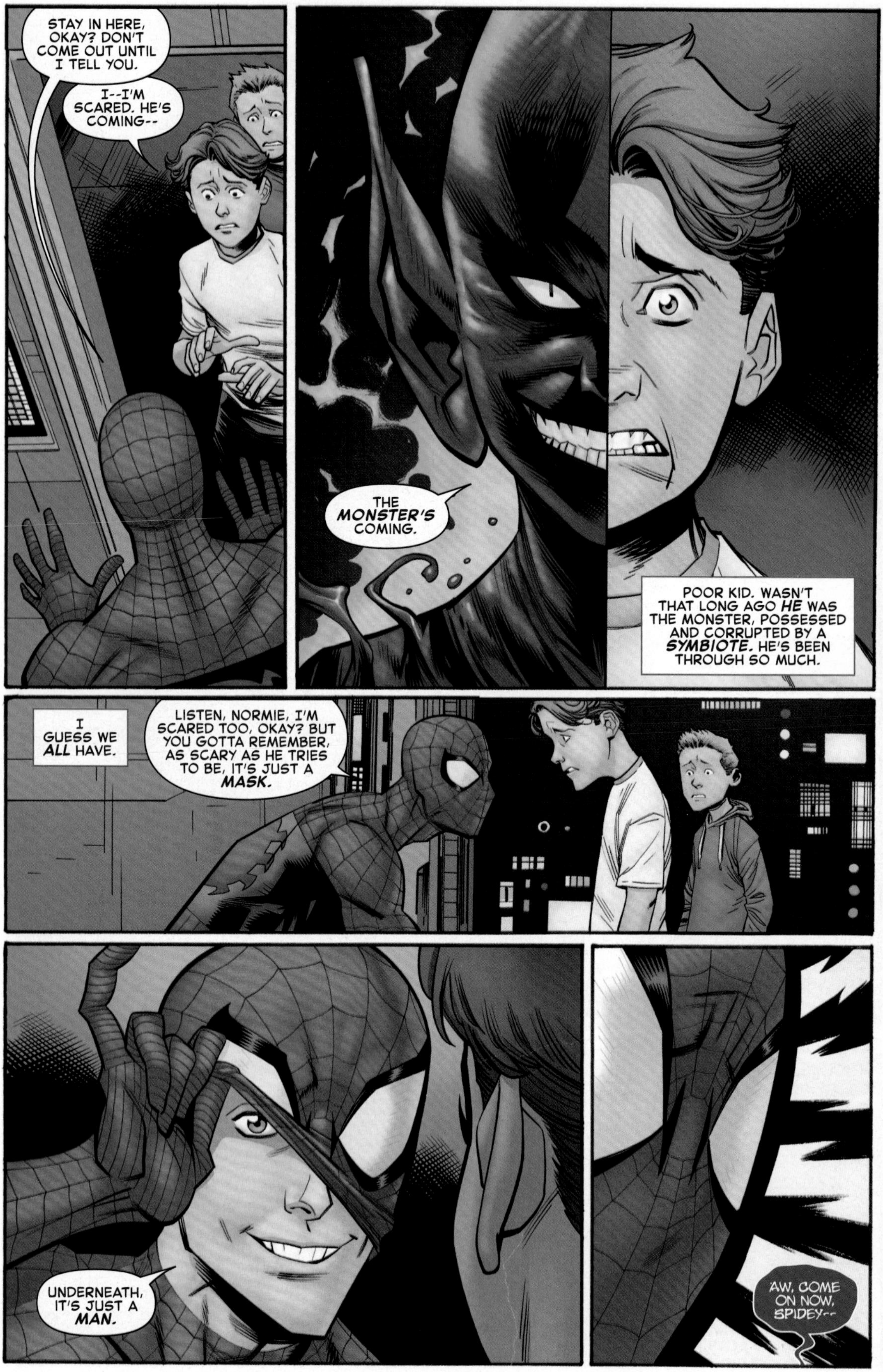
STAY IN HERE, OKAY? DON'T COME OUT UNTIL I TELL YOU.
I--I'M SCARED. HE'S COMING--
THE MONSTER'S COMING.
POOR KID. WASN'T THAT LONG AGO HE WAS THE MONSTER, POSSESSED AND CORRUPTED BY A SYMBIOTE. HE'S BEEN THROUGH SO MUCH.
I GUESS WE ALL HAVE.
LISTEN, NORMIE, I'M SCARED TOO, OKAY? BUT YOU GOTTA REMEMBER, AS SCARY AS HE TRIES TO BE, IT'S JUST A MASK.
UNDERNEATH, IT'S JUST A MAN.
AW, COME ON NOW, SPIDEY--

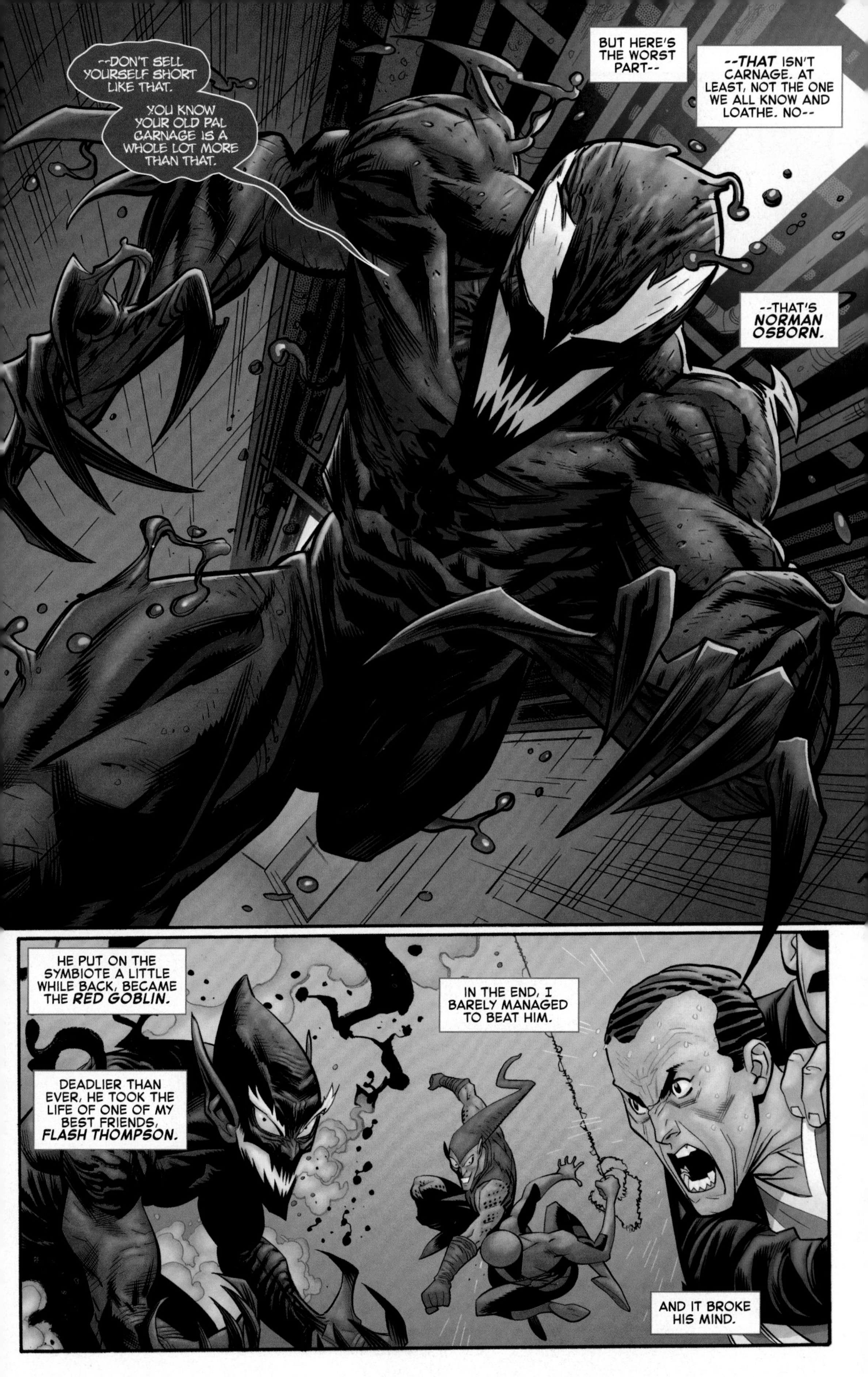
--DON'T SELL YOURSELF SHORT LIKE THAT.
YOU KNOW YOUR OLD PAL CARNAGE IS A WHOLE LOT MORE THAN THAT.
BUT HERE'S THE WORST PART--
--THAT ISN'T CARNAGE. AT LEAST, NOT THE ONE WE ALL KNOW AND LOATHE. NO--
--THAT'S NORMAN OSBORN.
HE PUT ON THE SYMBIOTE A LITTLE WHILE BACK, BECAME THE RED GOBLIN.
DEADLIER THAN EVER, HE TOOK THE LIFE OF ONE OF MY BEST FRIENDS, FLASH THOMPSON.
IN THE END, I BARELY MANAGED TO BEAT HIM.
AND IT BROKE HIS MIND.

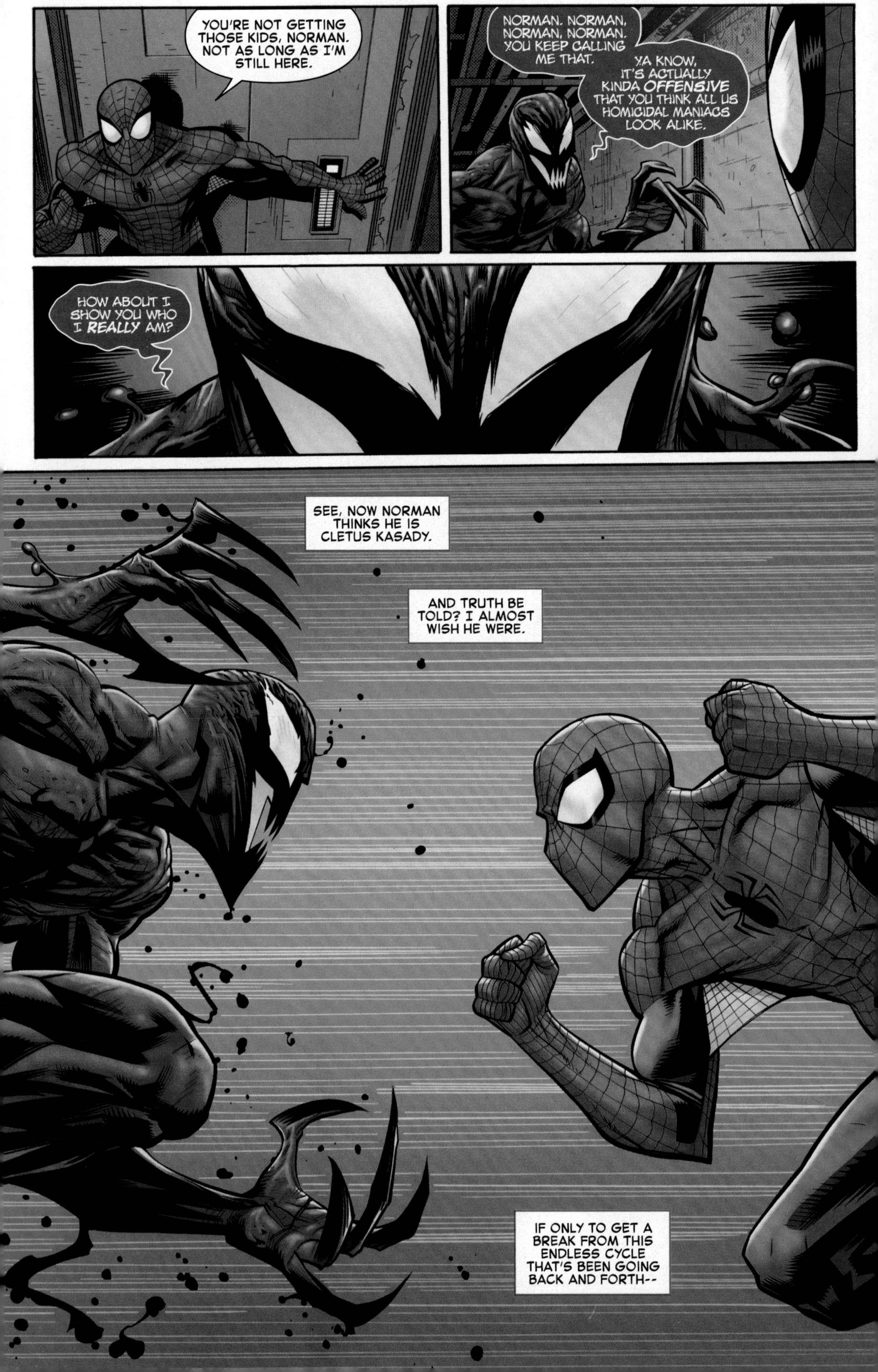

YOU'RE NOT GETTING THOSE KIDS, NORMAN. NOT AS LONG AS I'M STILL HERE.
NORMAN. NORMAN, NORMAN, NORMAN. YOU KEEP CALLING ME THAT.
YA KNOW, IT'S ACTUALLY KINDA OFFENSIVE THAT YOU THINK ALL US HOMICIDAL MANIACS LOOK ALIKE.
HOW ABOUT I SHOW YOU WHO I REALLY AM?
SEE, NOW NORMAN THINKS HE IS CLETUS KASADY.
AND TRUTH BE TOLD? I ALMOST WISH HE WERE.
IF ONLY TO GET A BREAK FROM THIS ENDLESS CYCLE THAT'S BEEN GOING BACK AND FORTH--

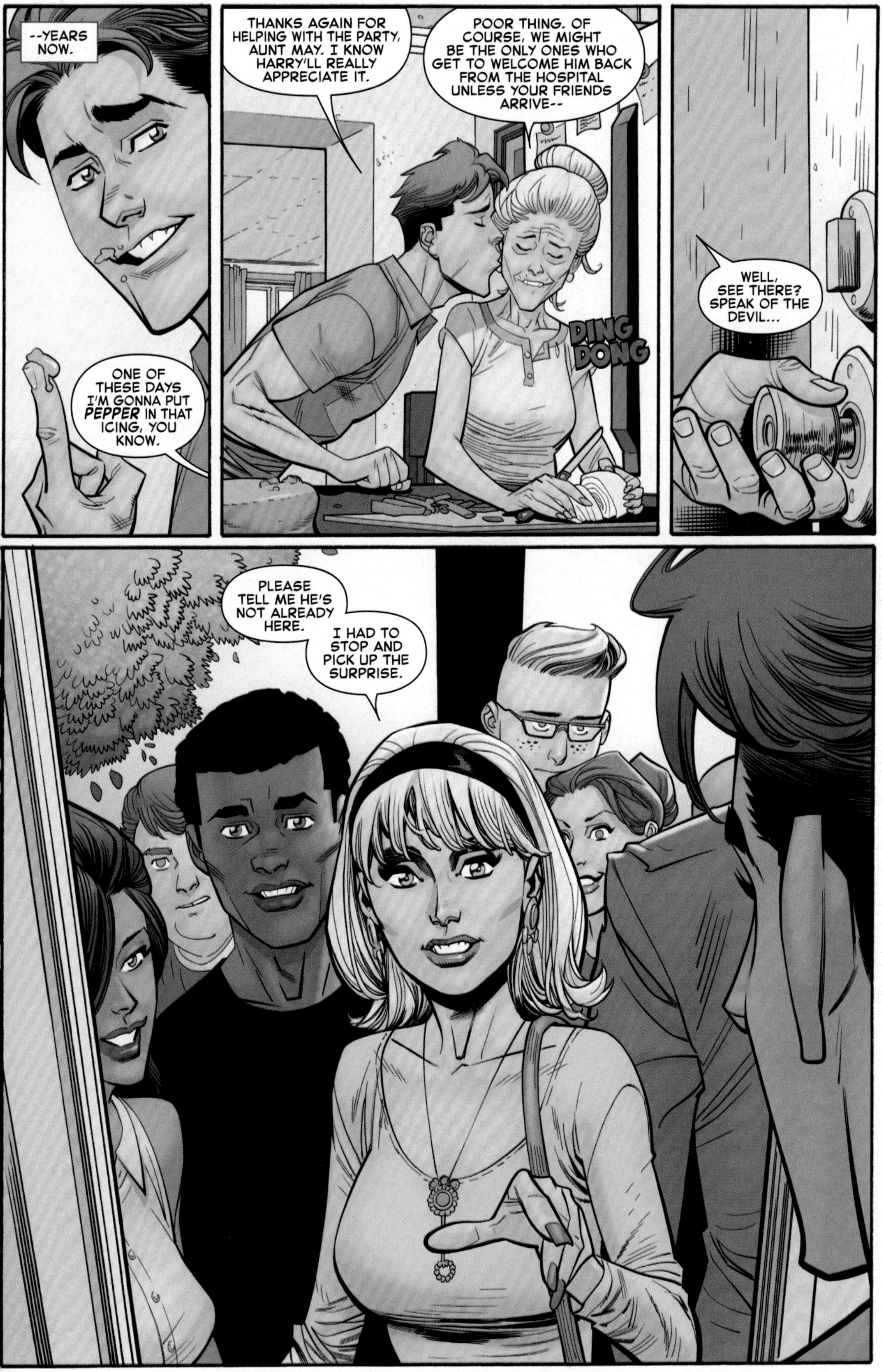
--YEARS NOW.
ONE OF THESE DAYS I'M GONNA PUT PEPPER IN THAT ICING, YOU KNOW.
THANKS AGAIN FOR HELPING WITH THE PARTY, AUNT MAY. I KNOW HARRY'LL REALLY APPRECIATE IT.
POOR THING. OF COURSE, WE MIGHT BE THE ONLY ONES WHO GET TO WELCOME HIM BACK FROM THE HOSPITAL UNLESS YOUR FRIENDS ARRIVE--
DING DONG
WELL, SEE THERE? SPEAK OF THE DEVIL...
PLEASE TELL ME HE'S NOT ALREADY HERE.
I HAD TO STOP AND PICK UP THE SURPRISE.

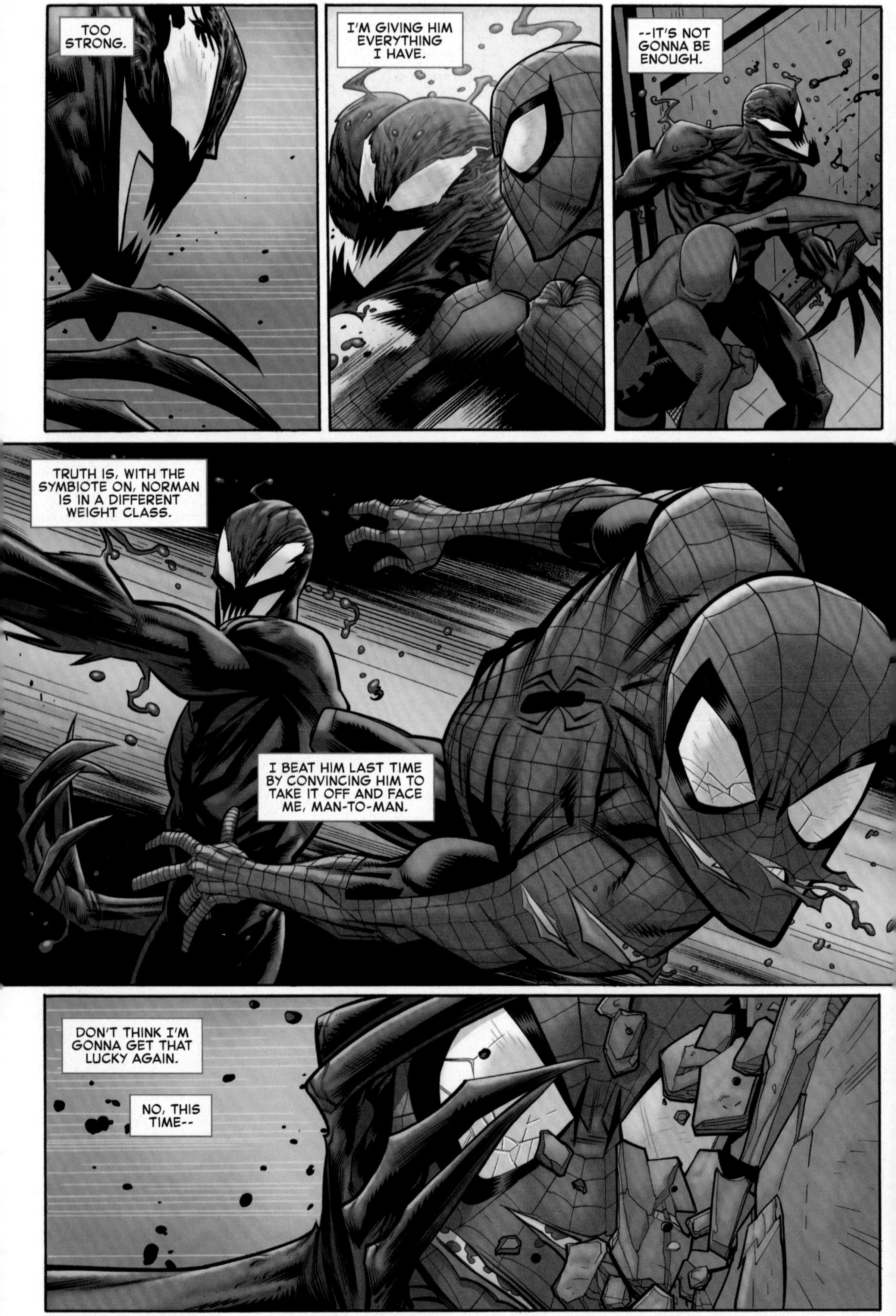
TOO STRONG.
I'M GIVING HIM EVERYTHING I HAVE.
--IT'S NOT GONNA BE ENOUGH.
TRUTH IS, WITH THE SYMBIOTE ON, NORMAN IS IN A DIFFERENT WEIGHT CLASS.
I BEAT HIM LAST TIME BY CONVINCING HIM TO TAKE IT OFF AND FACE ME, MAN-TO-MAN.
DON'T THINK I'M GONNA GET THAT LUCKY AGAIN.
NO, THIS TIME--

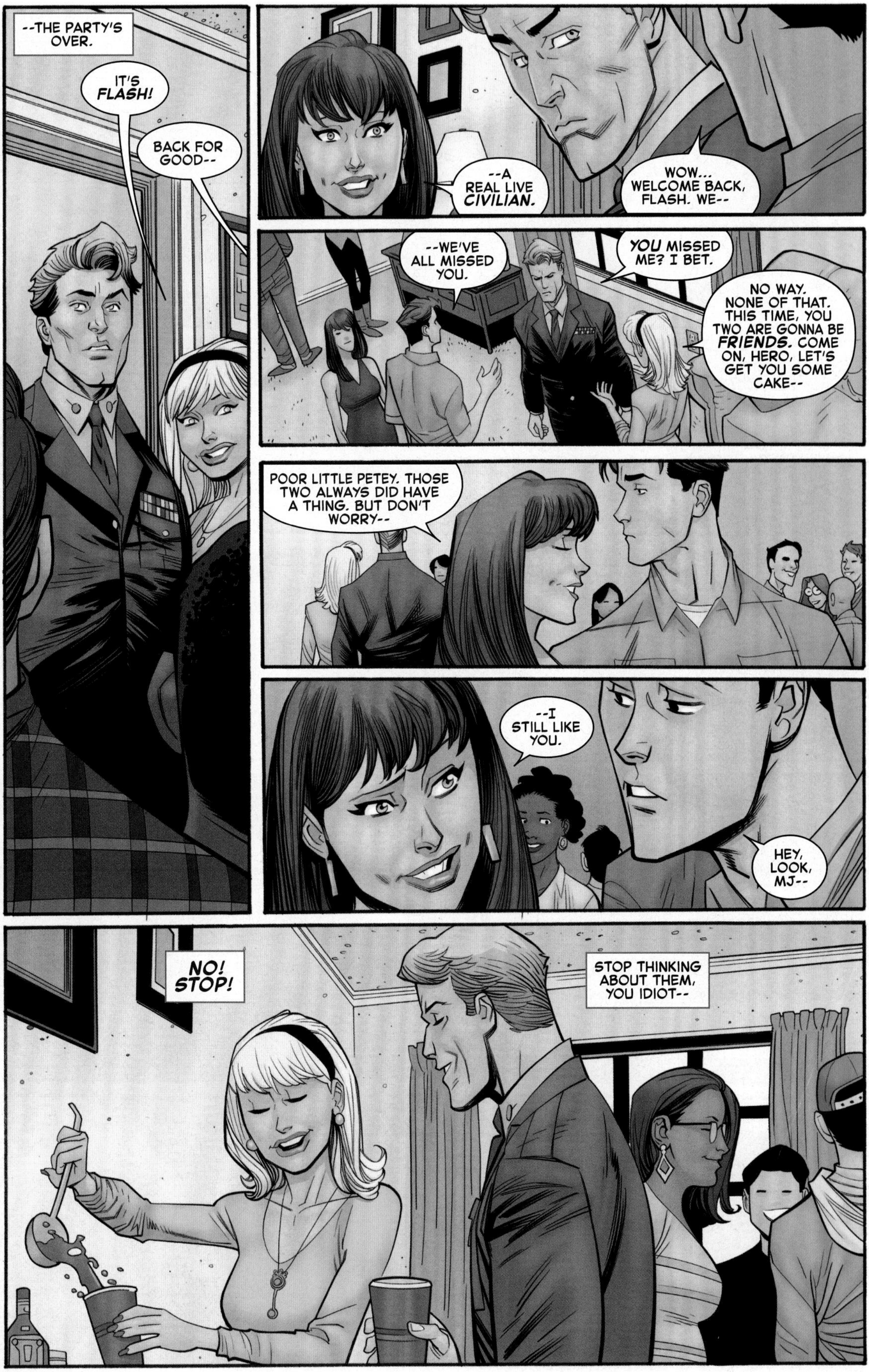
--THE PARTY'S OVER.
IT'S FLASH!
BACK FOR GOOD--
--A REAL LIVE CIVILIAN.
WOW... WELCOME BACK, FLASH. WE--
--WE'VE ALL MISSED YOU.
YOU MISSED ME? I BET.
NO WAY. NONE OF THAT. THIS TIME, YOU TWO ARE GONNA BE FRIENDS. COME ON, HERO, LET'S GET YOU SOME CAKE--
POOR LITTLE PETEY. THOSE TWO ALWAYS DID HAVE A THING. BUT DON'T WORRY--
--I STILL LIKE YOU.
HEY, LOOK, MJ--
NO! STOP!
STOP THINKING ABOUT THEM, YOU IDIOT--

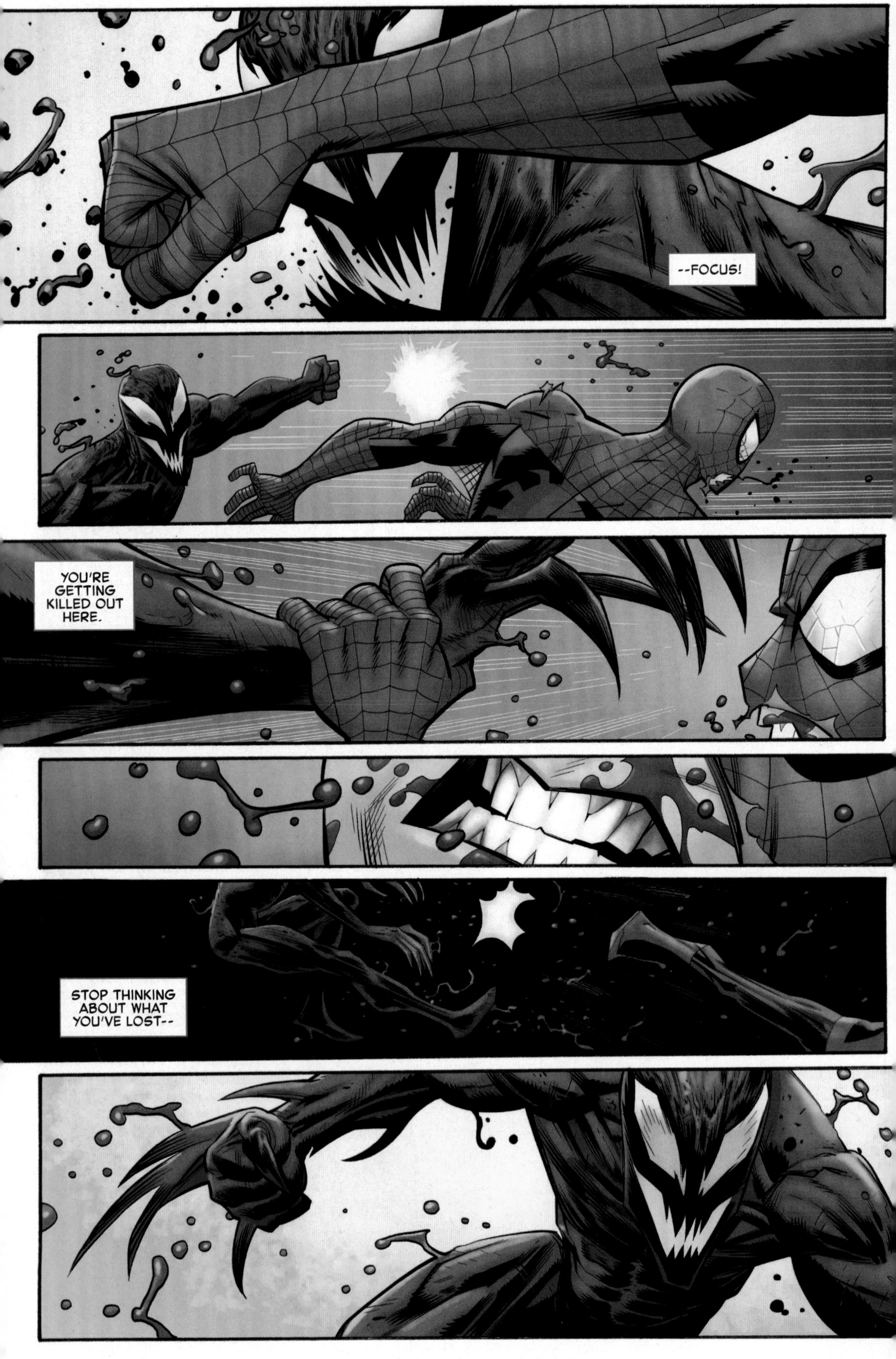
--FOCUS!
YOU'RE GETTING KILLED OUT HERE.
STOP THINKING ABOUT WHAT YOU'VE LOST--

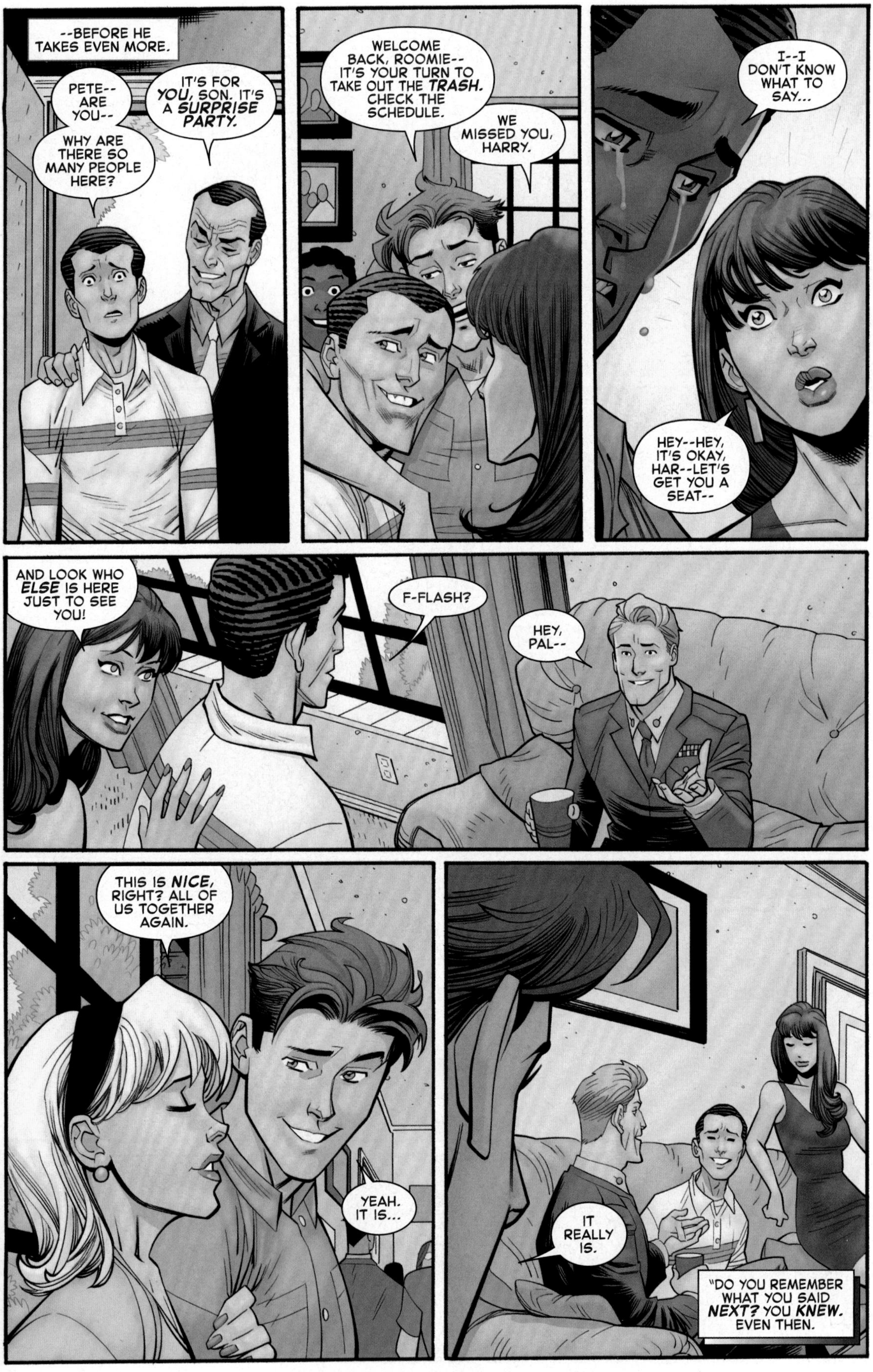
--BEFORE HE TAKES EVEN MORE.
PETE--ARE YOU--
WHY ARE THERE SO MANY PEOPLE HERE?
IT'S FOR YOU, SON. IT'S A SURPRISE PARTY.
WELCOME BACK, ROOMIE--IT'S YOUR TURN TO TAKE OUT THE TRASH. CHECK THE SCHEDULE.
WE MISSED YOU, HARRY.
I--I DON'T KNOW WHAT TO SAY...
HEY--HEY, IT'S OKAY, HAR--LET'S GET YOU A SEAT--
AND LOOK WHO ELSE IS HERE JUST TO SEE YOU!
F-FLASH?
HEY, PAL--
THIS IS NICE, RIGHT? ALL OF US TOGETHER AGAIN.
YEAH. IT IS...
IT REALLY IS.
"DO YOU REMEMBER WHAT YOU SAID NEXT? YOU KNEW. EVEN THEN.

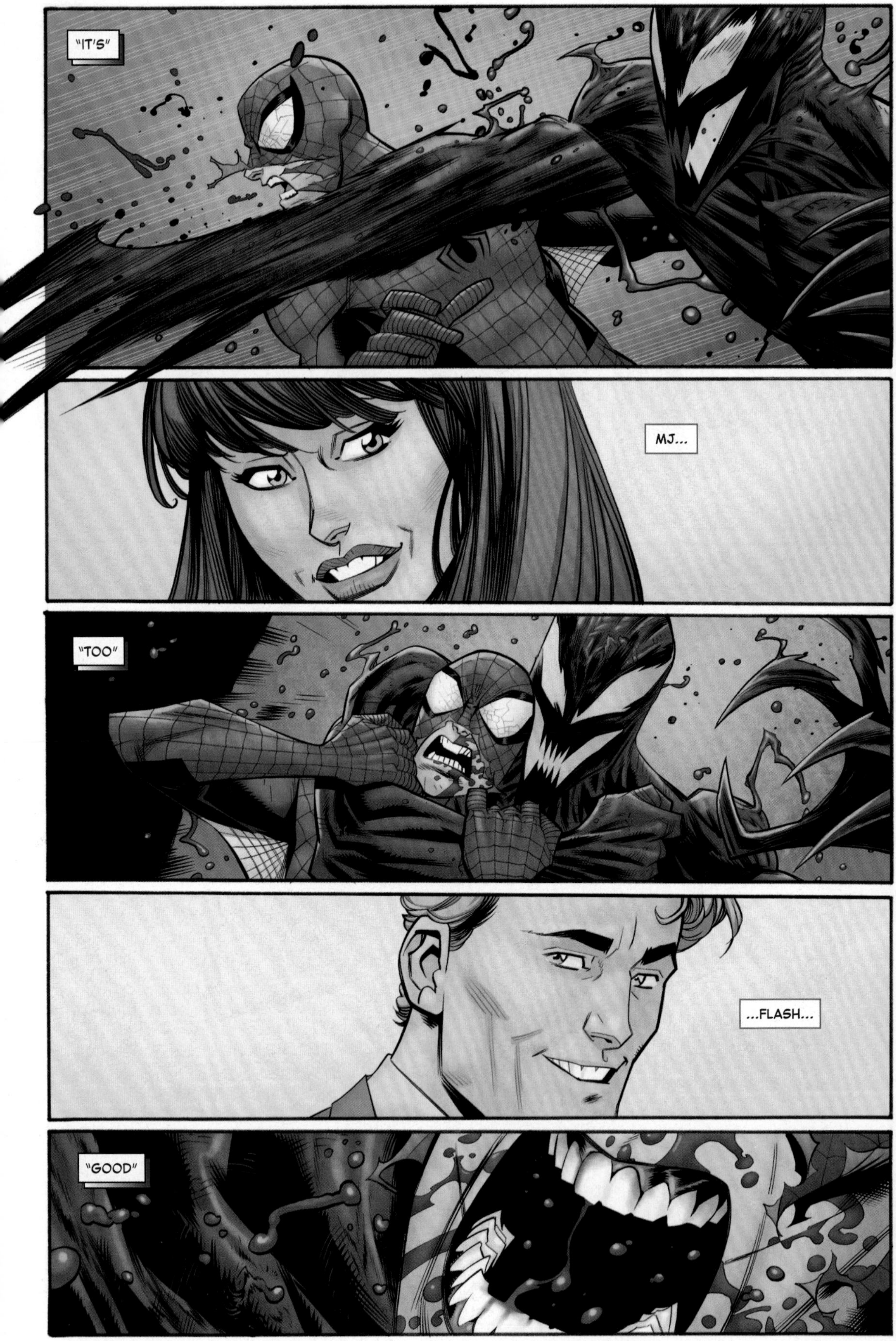
"IT'S"
MJ...
"TOO"
...FLASH...
"GOOD"

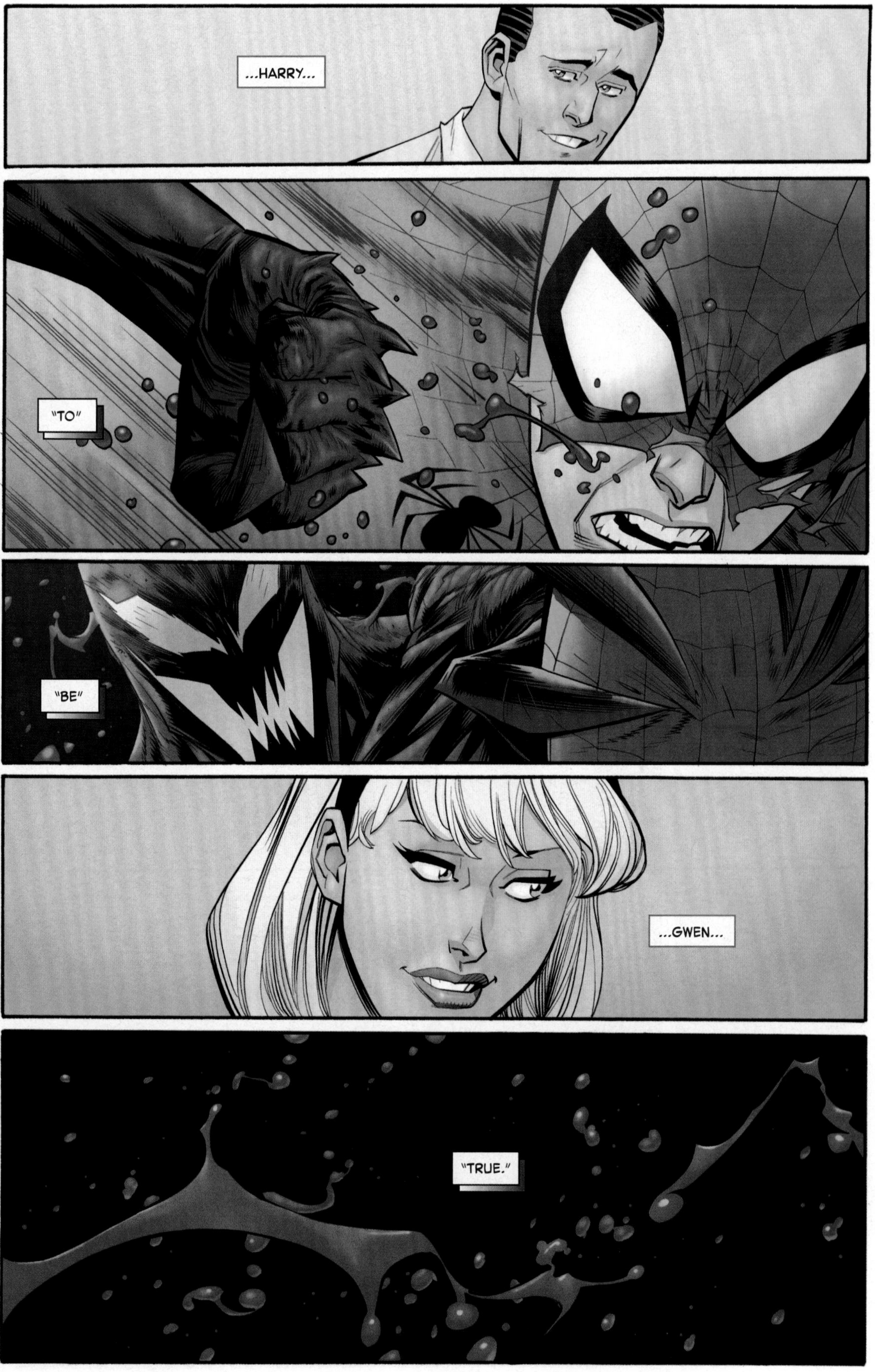

...HARRY...
"TO"
"BE"
...GWEN...
"TRUE."

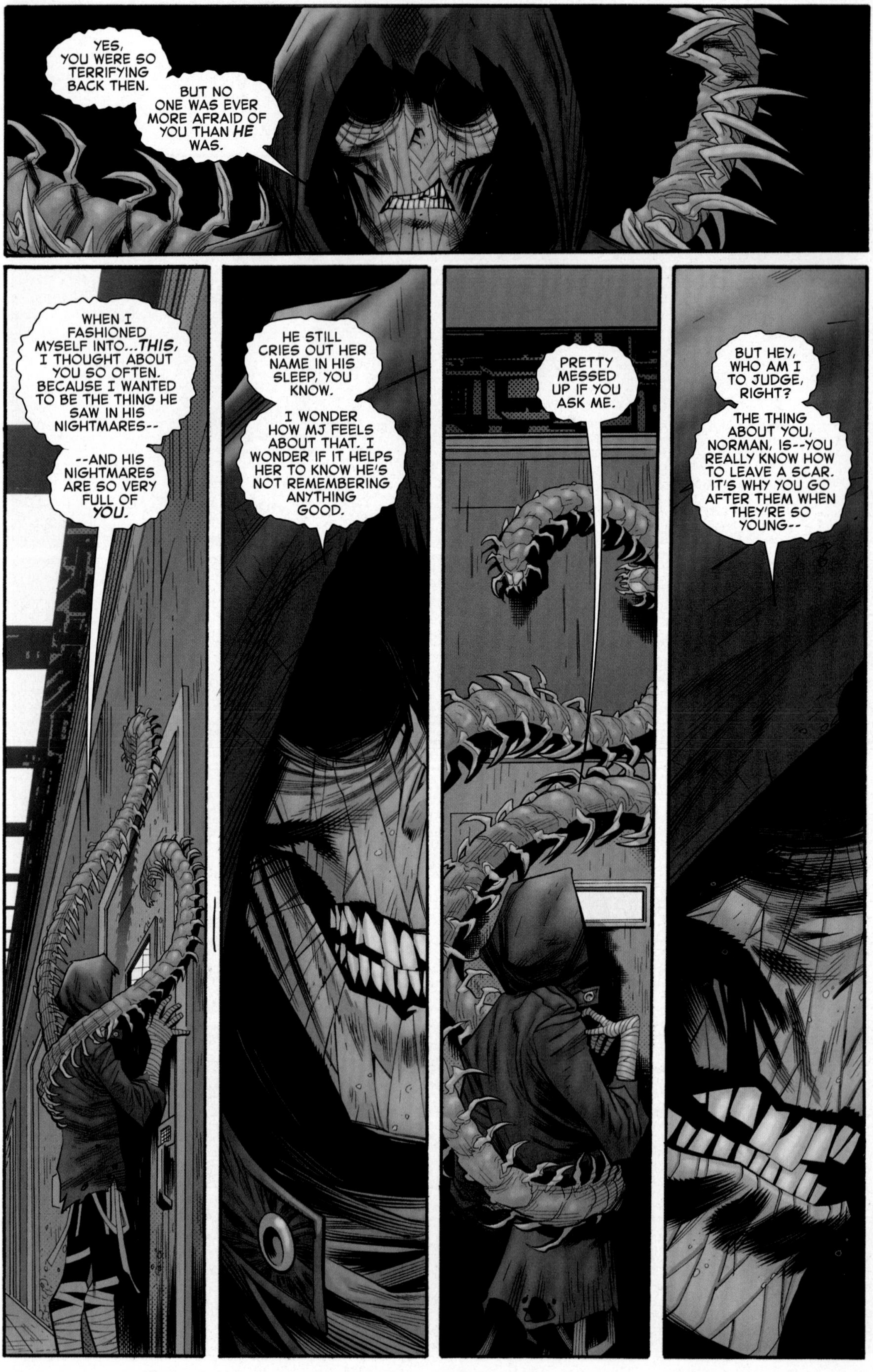
YES, YOU WERE SO TERRIFYING BACK THEN.
BUT NO ONE WAS EVER MORE AFRAID OF YOU THAN *HE* WAS.
WHEN I FASHIONED MYSELF INTO...*THIS,* I THOUGHT ABOUT YOU SO OFTEN. BECAUSE I WANTED TO BE THE THING HE SAW IN HIS NIGHTMARES--
--AND HIS NIGHTMARES ARE SO VERY FULL OF *YOU.*
HE STILL CRIES OUT HER NAME IN HIS SLEEP, YOU KNOW.
I WONDER HOW MJ FEELS ABOUT THAT. I WONDER IF IT HELPS HER TO KNOW HE'S NOT REMEMBERING ANYTHING GOOD.
PRETTY MESSED UP IF YOU ASK ME.
BUT HEY, WHO AM I TO JUDGE, RIGHT?
THE THING ABOUT YOU, NORMAN, IS--YOU REALLY KNOW HOW TO LEAVE A SCAR. IT'S WHY YOU GO AFTER THEM WHEN THEY'RE SO YOUNG--

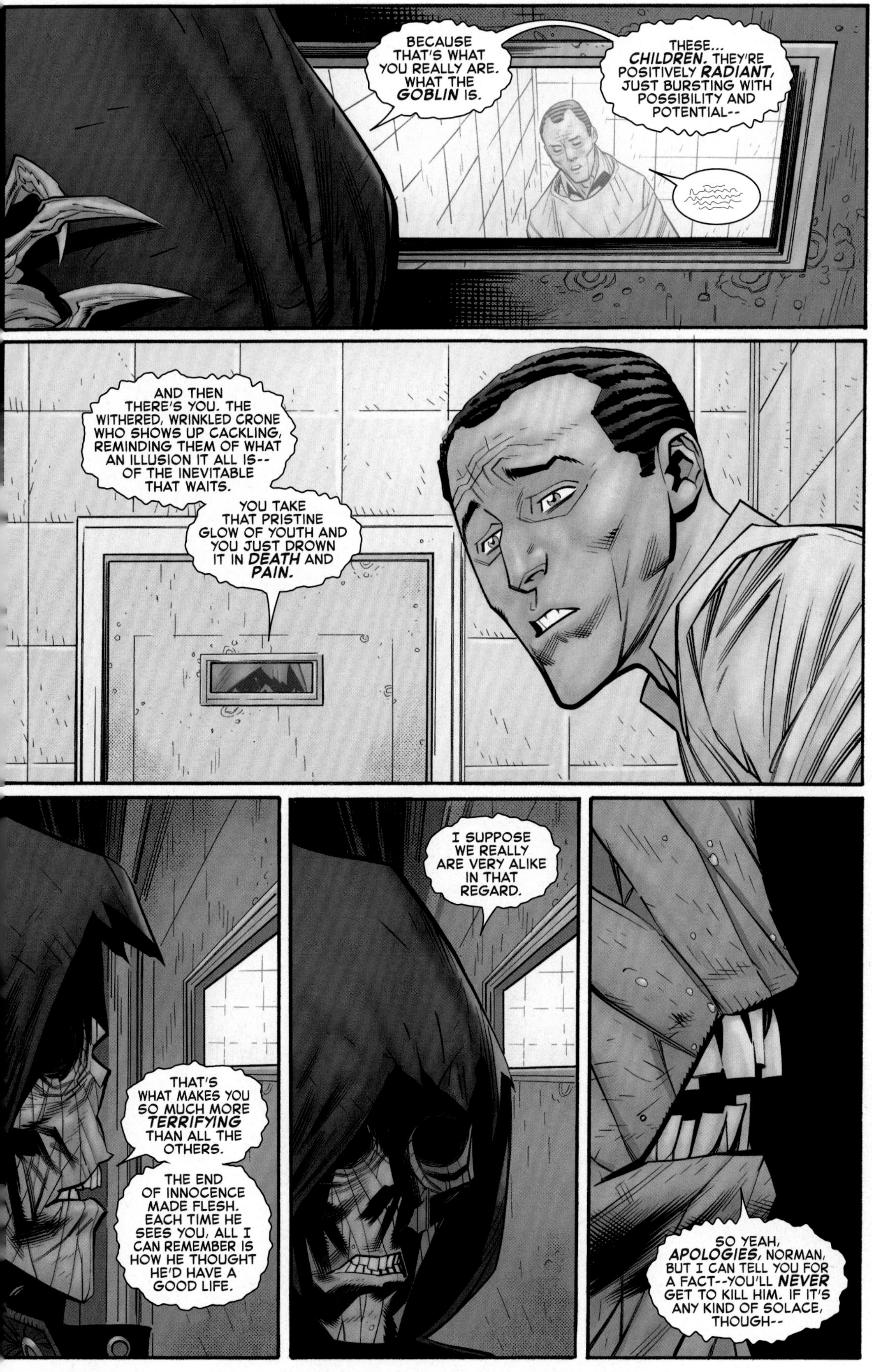
BECAUSE THAT'S WHAT YOU REALLY ARE. WHAT THE GOBLIN IS.
THESE... CHILDREN. THEY'RE POSITIVELY RADIANT, JUST BURSTING WITH POSSIBILITY AND POTENTIAL--
AND THEN THERE'S YOU. THE WITHERED, WRINKLED CRONE WHO SHOWS UP CACKLING, REMINDING THEM OF WHAT AN ILLUSION IT ALL IS-- OF THE INEVITABLE THAT WAITS.
YOU TAKE THAT PRISTINE GLOW OF YOUTH AND YOU JUST DROWN IT IN DEATH AND PAIN.
THAT'S WHAT MAKES YOU SO MUCH MORE TERRIFYING THAN ALL THE OTHERS.
THE END OF INNOCENCE MADE FLESH. EACH TIME HE SEES YOU, ALL I CAN REMEMBER IS HOW HE THOUGHT HE'D HAVE A GOOD LIFE.
I SUPPOSE WE REALLY ARE VERY ALIKE IN THAT REGARD.
SO YEAH, APOLOGIES, NORMAN, BUT I CAN TELL YOU FOR A FACT--YOU'LL NEVER GET TO KILL HIM. IF IT'S ANY KIND OF SOLACE, THOUGH--

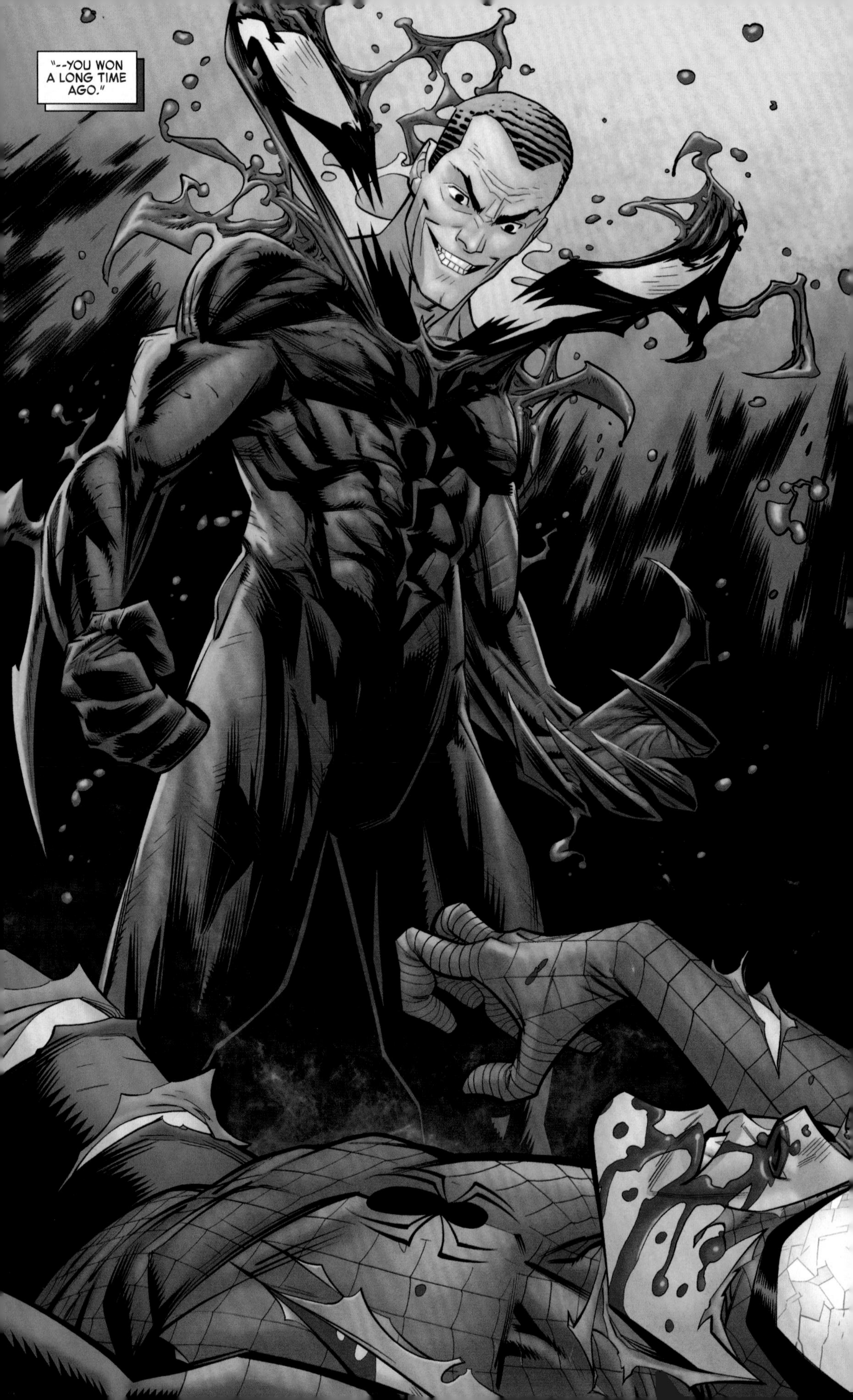
"--YOU WON A LONG TIME AGO."

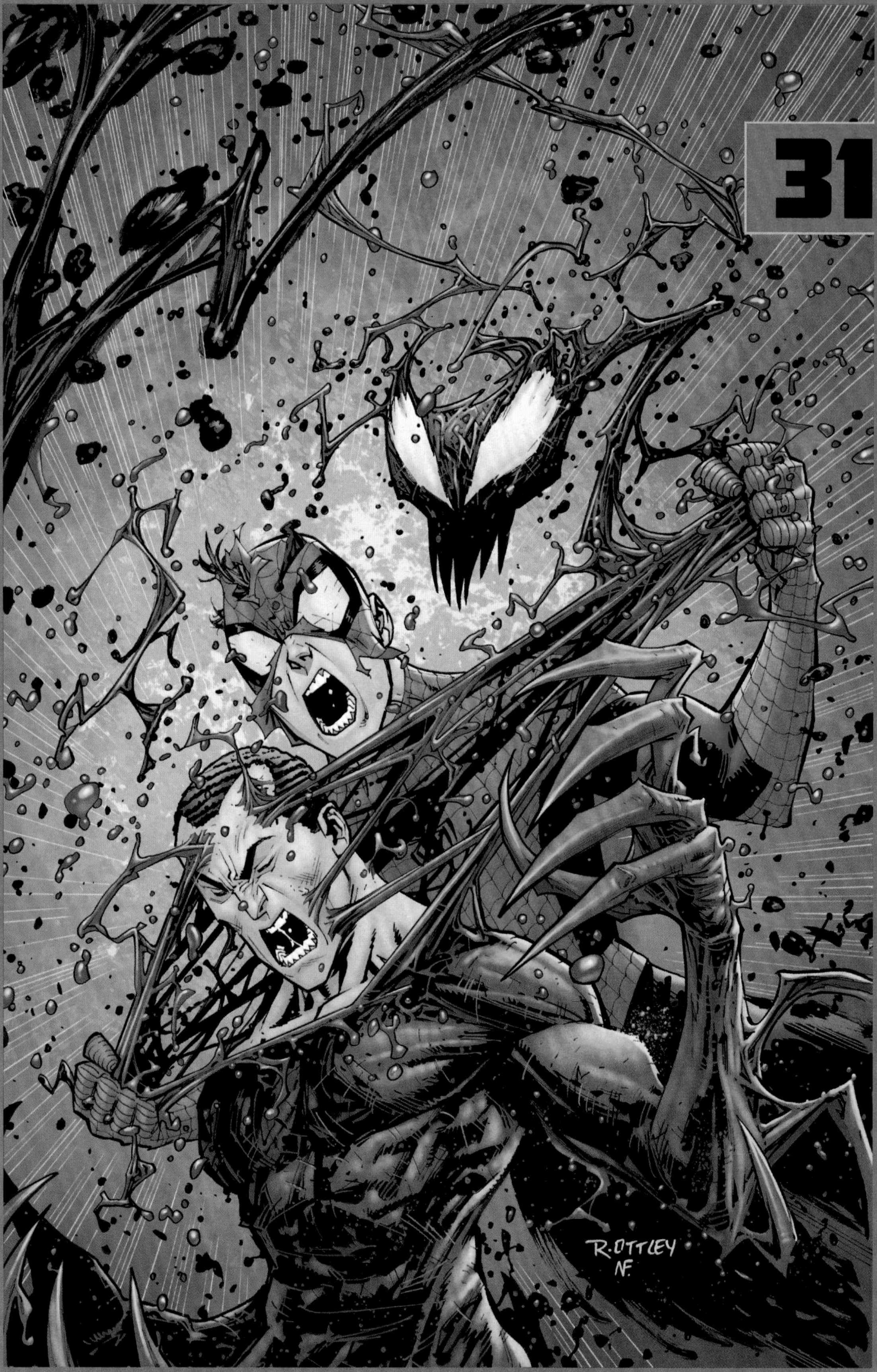
31
R. OTTLEY
NF.

ABSOLUTE CARNAGE PART 2

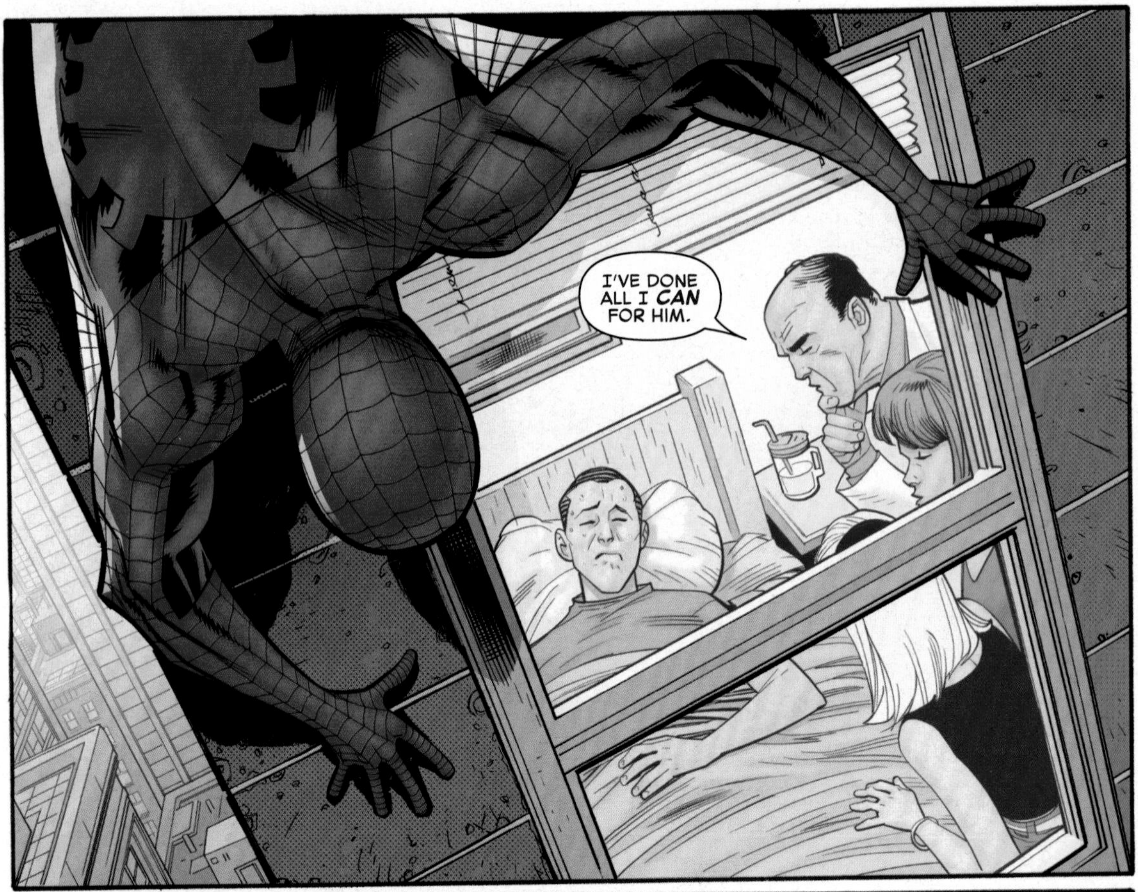
I'VE DONE ALL I CAN FOR HIM.

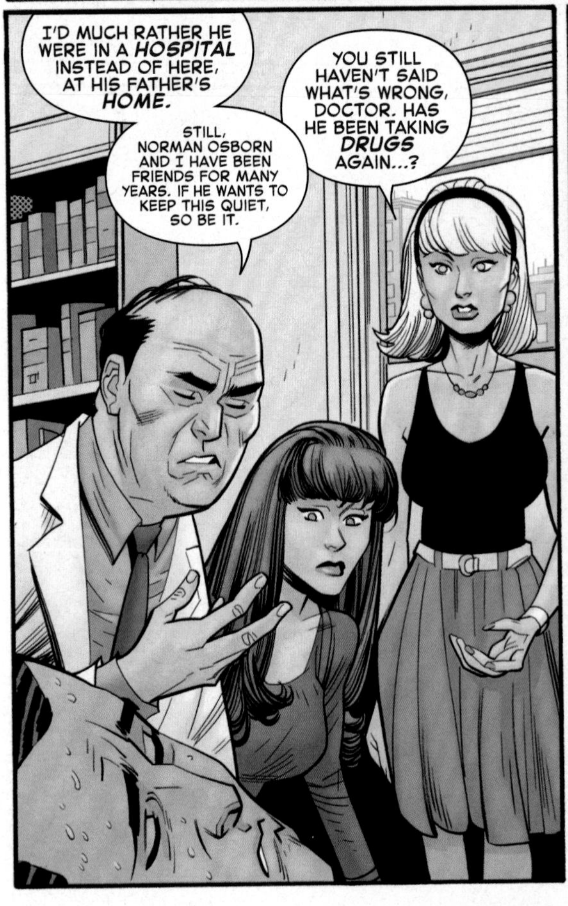
I'D MUCH RATHER HE WERE IN A HOSPITAL INSTEAD OF HERE, AT HIS FATHER'S HOME.
STILL, NORMAN OSBORN AND I HAVE BEEN FRIENDS FOR MANY YEARS. IF HE WANTS TO KEEP THIS QUIET, SO BE IT.
YOU STILL HAVEN'T SAID WHAT'S WRONG, DOCTOR. HAS HE BEEN TAKING DRUGS AGAIN...?

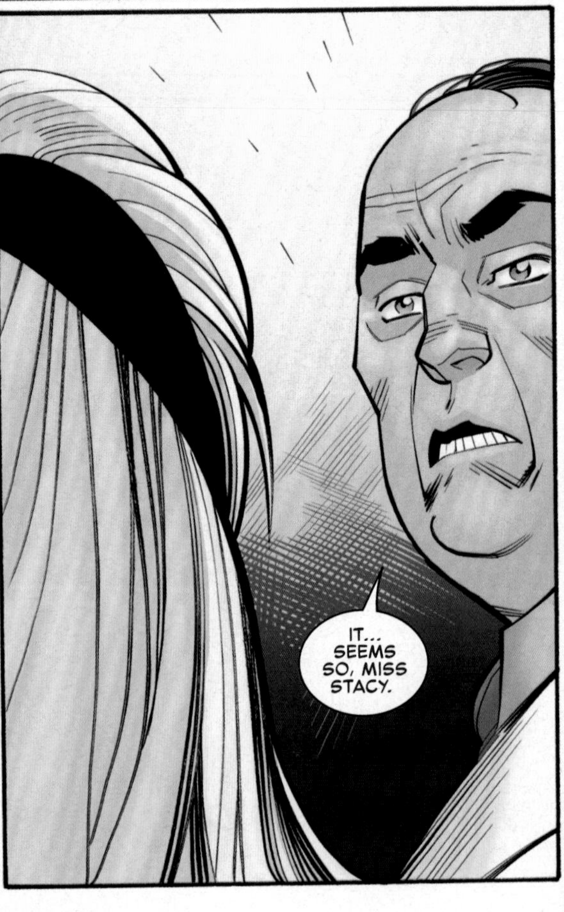
IT... SEEMS SO, MISS STACY.

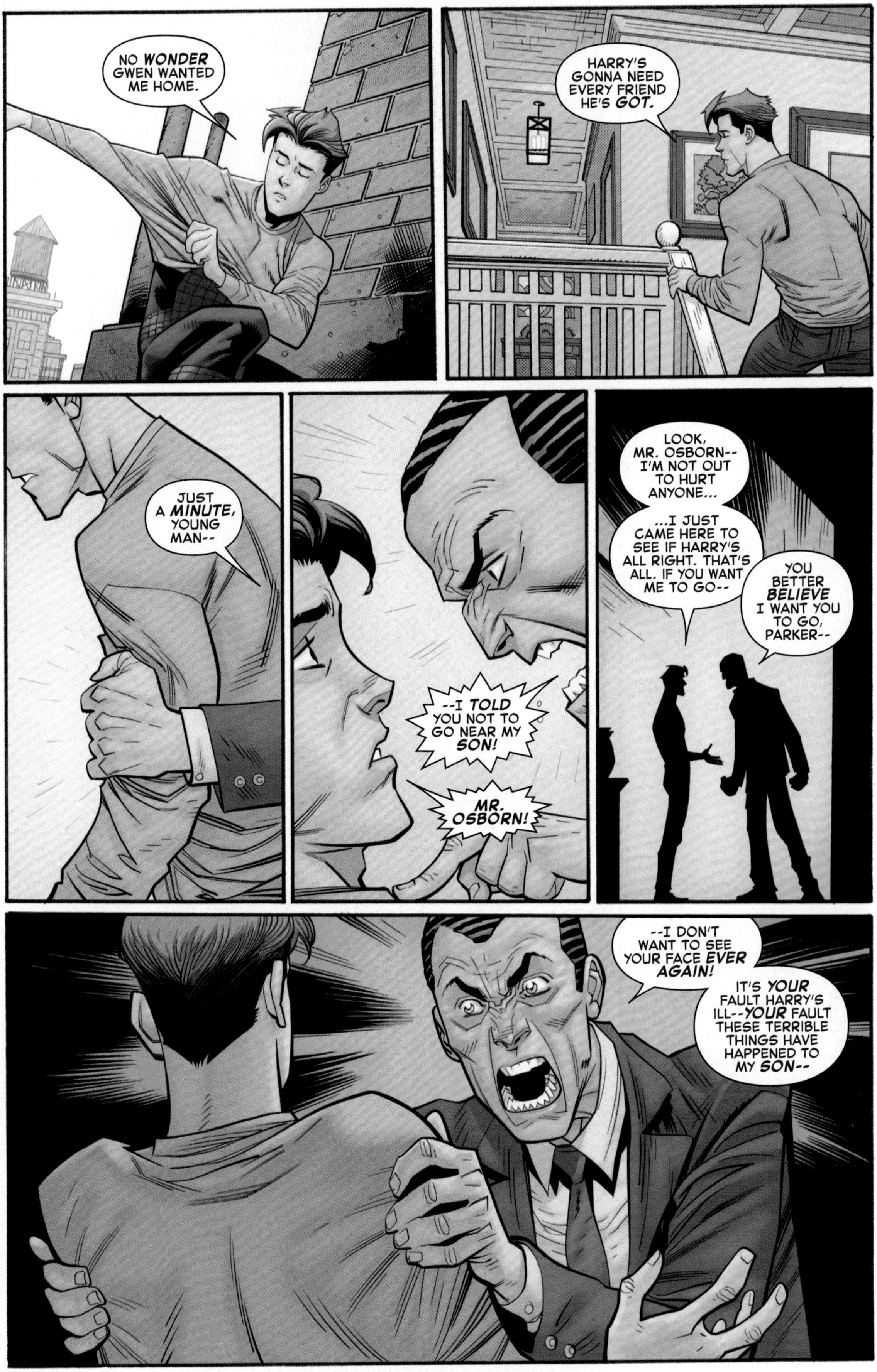
NO WONDER GWEN WANTED ME HOME.
HARRY'S GONNA NEED EVERY FRIEND HE'S GOT.
JUST A MINUTE, YOUNG MAN--
--I TOLD YOU NOT TO GO NEAR MY SON!
MR. OSBORN!
LOOK, MR. OSBORN-- I'M NOT OUT TO HURT ANYONE...
...I JUST CAME HERE TO SEE IF HARRY'S ALL RIGHT. THAT'S ALL. IF YOU WANT ME TO GO--
YOU BETTER BELIEVE I WANT YOU TO GO, PARKER--
--I DON'T WANT TO SEE YOUR FACE EVER AGAIN!
IT'S YOUR FAULT HARRY'S ILL--YOUR FAULT THESE TERRIBLE THINGS HAVE HAPPENED TO MY SON--

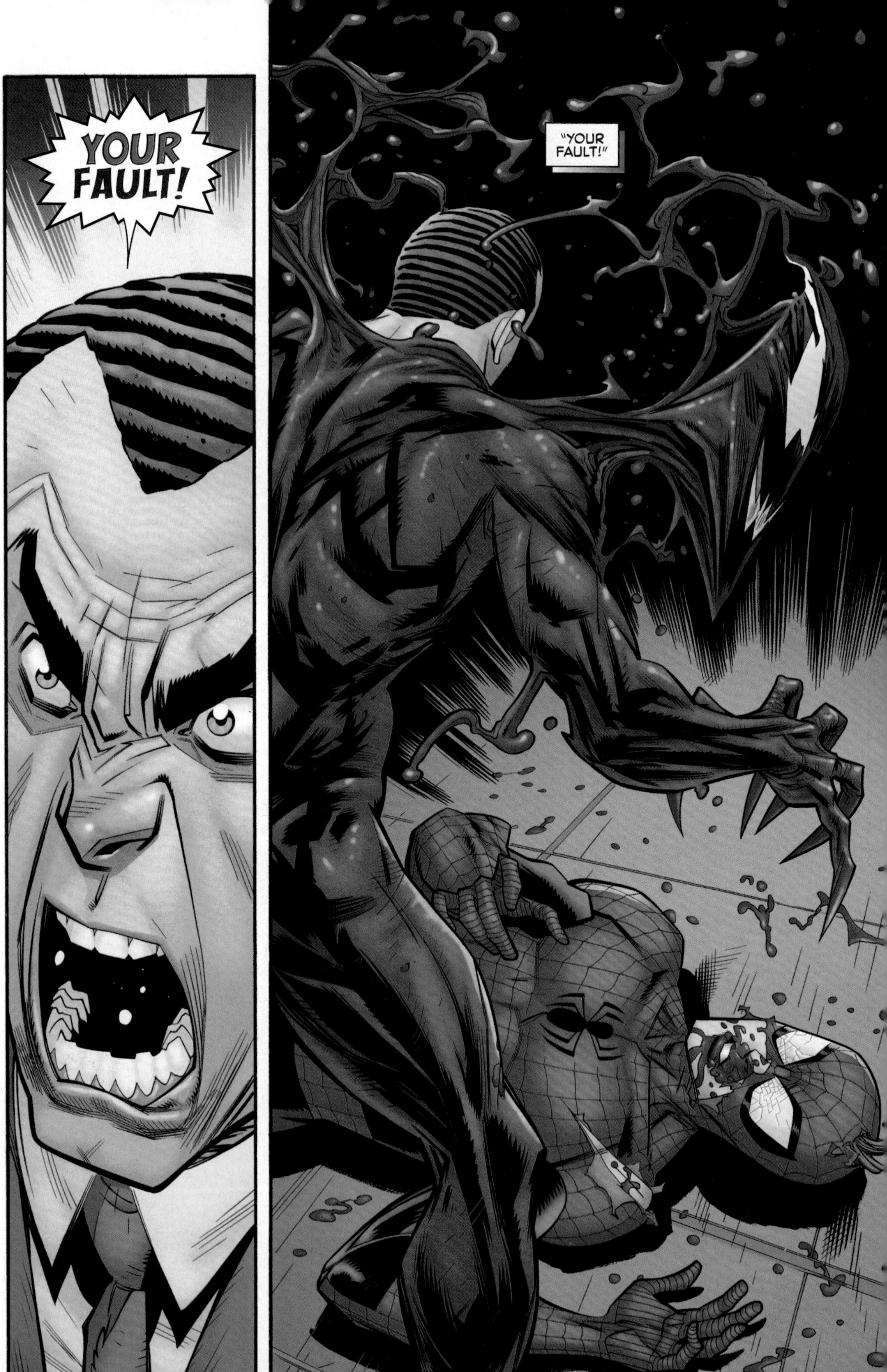
YOUR FAULT!
"YOUR FAULT!"
AND I'M SURE HE AGREES.

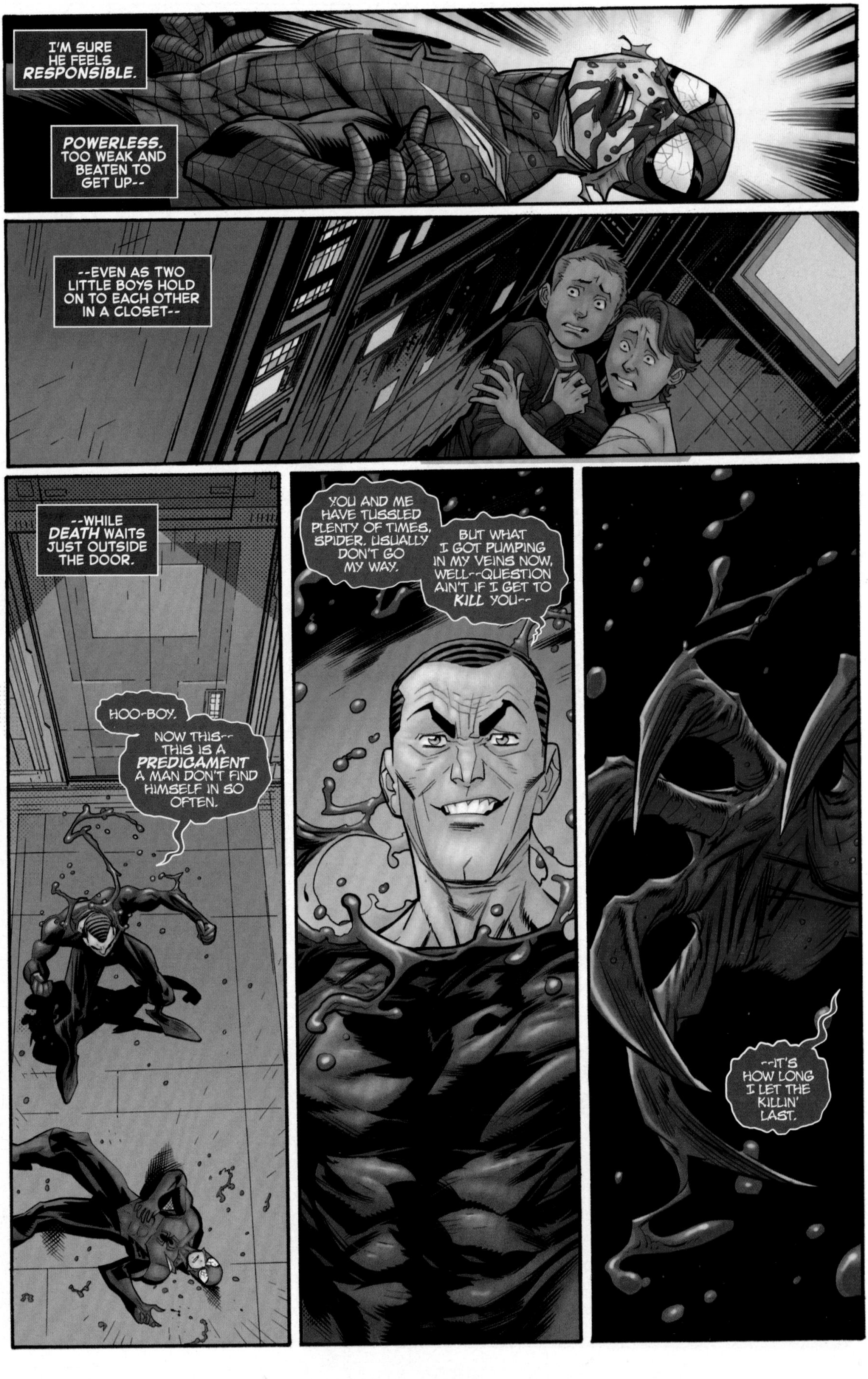
I'M SURE HE FEELS RESPONSIBLE.
POWERLESS. TOO WEAK AND BEATEN TO GET UP--
--EVEN AS TWO LITTLE BOYS HOLD ON TO EACH OTHER IN A CLOSET--
--WHILE DEATH WAITS JUST OUTSIDE THE DOOR.
HOO-BOY.
NOW THIS-- THIS IS A PREDICAMENT A MAN DON'T FIND HIMSELF IN SO OFTEN.
YOU AND ME HAVE TUSSLED PLENTY OF TIMES, SPIDER. USUALLY DON'T GO MY WAY.
BUT WHAT I GOT PUMPING IN MY VEINS NOW, WELL--QUESTION AIN'T IF I GET TO KILL YOU--
--IT'S HOW LONG I LET THE KILLIN' LAST.

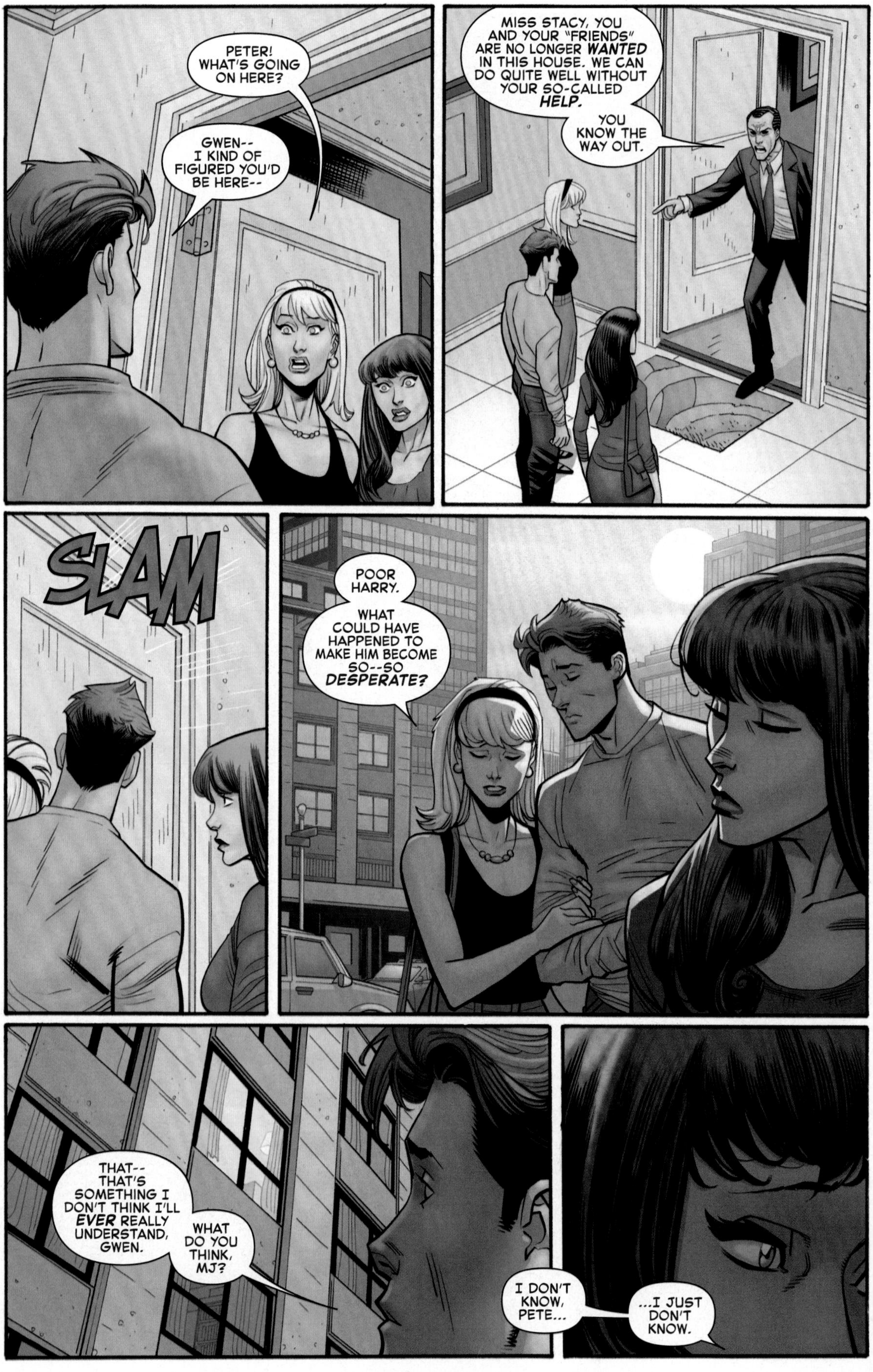
PETER! WHAT'S GOING ON HERE?
GWEN-- I KIND OF FIGURED YOU'D BE HERE--
MISS STACY, YOU AND YOUR "FRIENDS" ARE NO LONGER WANTED IN THIS HOUSE. WE CAN DO QUITE WELL WITHOUT YOUR SO-CALLED HELP.
YOU KNOW THE WAY OUT.
SLAM
POOR HARRY.
WHAT COULD HAVE HAPPENED TO MAKE HIM BECOME SO--SO DESPERATE?
THAT-- THAT'S SOMETHING I DON'T THINK I'LL EVER REALLY UNDERSTAND, GWEN.
WHAT DO YOU THINK, MJ?
I DON'T KNOW, PETE...
...I JUST DON'T KNOW.

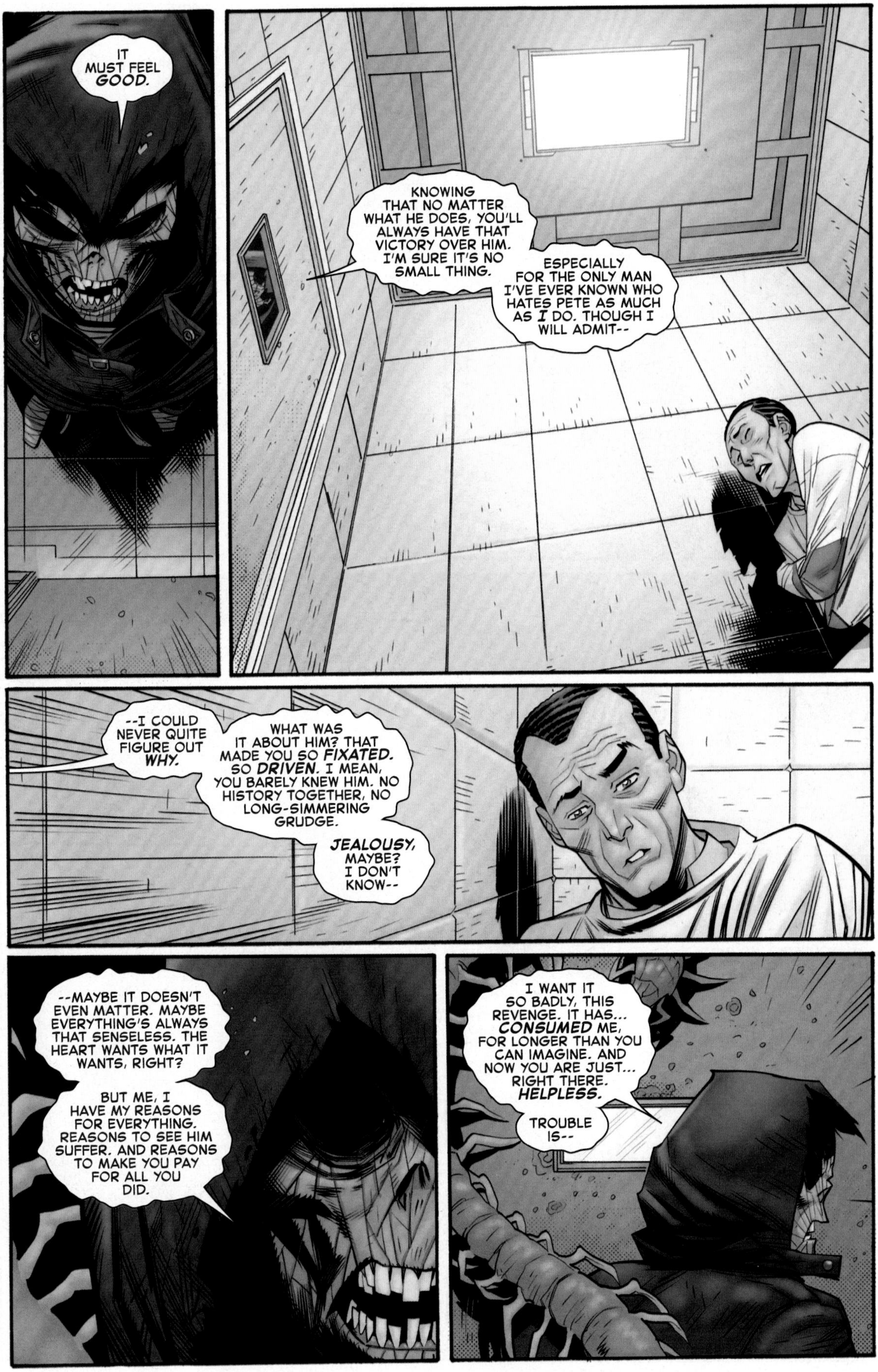
IT MUST FEEL GOOD.
KNOWING THAT NO MATTER WHAT HE DOES, YOU'LL ALWAYS HAVE THAT VICTORY OVER HIM. I'M SURE IT'S NO SMALL THING.
ESPECIALLY FOR THE ONLY MAN I'VE EVER KNOWN WHO HATES PETE AS MUCH AS I DO. THOUGH I WILL ADMIT--
--I COULD NEVER QUITE FIGURE OUT WHY.
WHAT WAS IT ABOUT HIM? THAT MADE YOU SO FIXATED. SO DRIVEN. I MEAN, YOU BARELY KNEW HIM. NO HISTORY TOGETHER, NO LONG-SIMMERING GRUDGE.
JEALOUSY, MAYBE? I DON'T KNOW--
--MAYBE IT DOESN'T EVEN MATTER. MAYBE EVERYTHING'S ALWAYS THAT SENSELESS. THE HEART WANTS WHAT IT WANTS, RIGHT?
BUT ME, I HAVE MY REASONS FOR EVERYTHING. REASONS TO SEE HIM SUFFER. AND REASONS TO MAKE YOU PAY FOR ALL YOU DID.
I WANT IT SO BADLY, THIS REVENGE. IT HAS... CONSUMED ME, FOR LONGER THAN YOU CAN IMAGINE. AND NOW YOU ARE JUST... RIGHT THERE. HELPLESS.
TROUBLE IS--

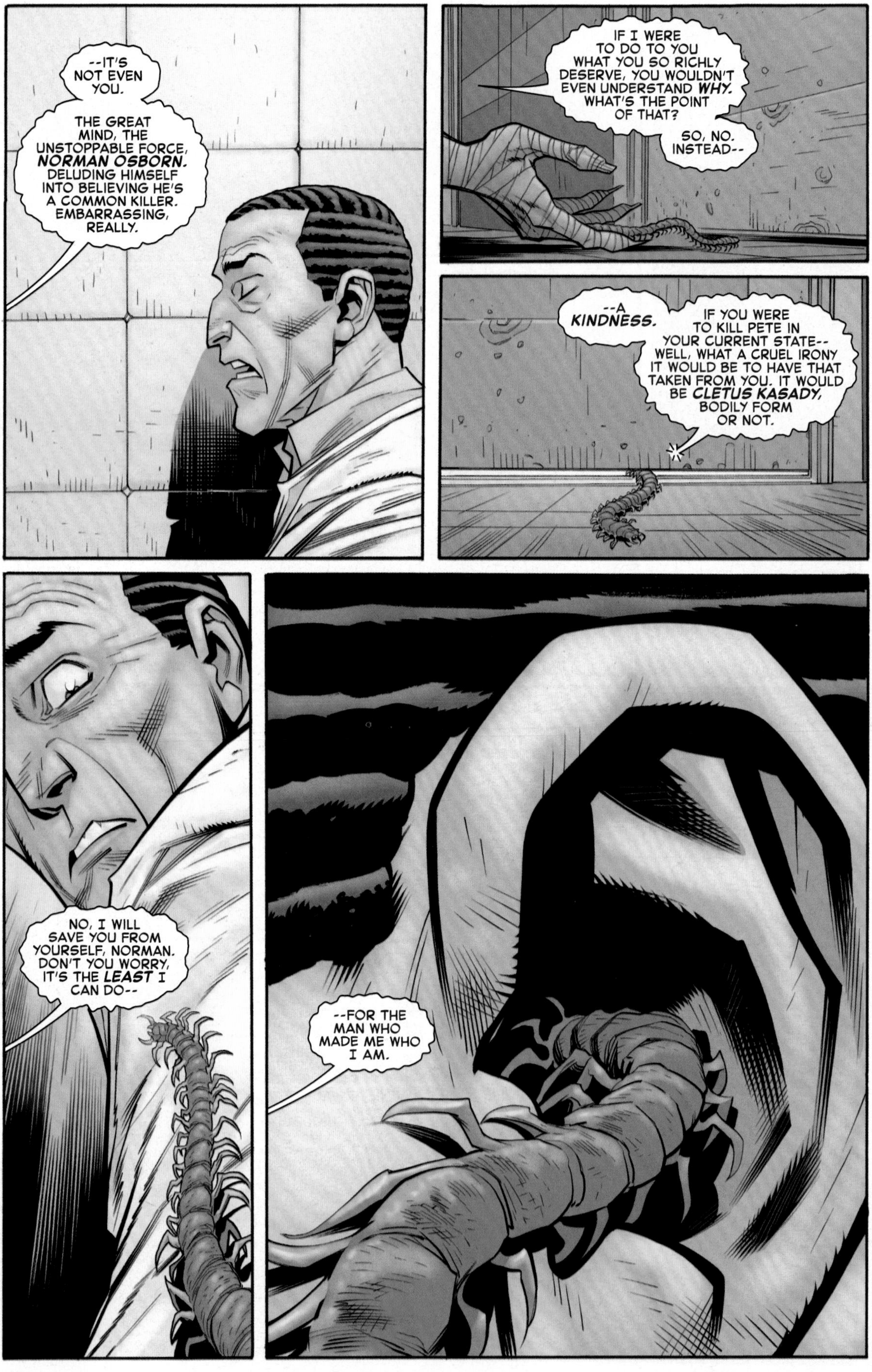
--IT'S NOT EVEN YOU.
THE GREAT MIND, THE UNSTOPPABLE FORCE, NORMAN OSBORN. DELUDING HIMSELF INTO BELIEVING HE'S A COMMON KILLER. EMBARRASSING, REALLY.
IF I WERE TO DO TO YOU WHAT YOU SO RICHLY DESERVE, YOU WOULDN'T EVEN UNDERSTAND WHY. WHAT'S THE POINT OF THAT?
SO, NO. INSTEAD--
--A KINDNESS.
IF YOU WERE TO KILL PETE IN YOUR CURRENT STATE-- WELL, WHAT A CRUEL IRONY IT WOULD BE TO HAVE THAT TAKEN FROM YOU. IT WOULD BE CLETUS KASADY, BODILY FORM OR NOT.
NO, I WILL SAVE YOU FROM YOURSELF, NORMAN. DON'T YOU WORRY, IT'S THE LEAST I CAN DO--
--FOR THE MAN WHO MADE ME WHO I AM.

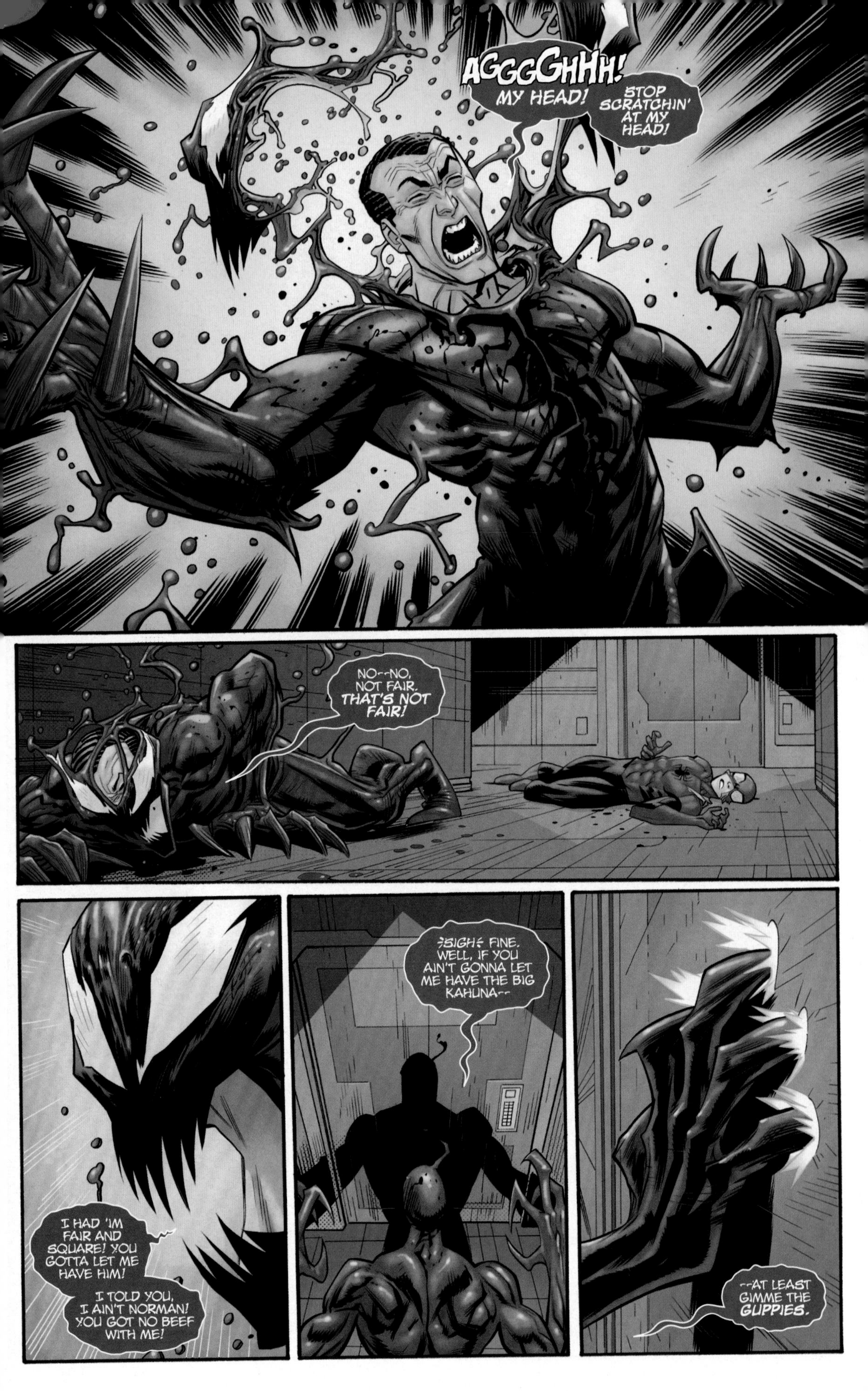
AGGGGHHH! MY HEAD!
STOP SCRATCHIN' AT MY HEAD!
NO--NO, NOT FAIR. THAT'S NOT FAIR!
I HAD 'IM FAIR AND SQUARE! YOU GOTTA LET ME HAVE HIM!
I TOLD YOU, I AIN'T NORMAN! YOU GOT NO BEEF WITH ME!
SIGH FINE. WELL, IF YOU AIN'T GONNA LET ME HAVE THE BIG KAHUNA--
--AT LEAST GIMME THE GUPPIES.

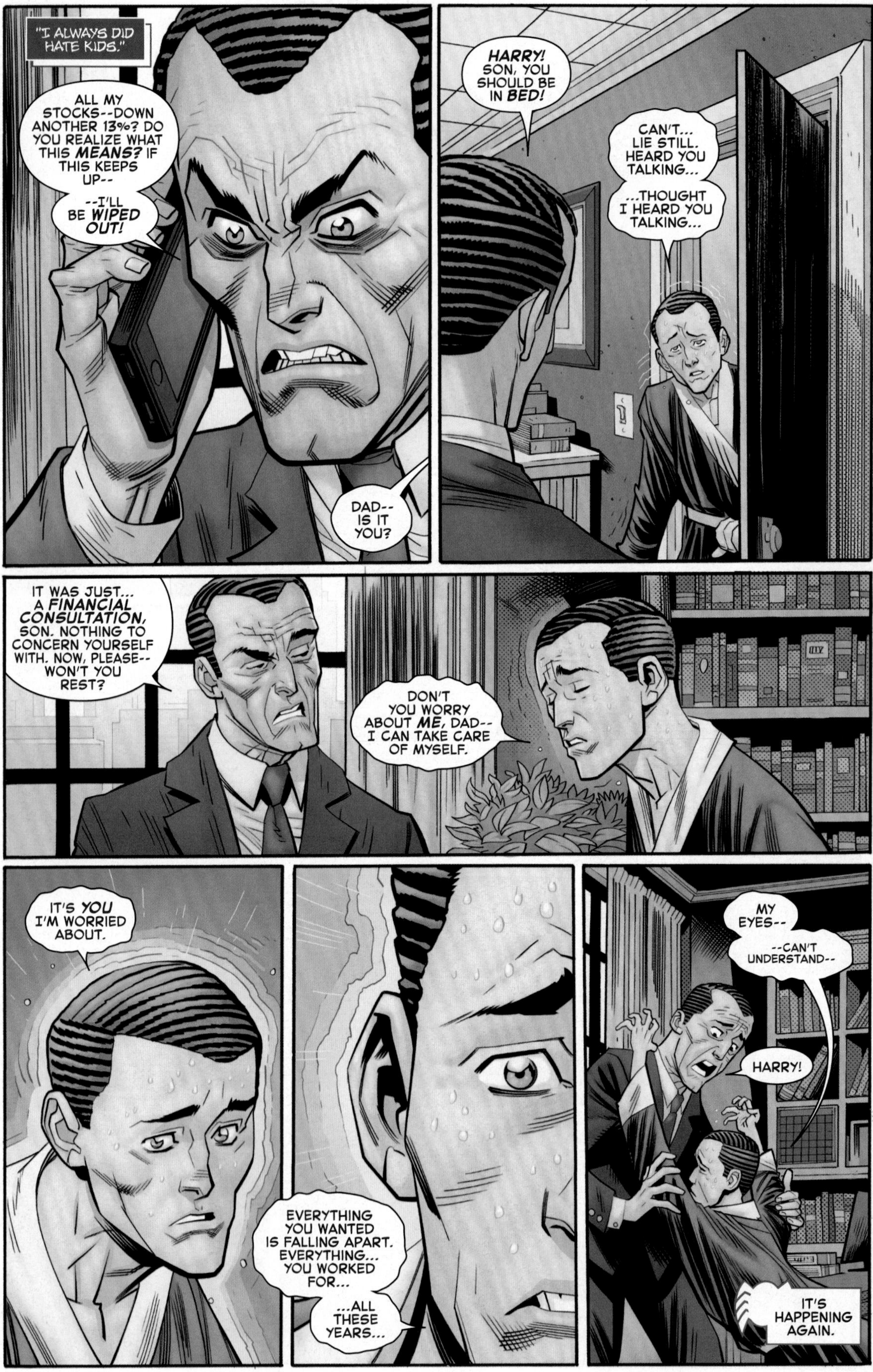
"I ALWAYS DID HATE KIDS."
ALL MY STOCKS--DOWN ANOTHER 13%? DO YOU REALIZE WHAT THIS MEANS? IF THIS KEEPS UP--
--I'LL BE WIPED OUT!
DAD-- IS IT YOU?
HARRY! SON, YOU SHOULD BE IN BED!
CAN'T... LIE STILL. HEARD YOU TALKING...
...THOUGHT I HEARD YOU TALKING...
IT WAS JUST... A FINANCIAL CONSULTATION, SON. NOTHING TO CONCERN YOURSELF WITH. NOW, PLEASE-- WON'T YOU REST?
DON'T YOU WORRY ABOUT ME, DAD-- I CAN TAKE CARE OF MYSELF.
IT'S YOU I'M WORRIED ABOUT.
EVERYTHING YOU WANTED IS FALLING APART. EVERYTHING... YOU WORKED FOR...
...ALL THESE YEARS...
MY EYES--
--CAN'T UNDERSTAND--
HARRY!
IT'S HAPPENING AGAIN.

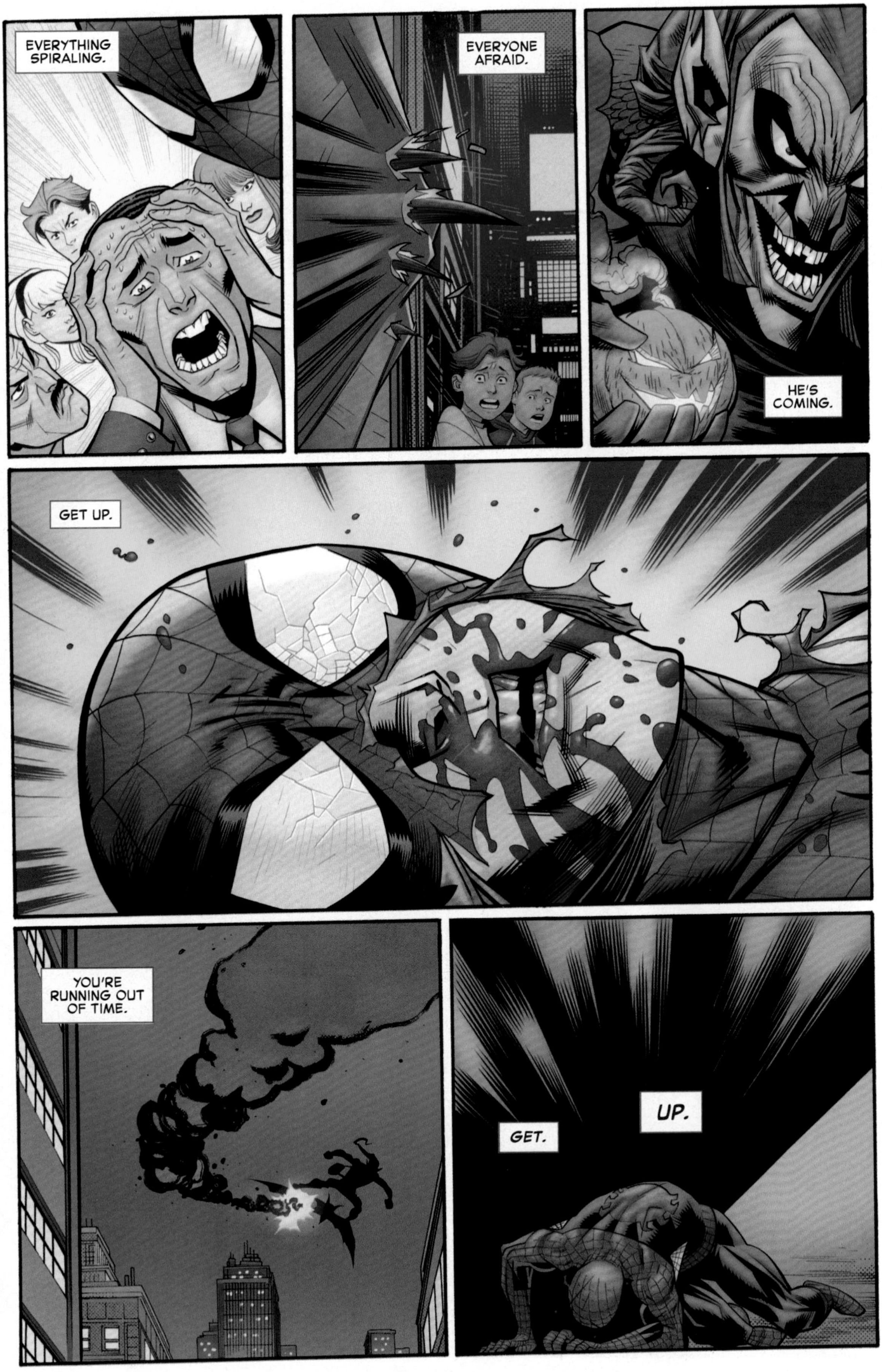
EVERYTHING SPIRALING.
EVERYONE AFRAID.
HE'S COMING.
GET UP.
YOU'RE RUNNING OUT OF TIME.
GET.
UP.

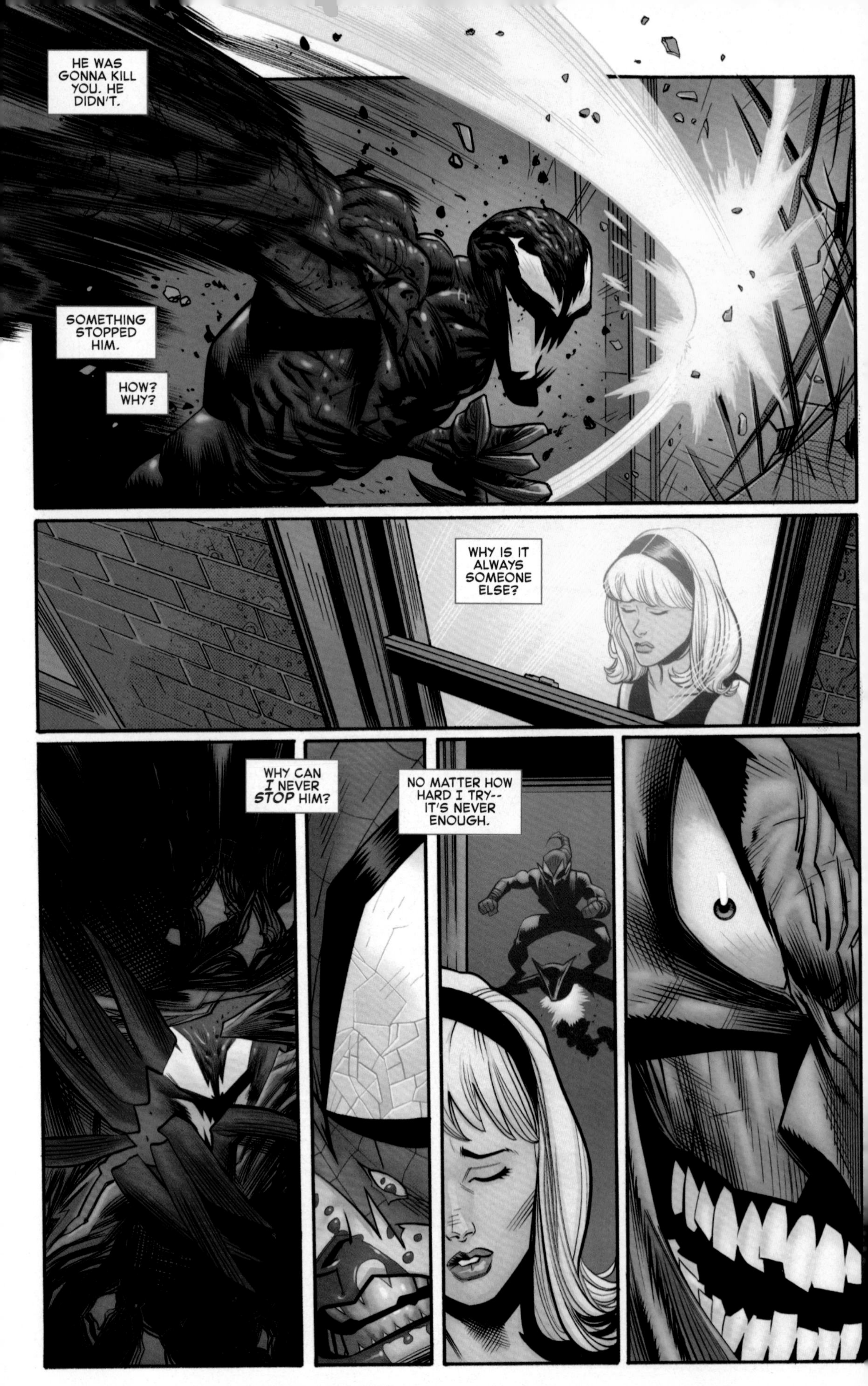
HE WAS GONNA KILL YOU. HE DIDN'T.
SOMETHING STOPPED HIM.
HOW? WHY?
WHY IS IT ALWAYS SOMEONE ELSE?
WHY CAN I NEVER STOP HIM?
NO MATTER HOW HARD I TRY-- IT'S NEVER ENOUGH.

THIS IS WHY.

THIS IS HOW YOU END UP HERE.

YOU WEREN'T ENOUGH.

YOU COULDN'T SAVE THEM.

SO THERE YOU WERE ON ANOTHER WORLD. AND THERE WAS THE MACHINE.

IF IT COULD MAKE YOU STRONGER... IF IT COULD MAKE YOU ENOUGH.

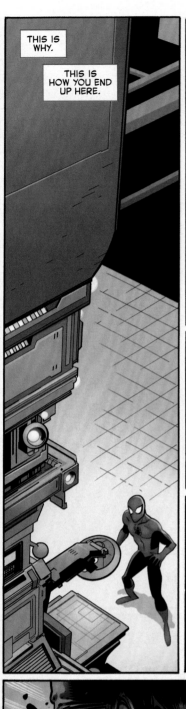

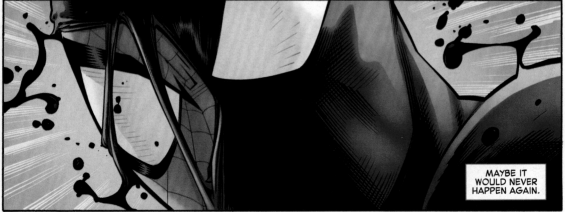

MAYBE IT WOULD NEVER HAPPEN AGAIN.

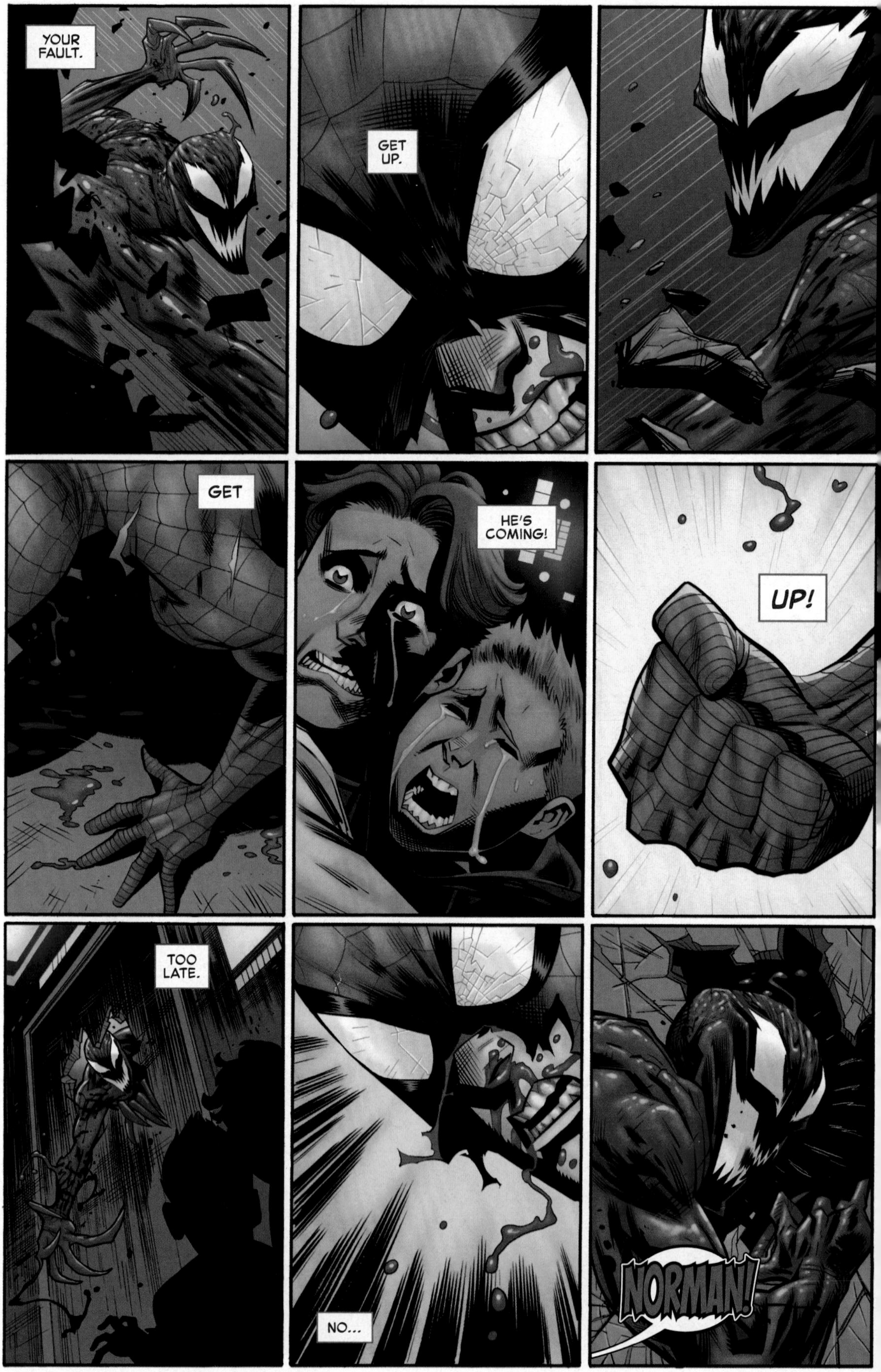

YOUR FAULT.
GET UP.
GET
HE'S COMING!
UP!
TOO LATE.
NO...
NORMAN!

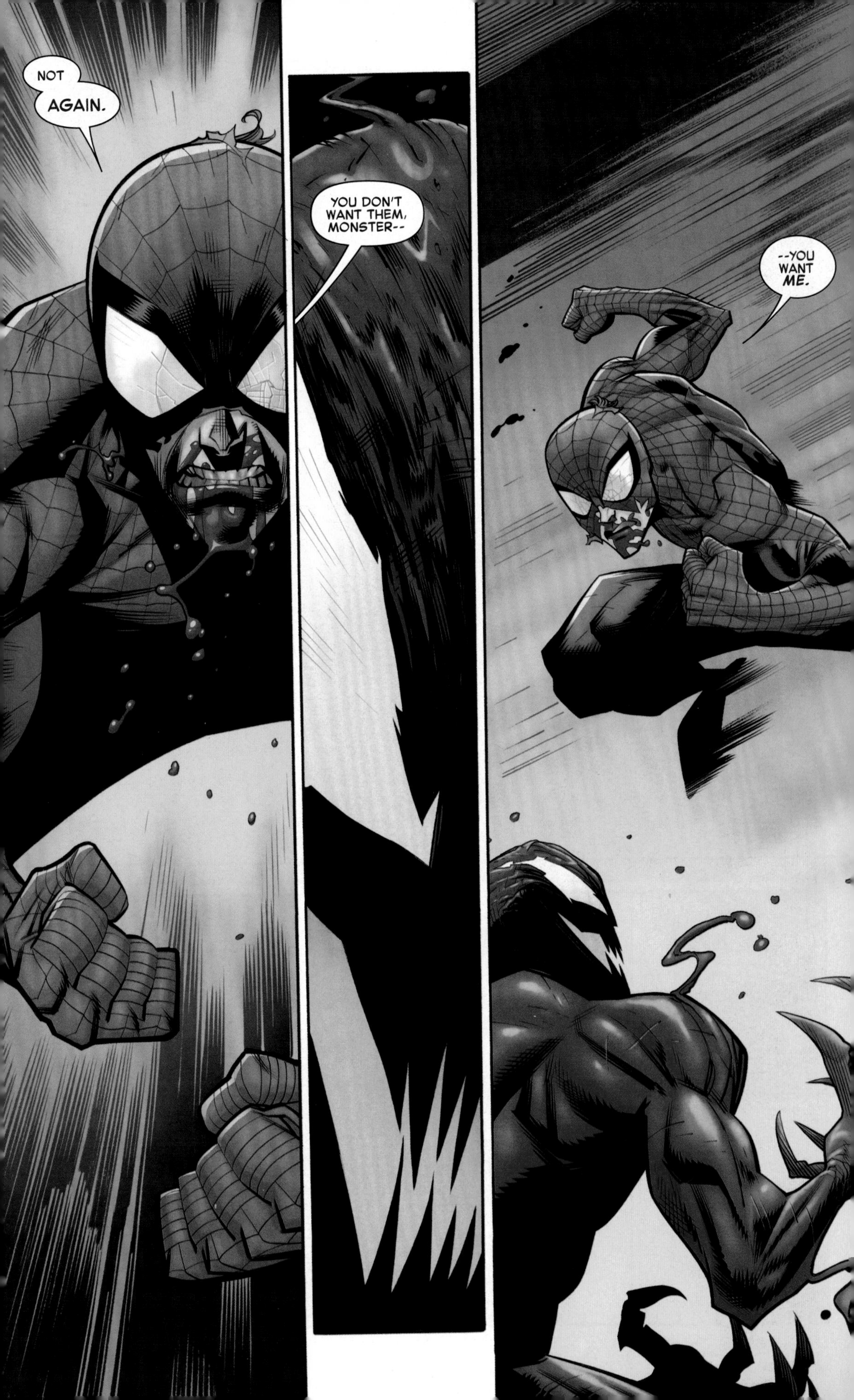
NOT AGAIN.
YOU DON'T WANT THEM, MONSTER--
--YOU WANT ME.

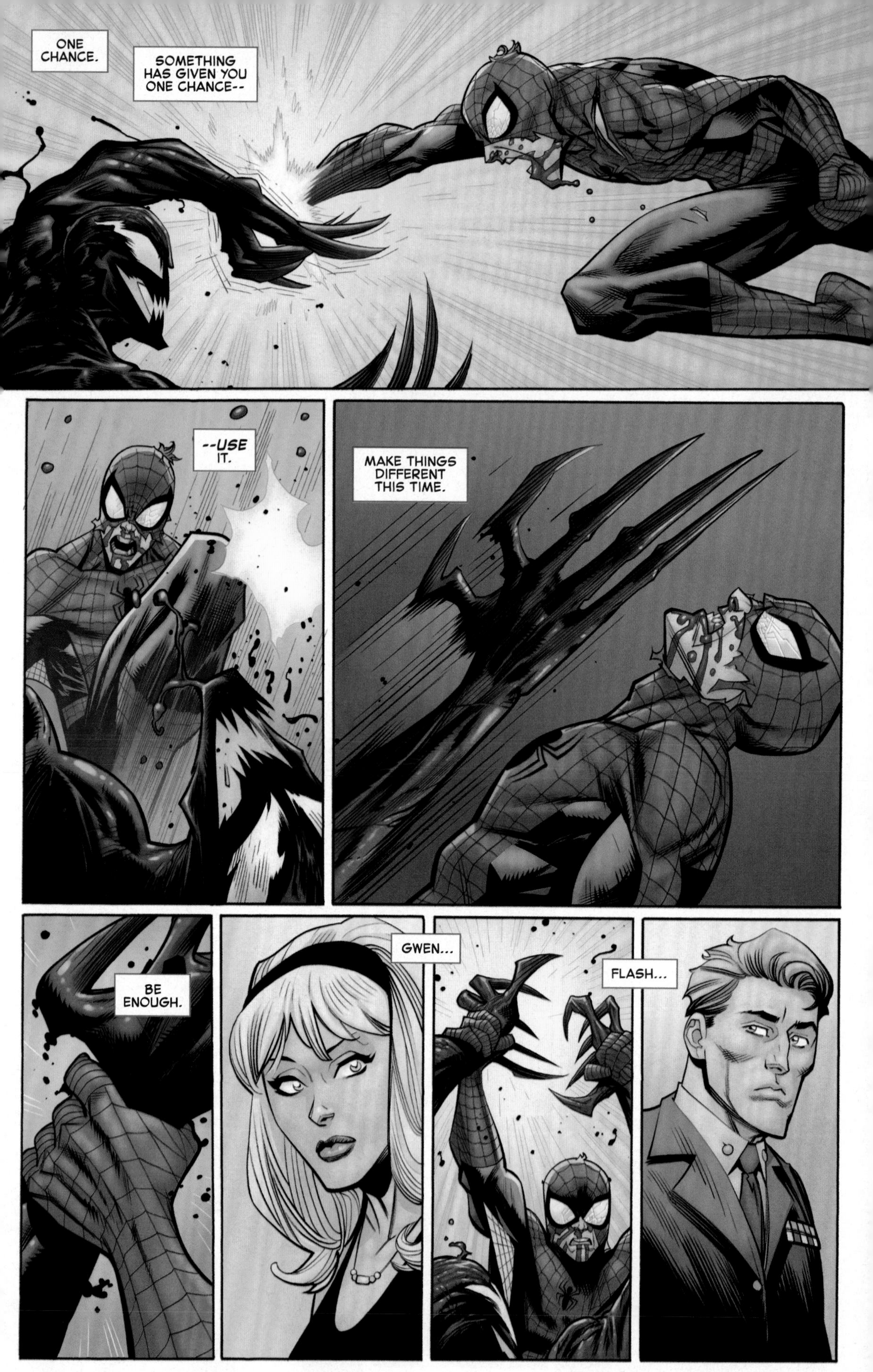
ONE CHANCE.
SOMETHING HAS GIVEN YOU ONE CHANCE--
--USE IT.
MAKE THINGS DIFFERENT THIS TIME.
BE ENOUGH.
GWEN...
FLASH...

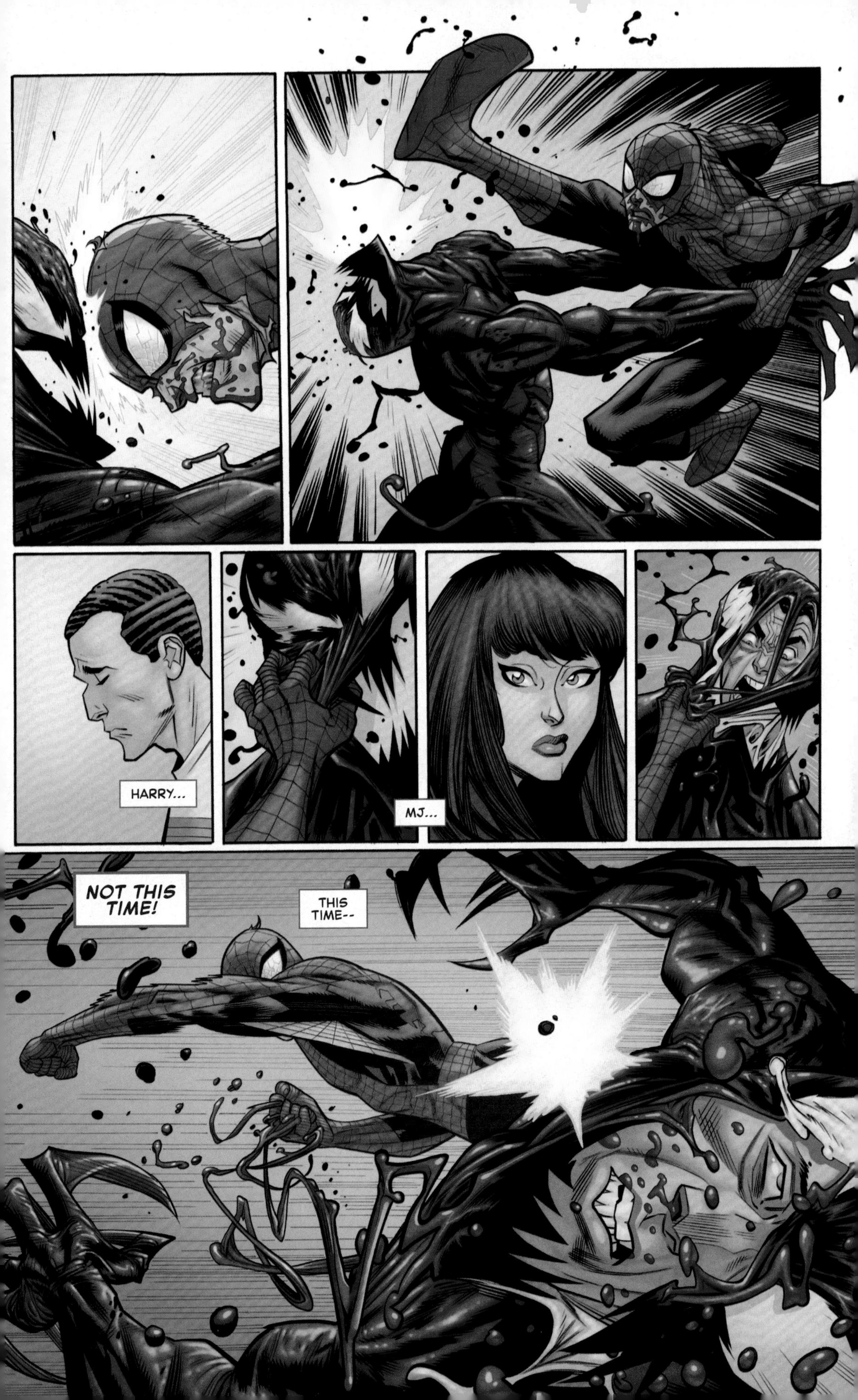
HARRY...
MJ...
NOT THIS TIME!
THIS TIME--

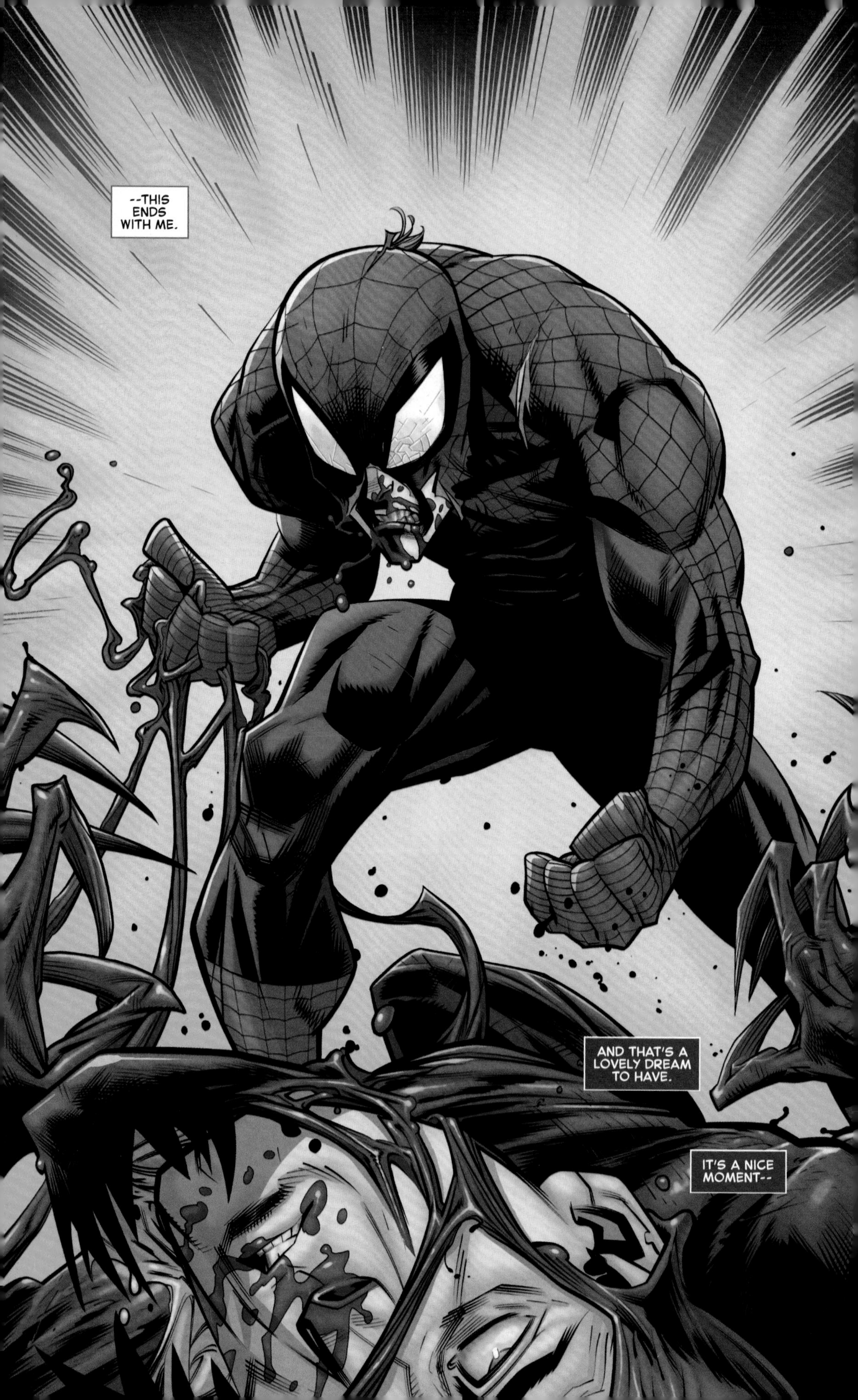
--THIS ENDS WITH ME.
AND THAT'S A LOVELY DREAM TO HAVE.
IT'S A NICE MOMENT--

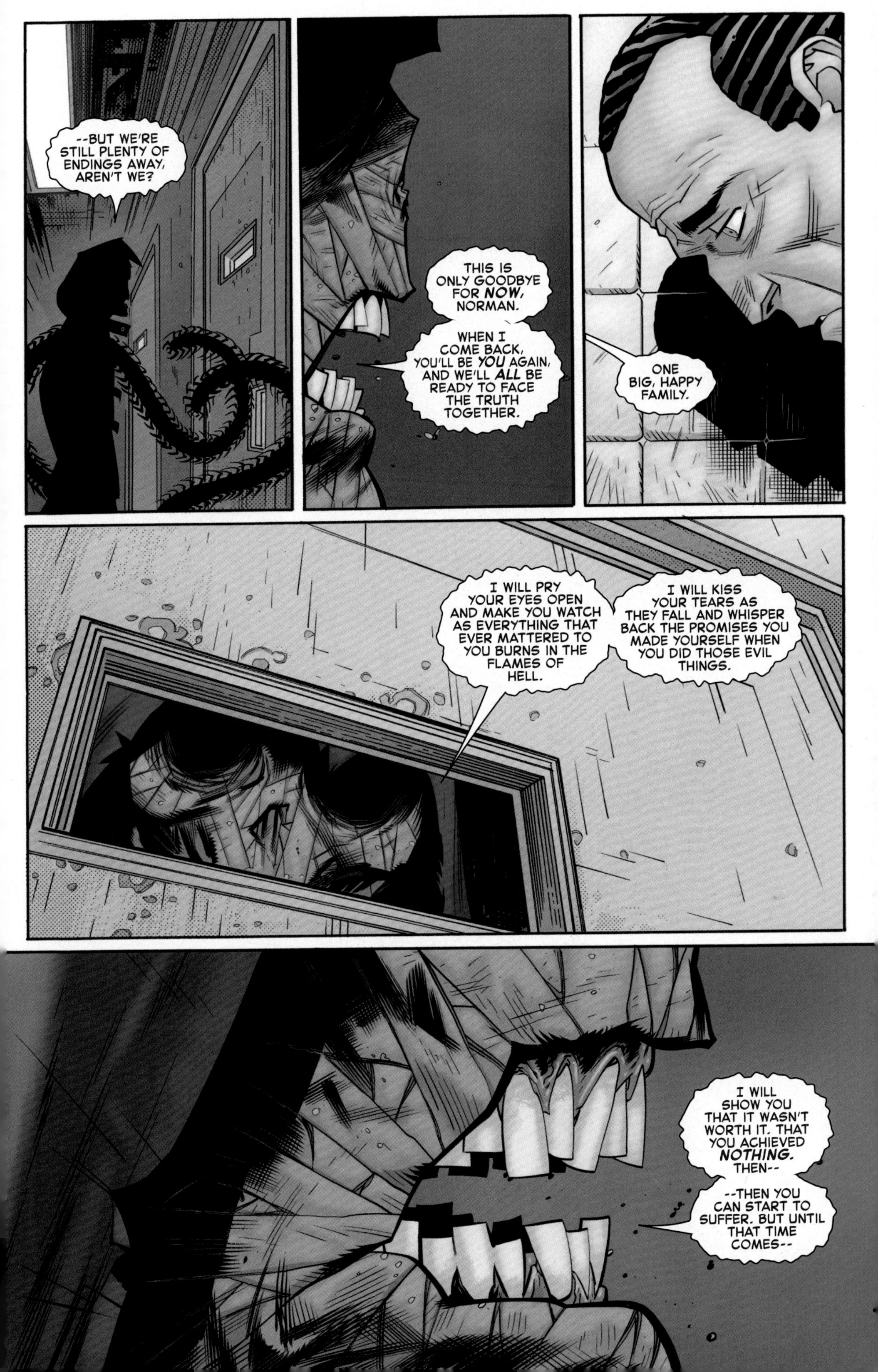
--BUT WE'RE STILL PLENTY OF ENDINGS AWAY, AREN'T WE?
THIS IS ONLY GOODBYE FOR NOW, NORMAN.
WHEN I COME BACK, YOU'LL BE YOU AGAIN, AND WE'LL ALL BE READY TO FACE THE TRUTH TOGETHER.
ONE BIG, HAPPY FAMILY.
I WILL PRY YOUR EYES OPEN AND MAKE YOU WATCH AS EVERYTHING THAT EVER MATTERED TO YOU BURNS IN THE FLAMES OF HELL.
I WILL KISS YOUR TEARS AS THEY FALL AND WHISPER BACK THE PROMISES YOU MADE YOURSELF WHEN YOU DID THOSE EVIL THINGS.
I WILL SHOW YOU THAT IT WASN'T WORTH IT. THAT YOU ACHIEVED NOTHING. THEN--
--THEN YOU CAN START TO SUFFER. BUT UNTIL THAT TIME COMES--

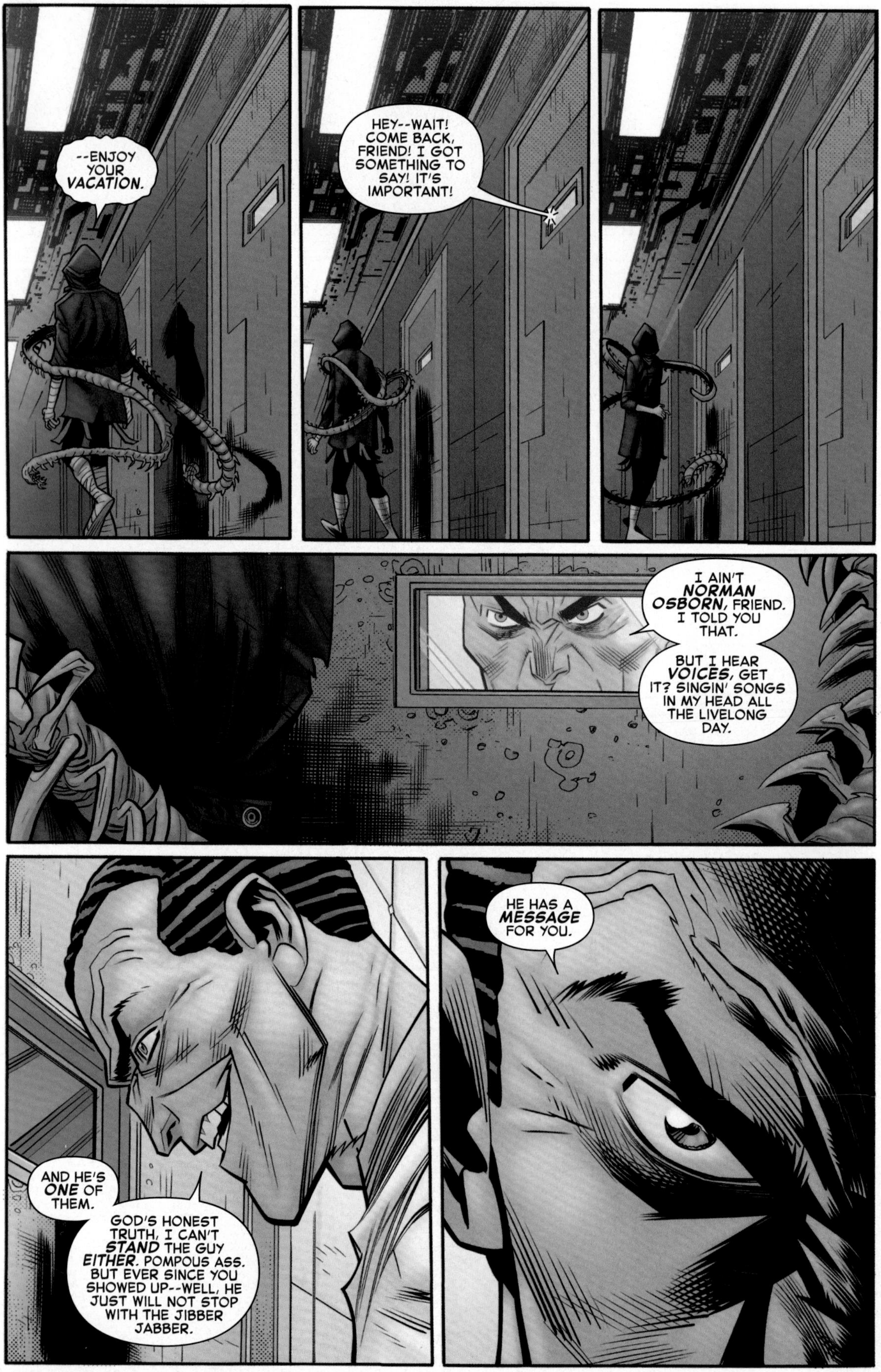
--ENJOY YOUR VACATION.
HEY--WAIT! COME BACK, FRIEND! I GOT SOMETHING TO SAY! IT'S IMPORTANT!
I AIN'T NORMAN OSBORN, FRIEND. I TOLD YOU THAT.
BUT I HEAR VOICES, GET IT? SINGIN' SONGS IN MY HEAD ALL THE LIVELONG DAY.
AND HE'S ONE OF THEM.
GOD'S HONEST TRUTH, I CAN'T STAND THE GUY EITHER. POMPOUS ASS. BUT EVER SINCE YOU SHOWED UP--WELL, HE JUST WILL NOT STOP WITH THE JIBBER JABBER.
HE HAS A MESSAGE FOR YOU.

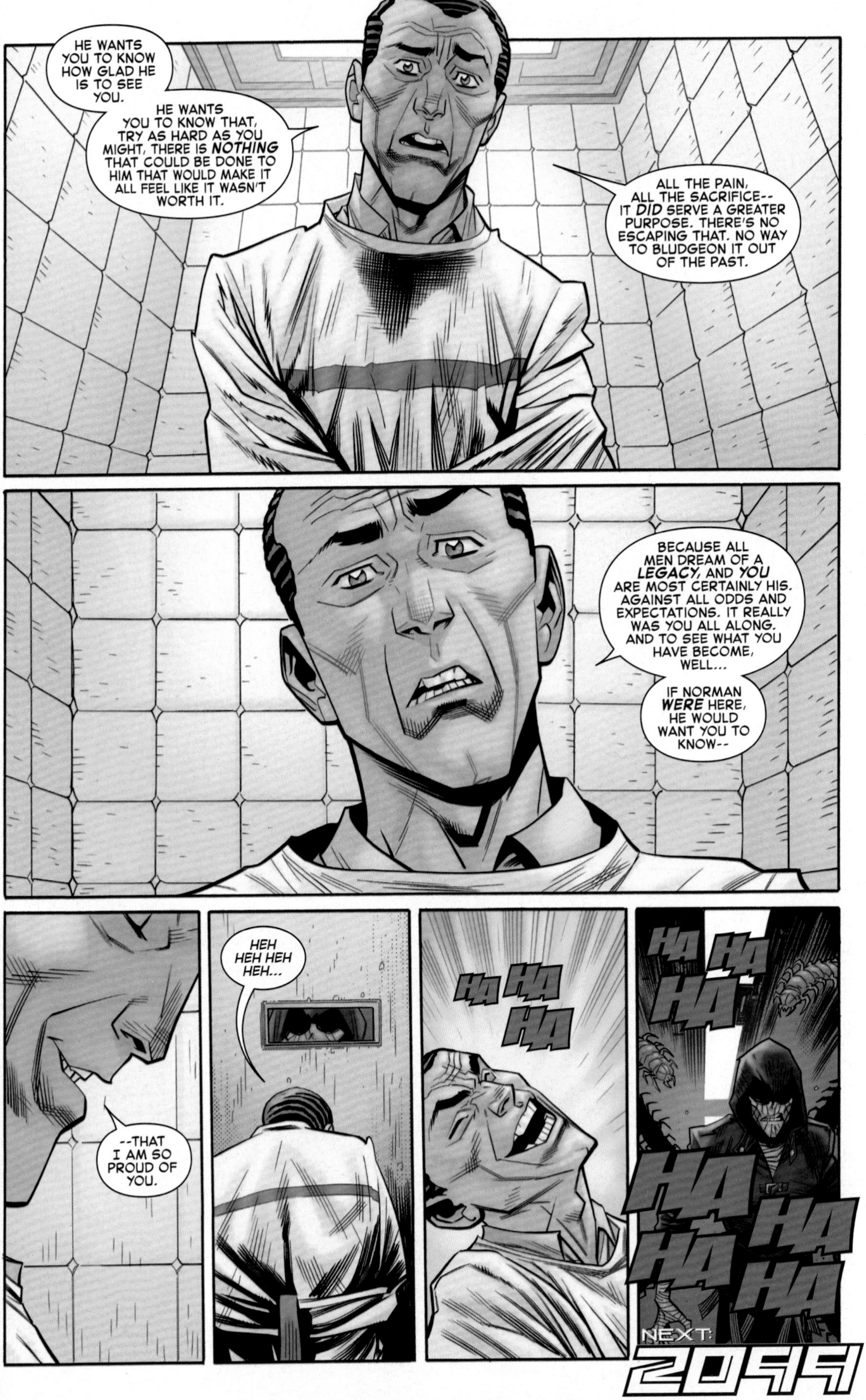

HE WANTS YOU TO KNOW HOW GLAD HE IS TO SEE YOU.
HE WANTS YOU TO KNOW THAT, TRY AS HARD AS YOU MIGHT, THERE IS NOTHING THAT COULD BE DONE TO HIM THAT WOULD MAKE IT ALL FEEL LIKE IT WASN'T WORTH IT.
ALL THE PAIN, ALL THE SACRIFICE-- IT DID SERVE A GREATER PURPOSE. THERE'S NO ESCAPING THAT. NO WAY TO BLUDGEON IT OUT OF THE PAST.
BECAUSE ALL MEN DREAM OF A LEGACY, AND YOU ARE MOST CERTAINLY HIS. AGAINST ALL ODDS AND EXPECTATIONS. IT REALLY WAS YOU ALL ALONG. AND TO SEE WHAT YOU HAVE BECOME, WELL...
IF NORMAN WERE HERE, HE WOULD WANT YOU TO KNOW--
--THAT I AM SO PROUD OF YOU.
HEH HEH HEH HEH...
HA HA HA
HA HA HA
HA HA HA HA HA HA
NEXT:
2099

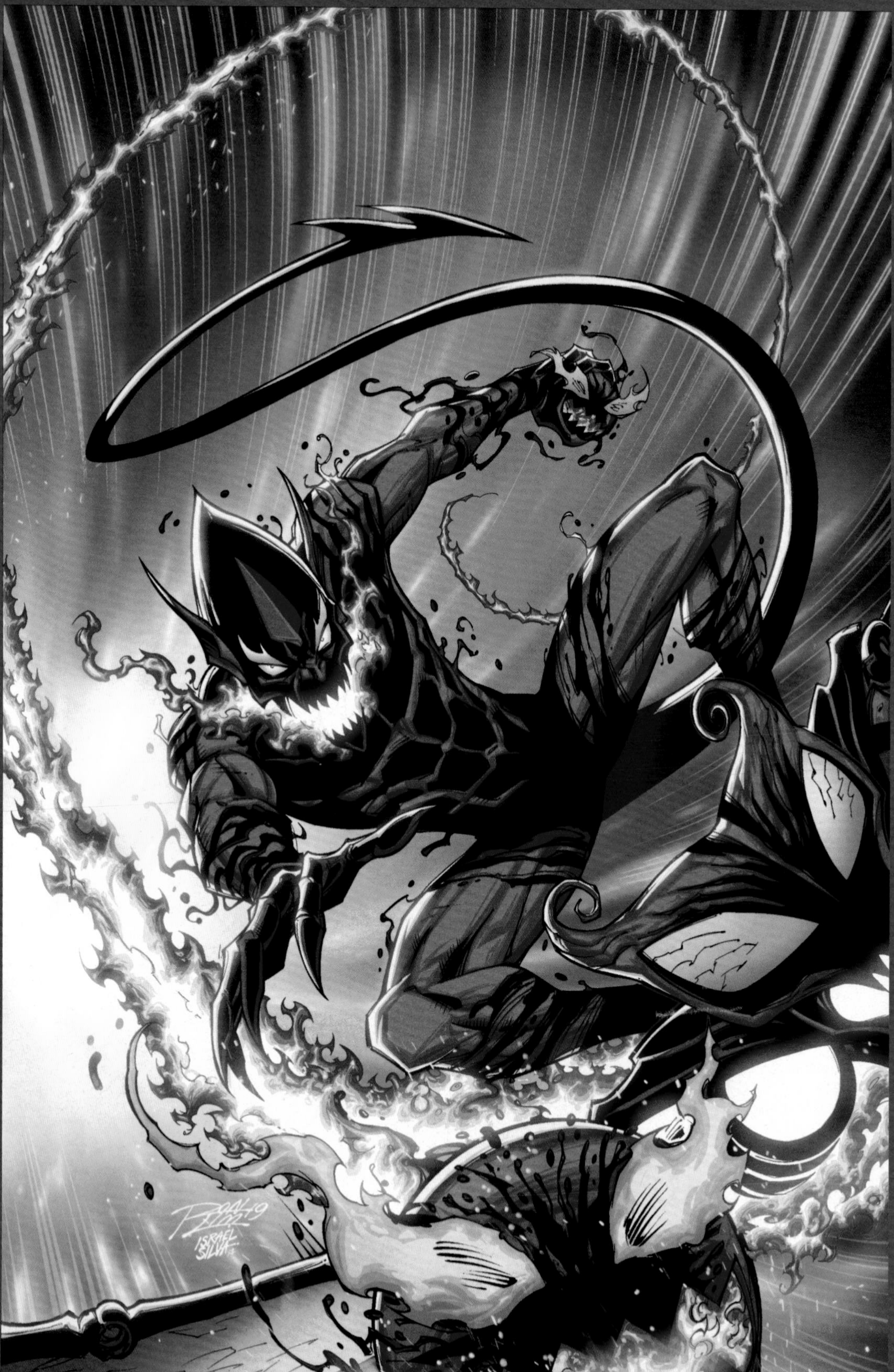

RED GOBLIN: RED DEATH #1 VARIANT BY RON LIM & ISRAEL SILVA

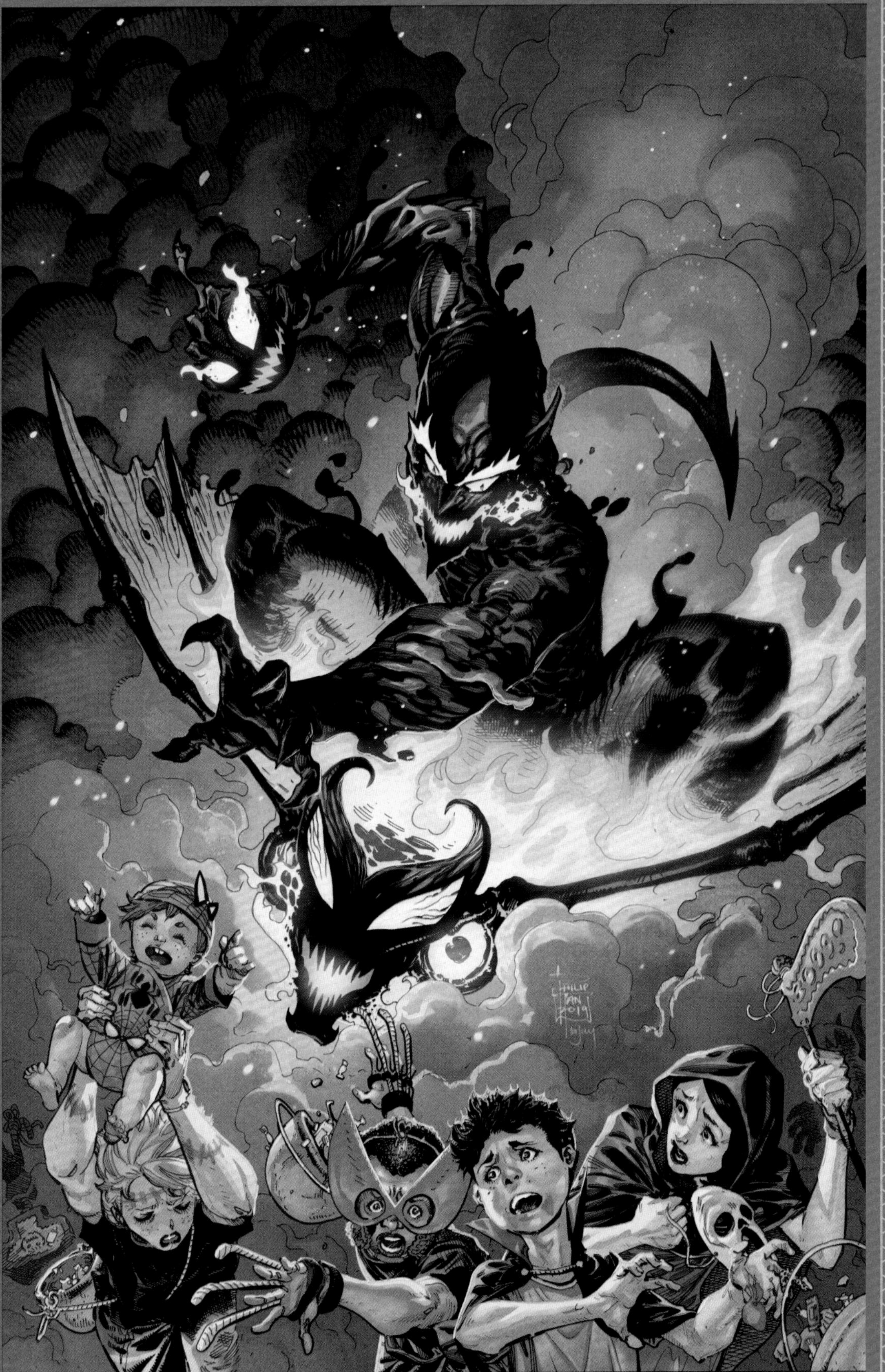

RED GOBLIN: RED DEATH

RED GOBLIN

RED DEATH

SPIDER-MAN CURED NORMAN OSBORN OF HIS GREEN GOBLIN SERUM-INDUCED INSANITY BY INJECTING HIM WITH AN ANTIDOTE...BUT THE CURE ALSO DEPOWERED NORMAN, AND IF THERE'S ONE THING NORMAN OSBORN WILL NEVER STAND FOR, IT'S LOSING POWER. SO HE FOUND THE ONE THING THAT COULD PURGE THE ANTIDOTE...THE CARNAGE SYMBIOTE. WITH HIS POWER AND HIS INSANITY RESTORED AND MIXED WITH THE ADDITIONAL POWERS OF THE CARNAGE SYMBIOTE, THE RED GOBLIN WAS BORN!

GREAT RESPONSIBILITY

ROB FEE WRITER
PETE WOODS ARTIST

BIG MOUTH

SEAN RYAN WRITER
PETE WOODS ARTIST

THE WAYSIDE DARKNESS

PATRICK GLEASON WRITER
RAY-ANTHONY HEIGHT PENCILS
MARC DEERING INKS
DONO SÁNCHEZ-ALMARA
WITH **PROTOBUNKER** COLORS

VC's JOE SABINO LETTERS
PHILIP TAN & JAY DAVID RAMOS
COVER ARTISTS

**CHRIS DAUGHTRY,
RON GARNEY &
DAVE STEWART;
PETE WOODS;
LOGAN LUBERA &
RACHELLE ROSENBERG;
RON LIM & ISRAEL SILVA**
VARIANT COVER ARTISTS

**CHRIS STEVENS
& JASON KEITH**
RECAP PAGE ARTISTS

ANTHONY GAMBINO
LOGO/GRAPHIC DESIGNER
LINDSEY COHICK
ASSISTANT EDITOR
JAKE THOMAS
EDITOR

C.B. CEBULSKI
EDITOR IN CHIEF
JOE QUESADA
CHIEF CREATIVE OFFICER
DAN BUCKLEY
PRESIDENT
ALAN FINE
EXECUTIVE PRODUCER

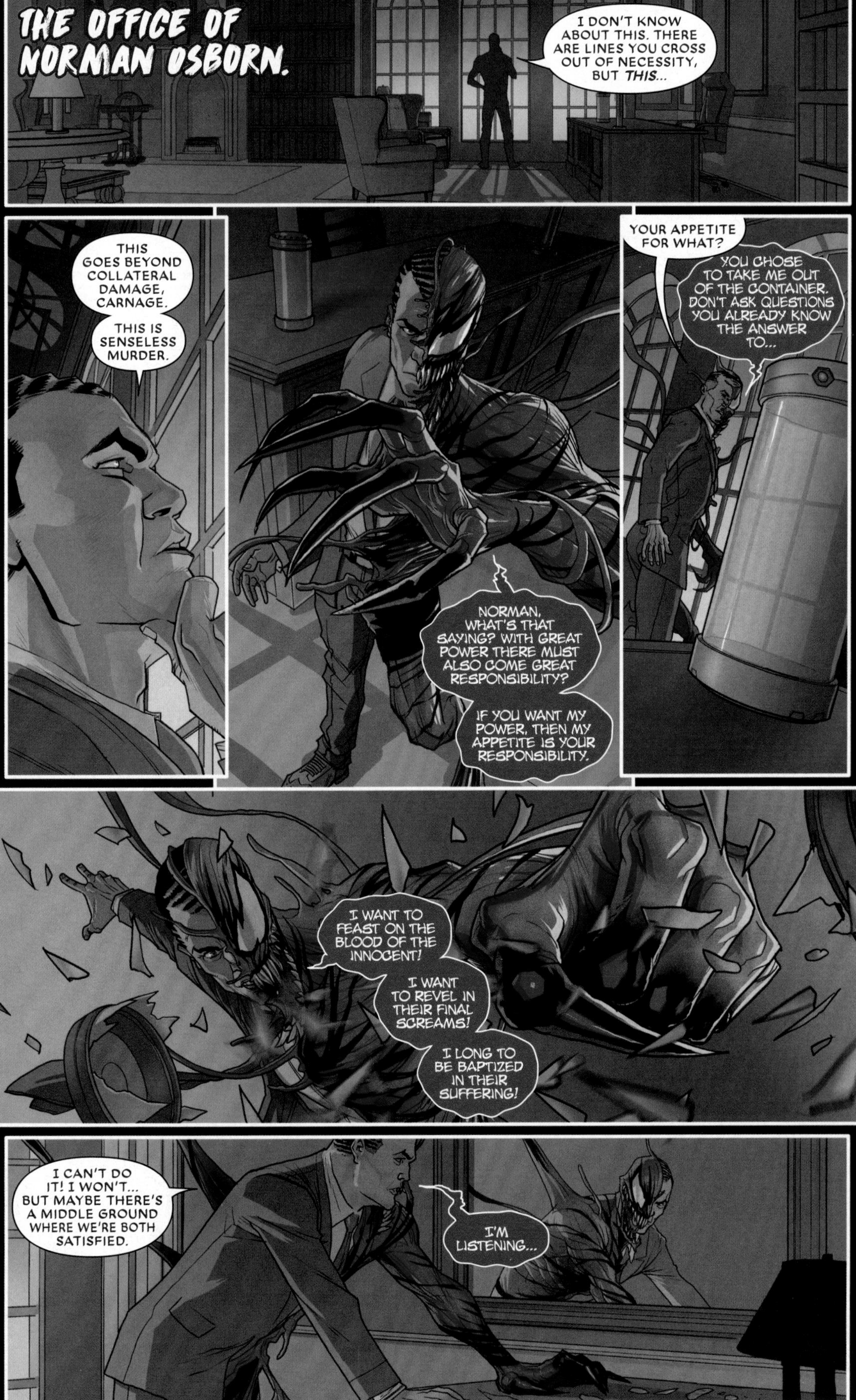
THE OFFICE OF NORMAN OSBORN.
I DON'T KNOW ABOUT THIS. THERE ARE LINES YOU CROSS OUT OF NECESSITY, BUT THIS...
THIS GOES BEYOND COLLATERAL DAMAGE, CARNAGE.
THIS IS SENSELESS MURDER.
NORMAN, WHAT'S THAT SAYING? WITH GREAT POWER THERE MUST ALSO COME GREAT RESPONSIBILITY?
IF YOU WANT MY POWER, THEN MY APPETITE IS YOUR RESPONSIBILITY.
YOUR APPETITE FOR WHAT?
YOU CHOSE TO TAKE ME OUT OF THE CONTAINER. DON'T ASK QUESTIONS YOU ALREADY KNOW THE ANSWER TO...
I WANT TO FEAST ON THE BLOOD OF THE INNOCENT!
I WANT TO REVEL IN THEIR FINAL SCREAMS!
I LONG TO BE BAPTIZED IN THEIR SUFFERING!
I CAN'T DO IT! I WON'T... BUT MAYBE THERE'S A MIDDLE GROUND WHERE WE'RE BOTH SATISFIED.
I'M LISTENING...

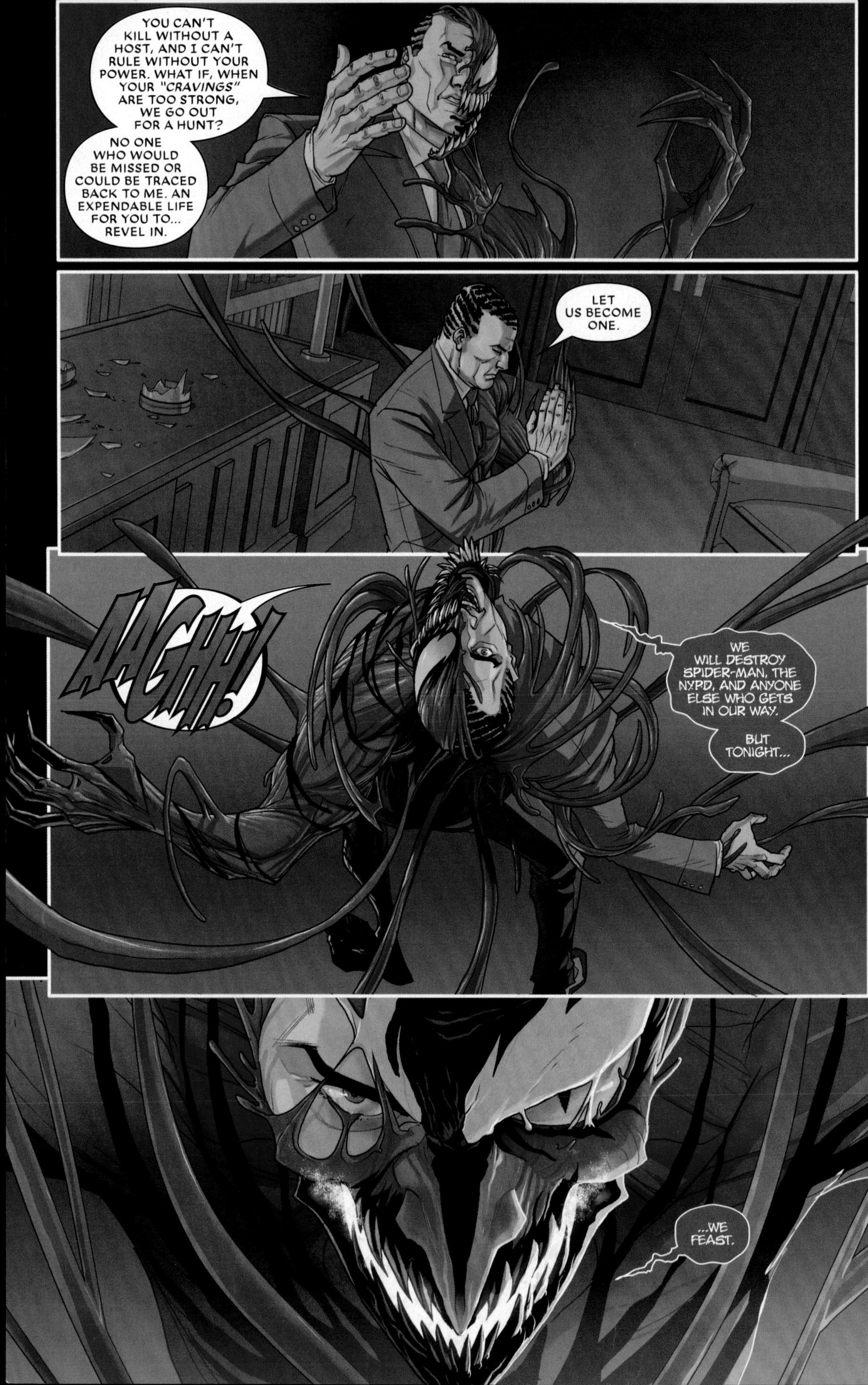
YOU CAN'T KILL WITHOUT A HOST, AND I CAN'T RULE WITHOUT YOUR POWER. WHAT IF, WHEN YOUR "CRAVINGS" ARE TOO STRONG, WE GO OUT FOR A HUNT?
NO ONE WHO WOULD BE MISSED OR COULD BE TRACED BACK TO ME. AN EXPENDABLE LIFE FOR YOU TO... REVEL IN.
LET US BECOME ONE.
AAGH!
WE WILL DESTROY SPIDER-MAN, THE NYPD, AND ANYONE ELSE WHO GETS IN OUR WAY.
BUT TONIGHT...
...WE FEAST.

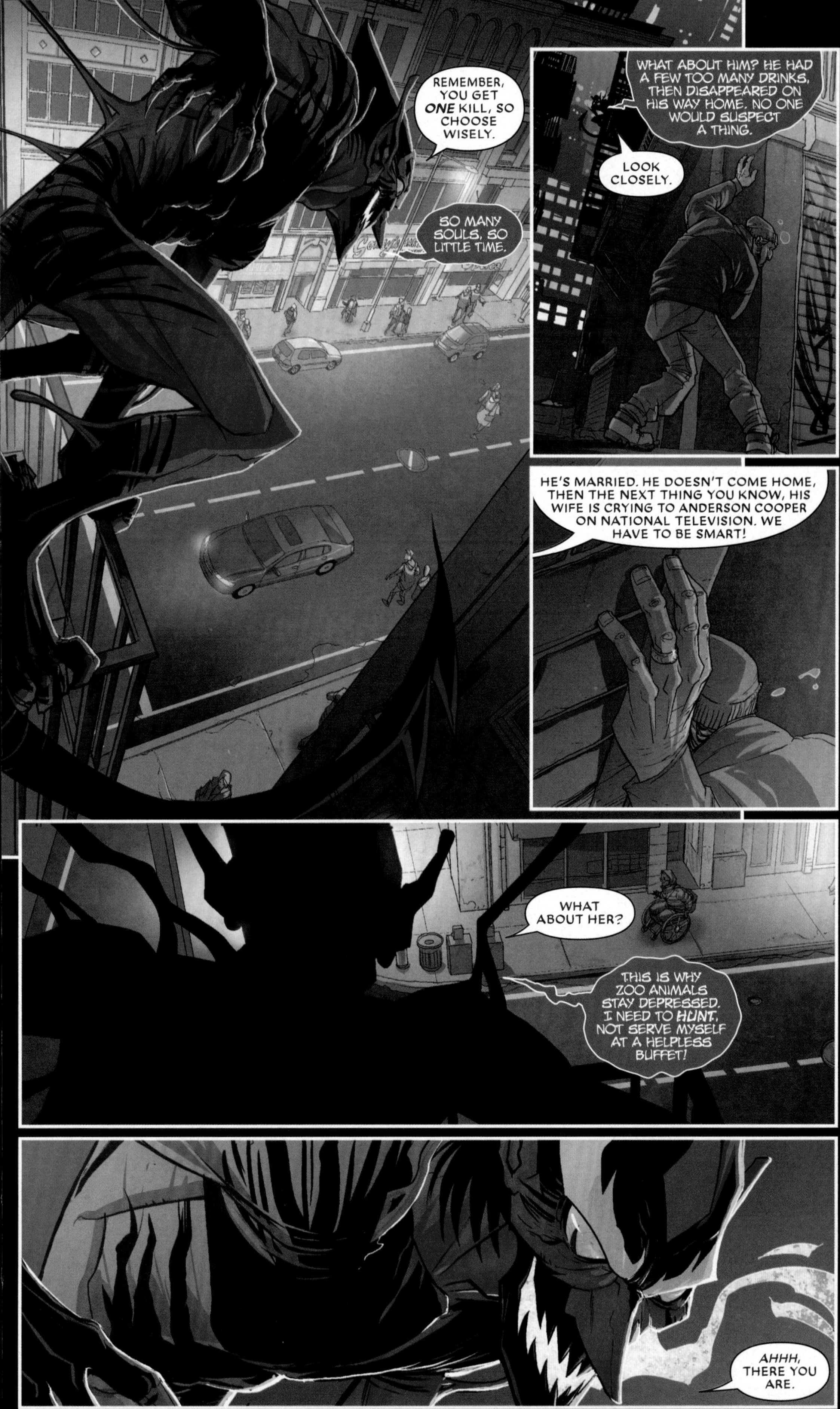
REMEMBER, YOU GET ONE KILL, SO CHOOSE WISELY.
SO MANY SOULS, SO LITTLE TIME.
WHAT ABOUT HIM? HE HAD A FEW TOO MANY DRINKS, THEN DISAPPEARED ON HIS WAY HOME. NO ONE WOULD SUSPECT A THING.
LOOK CLOSELY.
HE'S MARRIED. HE DOESN'T COME HOME, THEN THE NEXT THING YOU KNOW, HIS WIFE IS CRYING TO ANDERSON COOPER ON NATIONAL TELEVISION. WE HAVE TO BE SMART!
WHAT ABOUT HER?
THIS IS WHY ZOO ANIMALS STAY DEPRESSED. I NEED TO HUNT, NOT SERVE MYSELF AT A HELPLESS BUFFET!
AHHH, THERE YOU ARE.

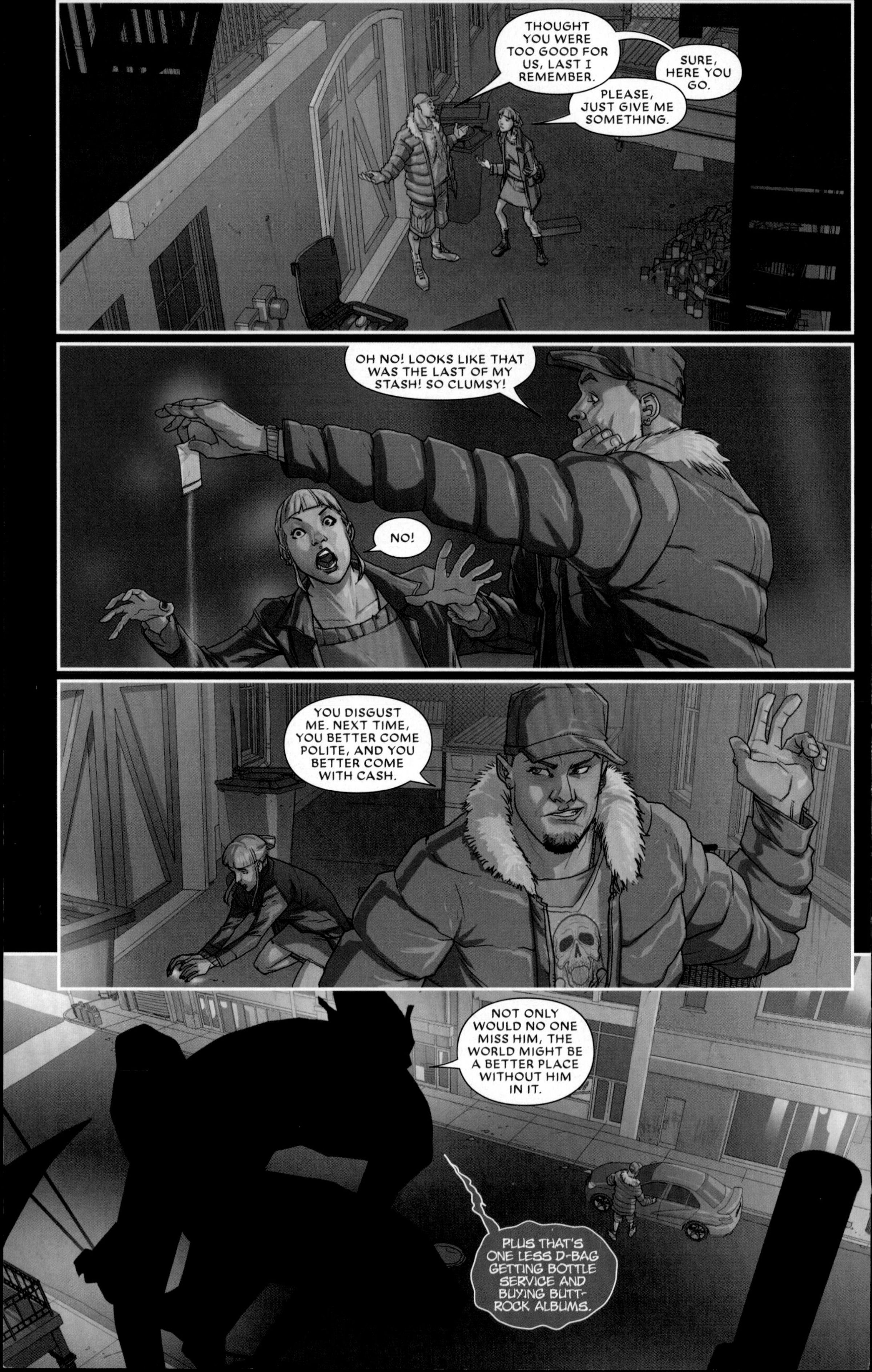
THOUGHT YOU WERE TOO GOOD FOR US, LAST I REMEMBER.
PLEASE, JUST GIVE ME SOMETHING.
SURE, HERE YOU GO.
OH NO! LOOKS LIKE THAT WAS THE LAST OF MY STASH! SO CLUMSY!
NO!
YOU DISGUST ME. NEXT TIME, YOU BETTER COME POLITE, AND YOU BETTER COME WITH CASH.
NOT ONLY WOULD NO ONE MISS HIM, THE WORLD MIGHT BE A BETTER PLACE WITHOUT HIM IN IT.
PLUS THAT'S ONE LESS D-BAG GETTING BOTTLE SERVICE AND BUYING BUTT-ROCK ALBUMS.

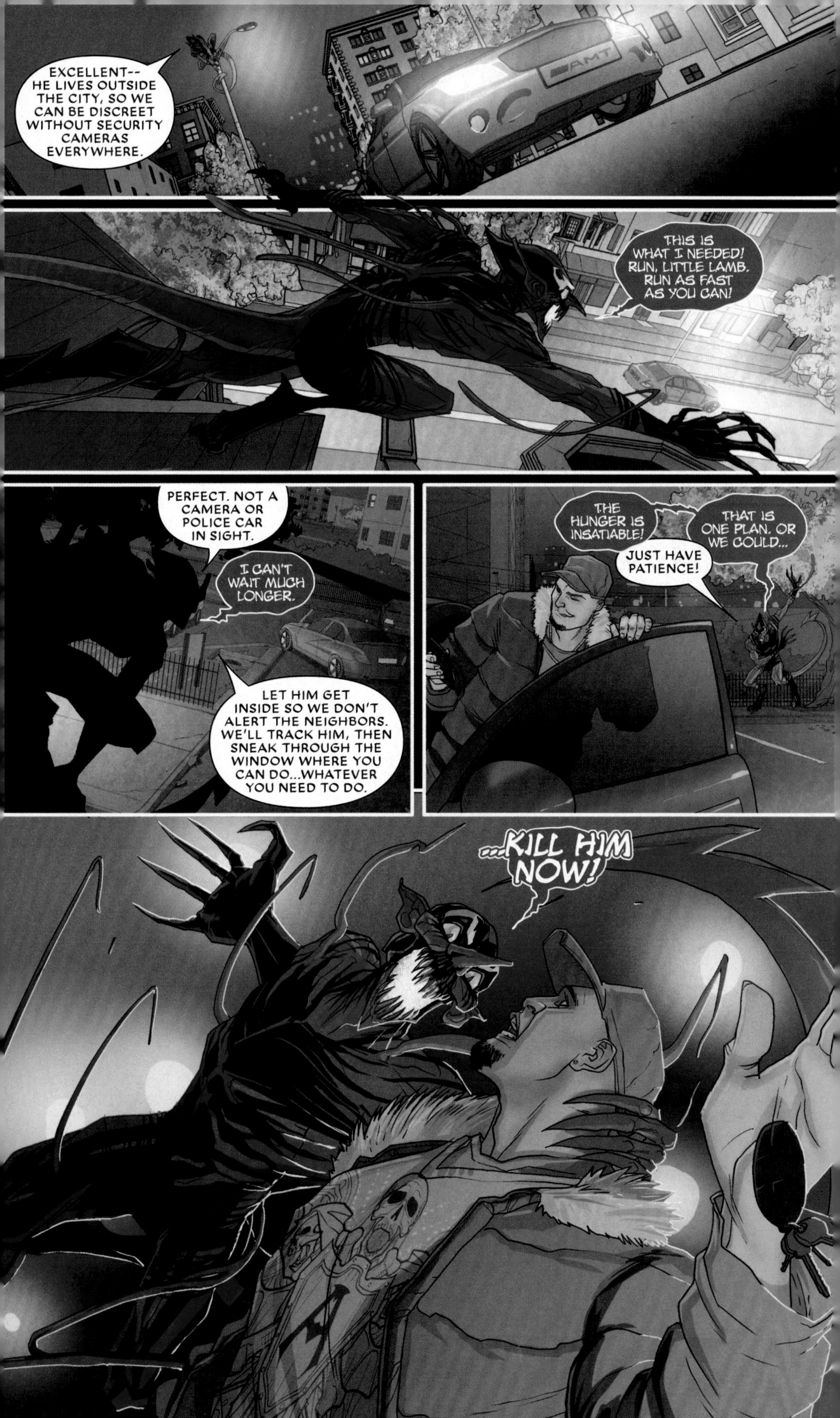
EXCELLENT-- HE LIVES OUTSIDE THE CITY, SO WE CAN BE DISCREET WITHOUT SECURITY CAMERAS EVERYWHERE.
AMT
THIS IS WHAT I NEEDED! RUN, LITTLE LAMB. RUN AS FAST AS YOU CAN!
PERFECT. NOT A CAMERA OR POLICE CAR IN SIGHT.
I CAN'T WAIT MUCH LONGER.
LET HIM GET INSIDE SO WE DON'T ALERT THE NEIGHBORS. WE'LL TRACK HIM, THEN SNEAK THROUGH THE WINDOW WHERE YOU CAN DO...WHATEVER YOU NEED TO DO.
THE HUNGER IS INSATIABLE!
JUST HAVE PATIENCE!
THAT IS ONE PLAN. OR WE COULD...
...KILL HIM NOW!

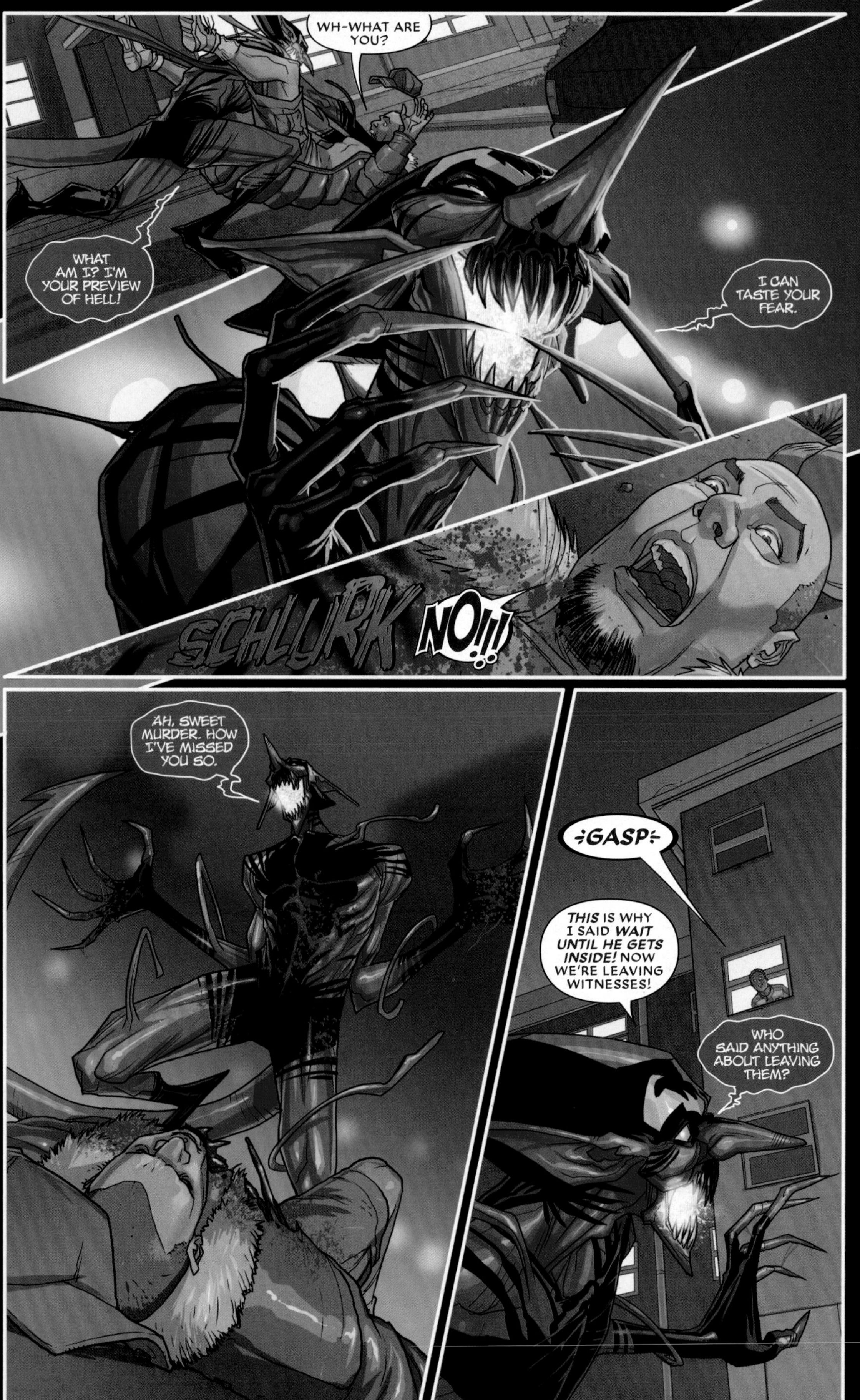
WH-WHAT ARE YOU?
WHAT AM I? I'M YOUR PREVIEW OF HELL!
I CAN TASTE YOUR FEAR.
SCHLURK
NO!!!
AH, SWEET MURDER. HOW I'VE MISSED YOU SO.
GASP
THIS IS WHY I SAID WAIT UNTIL HE GETS INSIDE! NOW WE'RE LEAVING WITNESSES!
WHO SAID ANYTHING ABOUT LEAVING THEM?

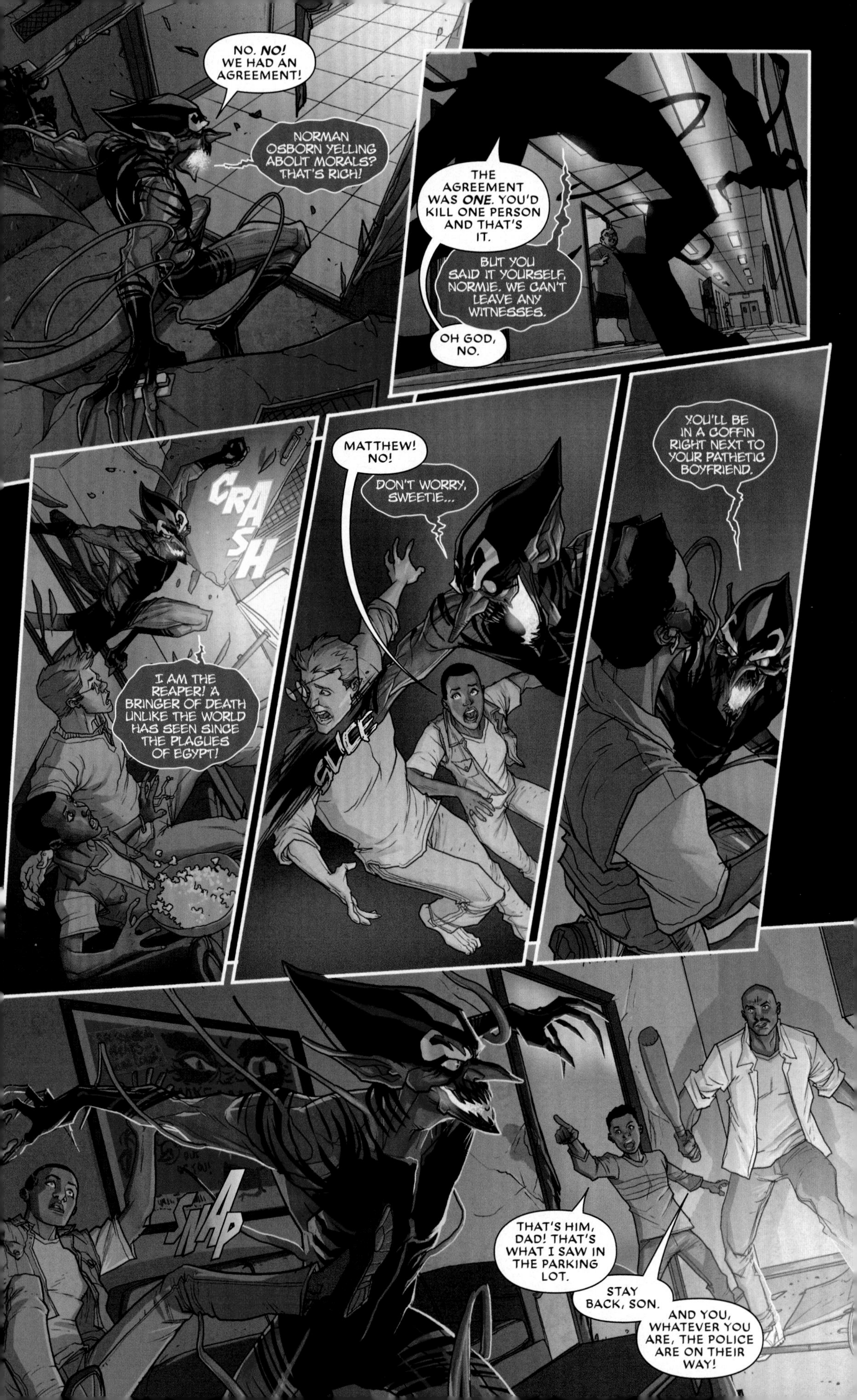
NO. *NO!* WE HAD AN AGREEMENT!
NORMAN OSBORN YELLING ABOUT MORALS? THAT'S RICH!
THE AGREEMENT WAS *ONE*. YOU'D KILL ONE PERSON AND THAT'S IT.
BUT YOU SAID IT YOURSELF, NORMIE. WE CAN'T LEAVE ANY WITNESSES.
OH GOD, NO.
CRASH
I AM THE REAPER! A BRINGER OF DEATH UNLIKE THE WORLD HAS SEEN SINCE THE PLAGUES OF EGYPT!
MATTHEW! NO!
DON'T WORRY, SWEETIE...
SLICE
YOU'LL BE IN A COFFIN RIGHT NEXT TO YOUR PATHETIC BOYFRIEND.
SNAP
THAT'S HIM, DAD! THAT'S WHAT I SAW IN THE PARKING LOT.
STAY BACK, SON.
AND YOU, WHATEVER YOU ARE, THE POLICE ARE ON THEIR WAY!

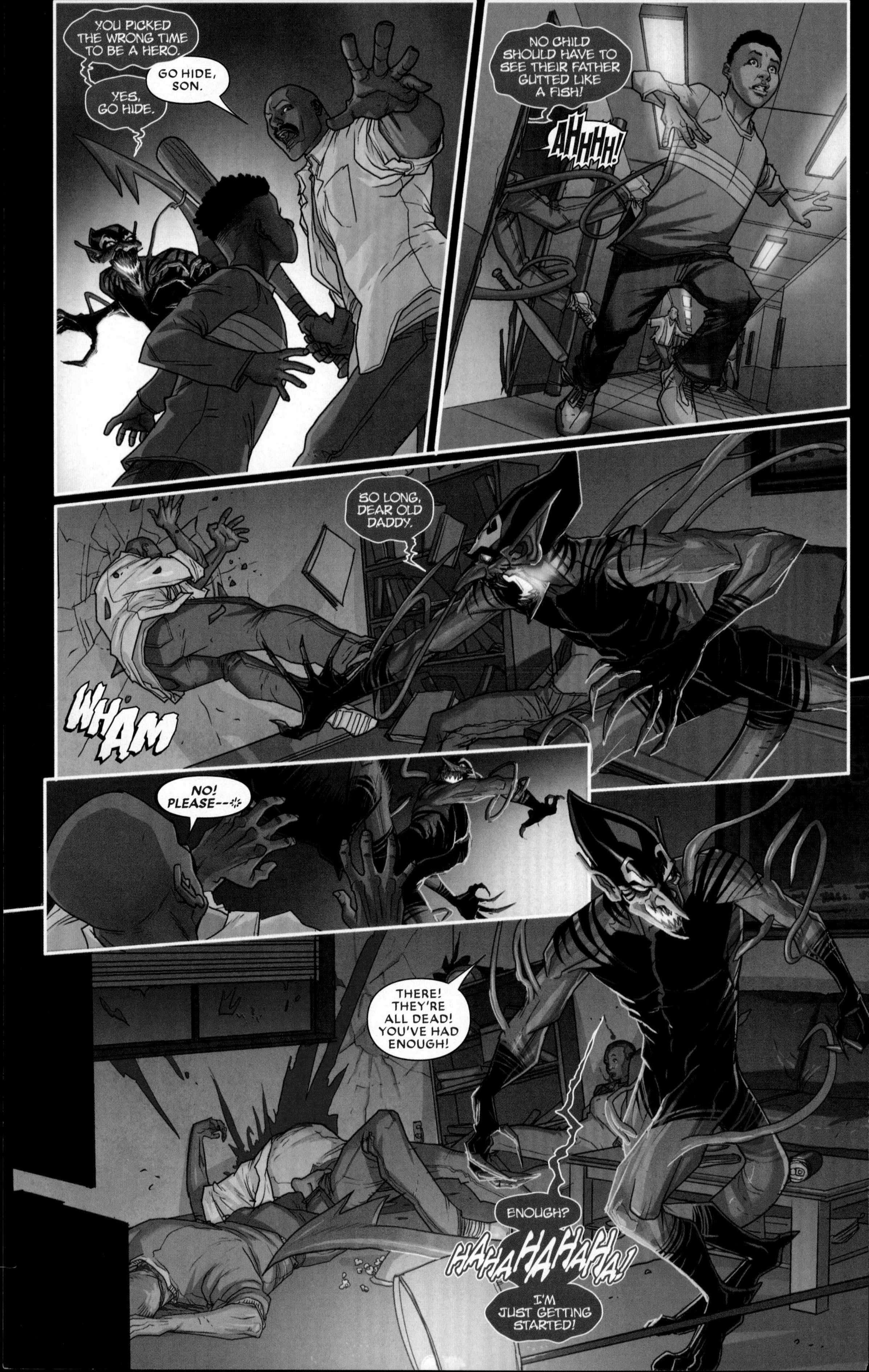
YOU PICKED THE WRONG TIME TO BE A HERO.
GO HIDE, SON.
YES, GO HIDE.
NO CHILD SHOULD HAVE TO SEE THEIR FATHER GUTTED LIKE A FISH!
AHHHH!
SO LONG, DEAR OLD DADDY.
WHAM
NO! PLEASE--
THERE! THEY'RE ALL DEAD! YOU'VE HAD ENOUGH!
ENOUGH?
HAHAHAHAHAHA!
I'M JUST GETTING STARTED!

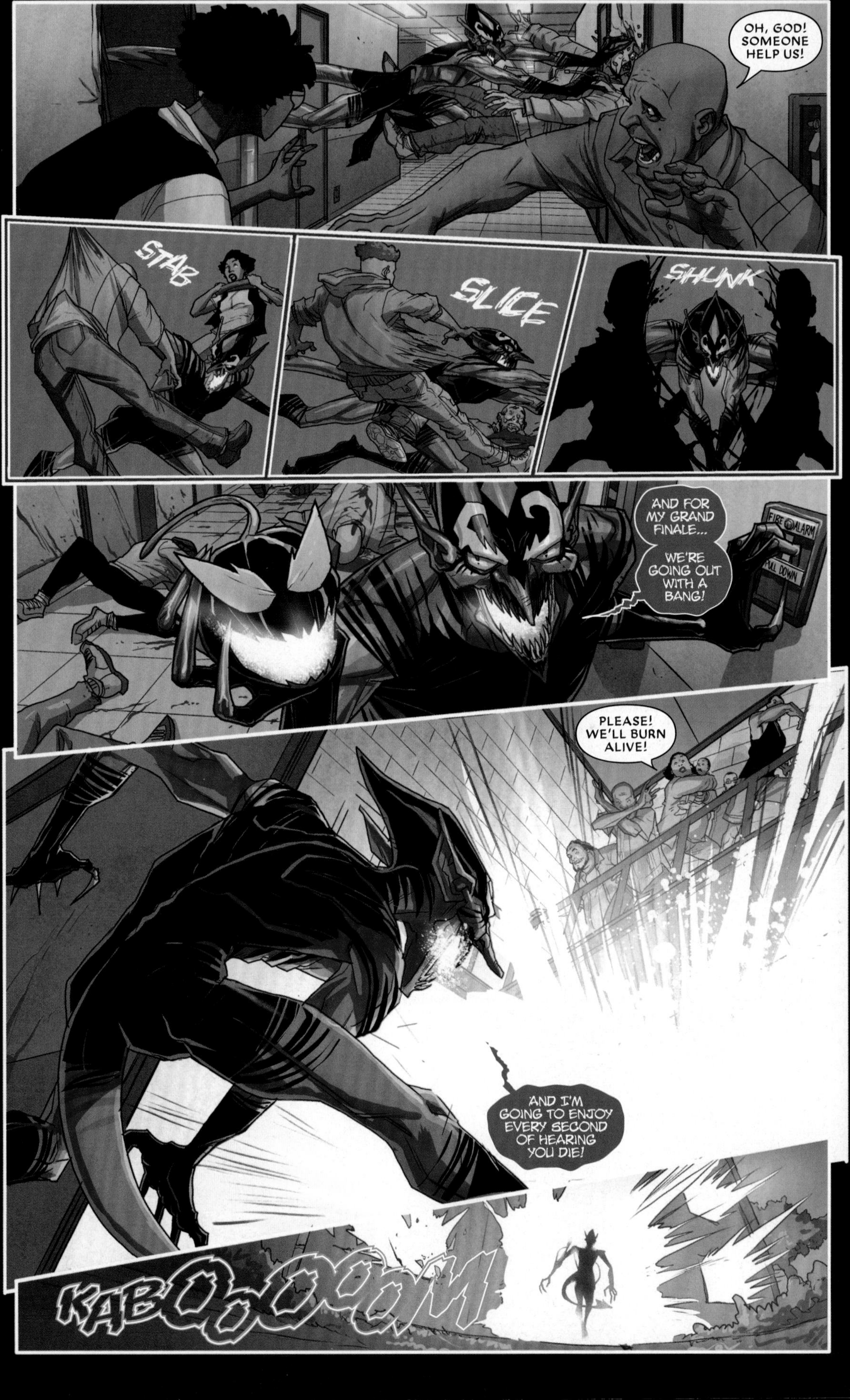
OH, GOD! SOMEONE HELP US!
STAB
SLICE
SHUNK
AND FOR MY GRAND FINALE...
WE'RE GOING OUT WITH A BANG!
FIRE ALARM
PULL DOWN
PLEASE! WE'LL BURN ALIVE!
AND I'M GOING TO ENJOY EVERY SECOND OF HEARING YOU DIE!
KABOOOOOM

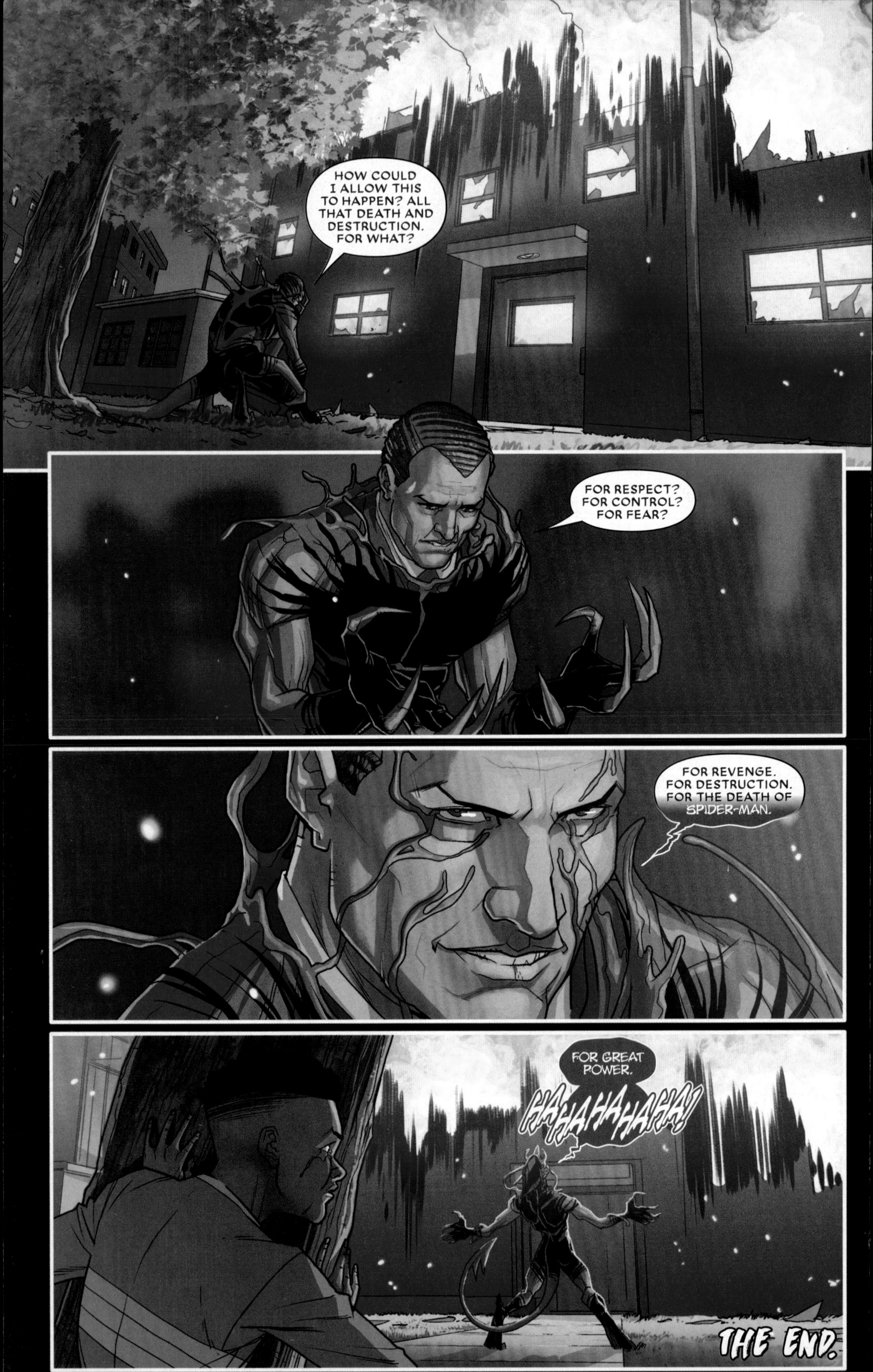
HOW COULD I ALLOW THIS TO HAPPEN? ALL THAT DEATH AND DESTRUCTION. FOR WHAT?
FOR RESPECT? FOR CONTROL? FOR FEAR?
FOR REVENGE. FOR DESTRUCTION. FOR THE DEATH OF SPIDER-MAN.
FOR GREAT POWER.
HAHAHAHAHAHA!
THE END.

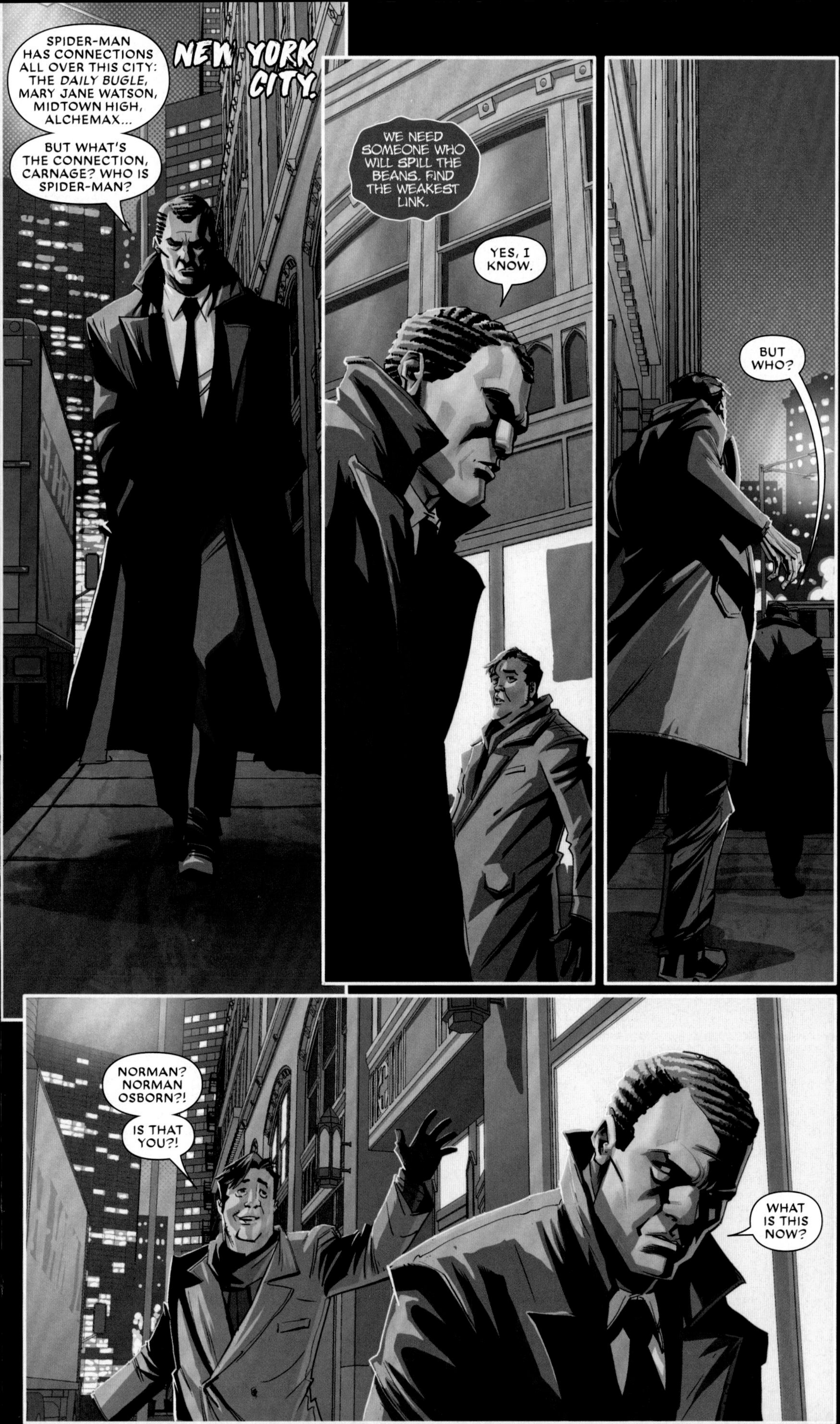
NEW YORK CITY.
SPIDER-MAN HAS CONNECTIONS ALL OVER THIS CITY: THE *DAILY BUGLE*, MARY JANE WATSON, MIDTOWN HIGH, ALCHEMAX...
BUT WHAT'S THE CONNECTION, CARNAGE? WHO IS SPIDER-MAN?
WE NEED SOMEONE WHO WILL SPILL THE BEANS. FIND THE WEAKEST LINK.
YES, I KNOW.
BUT WHO?
NORMAN? NORMAN OSBORN?!
IS THAT YOU?!
WHAT IS THIS NOW?

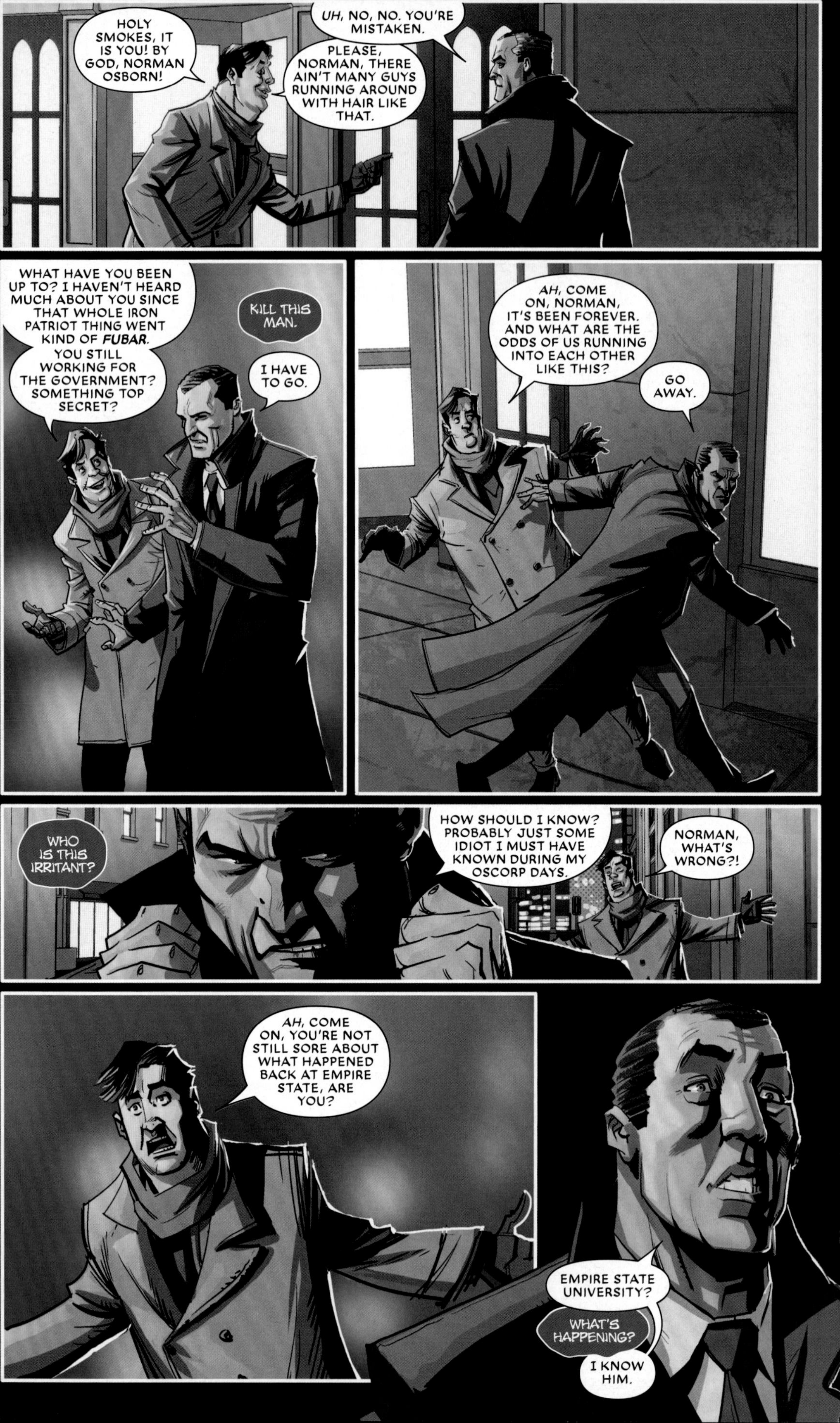
HOLY SMOKES, IT IS YOU! BY GOD, NORMAN OSBORN!
UH, NO, NO. YOU'RE MISTAKEN.
PLEASE, NORMAN, THERE AIN'T MANY GUYS RUNNING AROUND WITH HAIR LIKE THAT.
WHAT HAVE YOU BEEN UP TO? I HAVEN'T HEARD MUCH ABOUT YOU SINCE THAT WHOLE IRON PATRIOT THING WENT KIND OF FUBAR.
YOU STILL WORKING FOR THE GOVERNMENT? SOMETHING TOP SECRET?
KILL THIS MAN.
I HAVE TO GO.
AH, COME ON, NORMAN, IT'S BEEN FOREVER. AND WHAT ARE THE ODDS OF US RUNNING INTO EACH OTHER LIKE THIS?
GO AWAY.
WHO IS THIS IRRITANT?
HOW SHOULD I KNOW? PROBABLY JUST SOME IDIOT I MUST HAVE KNOWN DURING MY OSCORP DAYS.
NORMAN, WHAT'S WRONG?!
AH, COME ON, YOU'RE NOT STILL SORE ABOUT WHAT HAPPENED BACK AT EMPIRE STATE, ARE YOU?
EMPIRE STATE UNIVERSITY?
WHAT'S HAPPENING?
I KNOW HIM.

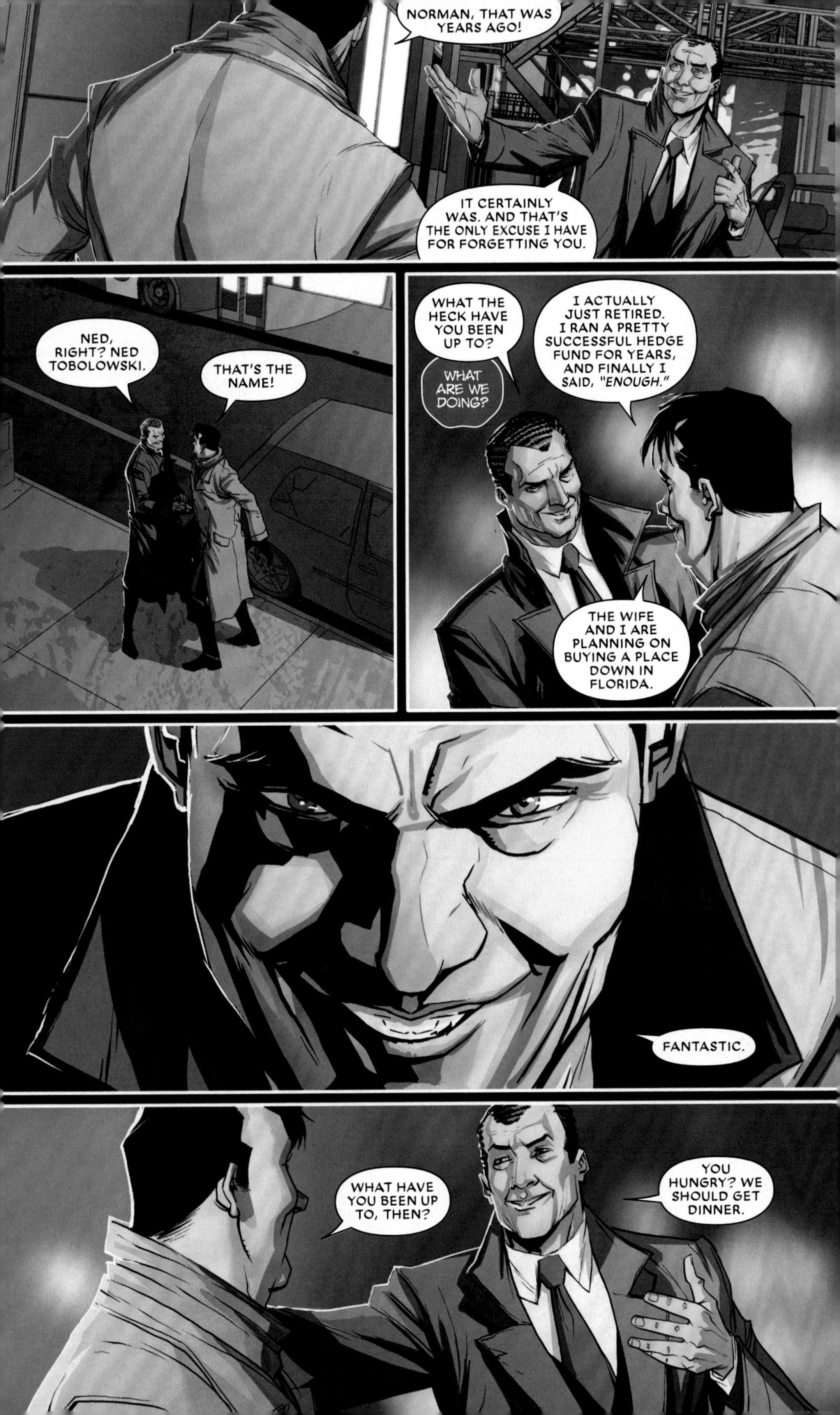
NORMAN, THAT WAS YEARS AGO!
IT CERTAINLY WAS. AND THAT'S THE ONLY EXCUSE I HAVE FOR FORGETTING YOU.
NED, RIGHT? NED TOBOLOWSKI.
THAT'S THE NAME!
WHAT THE HECK HAVE YOU BEEN UP TO?
WHAT ARE WE DOING?
I ACTUALLY JUST RETIRED. I RAN A PRETTY SUCCESSFUL HEDGE FUND FOR YEARS, AND FINALLY I SAID, "ENOUGH."
THE WIFE AND I ARE PLANNING ON BUYING A PLACE DOWN IN FLORIDA.
FANTASTIC.
WHAT HAVE YOU BEEN UP TO, THEN?
YOU HUNGRY? WE SHOULD GET DINNER.

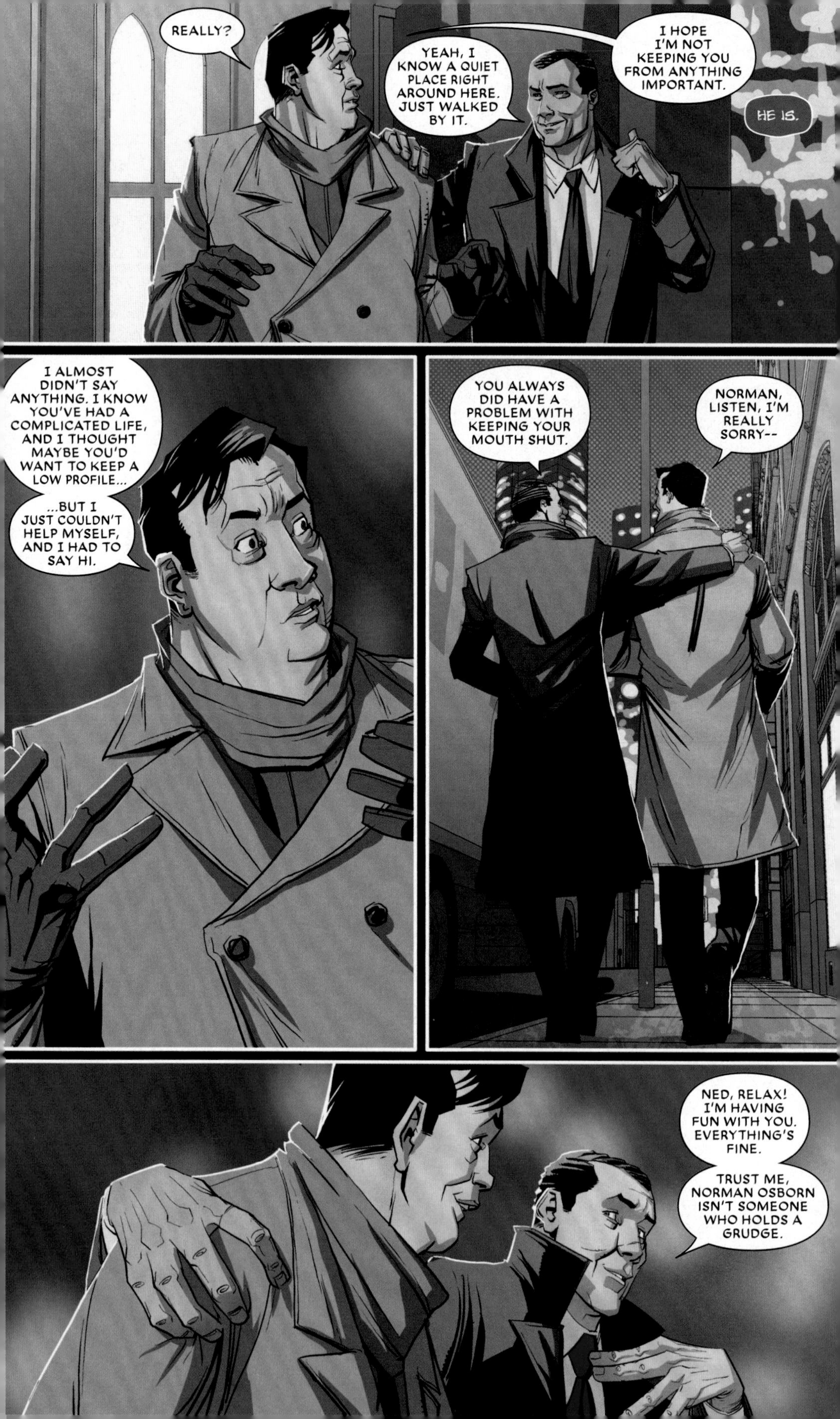
REALLY?
YEAH, I KNOW A QUIET PLACE RIGHT AROUND HERE. JUST WALKED BY IT.
I HOPE I'M NOT KEEPING YOU FROM ANYTHING IMPORTANT.
HE IS.
I ALMOST DIDN'T SAY ANYTHING. I KNOW YOU'VE HAD A COMPLICATED LIFE, AND I THOUGHT MAYBE YOU'D WANT TO KEEP A LOW PROFILE...
...BUT I JUST COULDN'T HELP MYSELF, AND I HAD TO SAY HI.
YOU ALWAYS DID HAVE A PROBLEM WITH KEEPING YOUR MOUTH SHUT.
NORMAN, LISTEN, I'M REALLY SORRY--
NED, RELAX! I'M HAVING FUN WITH YOU. EVERYTHING'S FINE.
TRUST ME, NORMAN OSBORN ISN'T SOMEONE WHO HOLDS A GRUDGE.

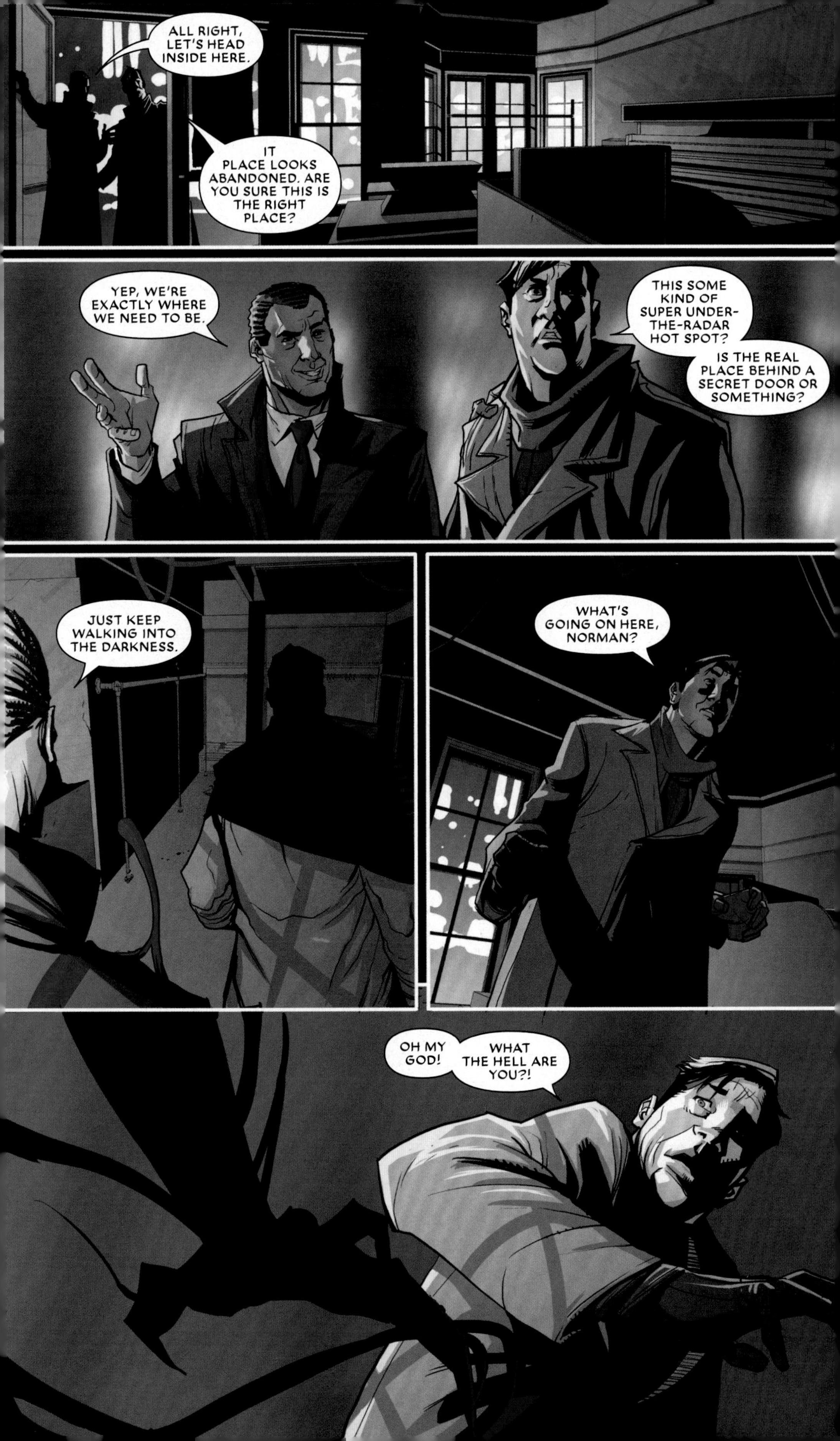
ALL RIGHT, LET'S HEAD INSIDE HERE.
IT PLACE LOOKS ABANDONED. ARE YOU SURE THIS IS THE RIGHT PLACE?
YEP, WE'RE EXACTLY WHERE WE NEED TO BE.
THIS SOME KIND OF SUPER UNDER-THE-RADAR HOT SPOT?
IS THE REAL PLACE BEHIND A SECRET DOOR OR SOMETHING?
JUST KEEP WALKING INTO THE DARKNESS.
WHAT'S GOING ON HERE, NORMAN?
OH MY GOD!
WHAT THE HELL ARE YOU?!

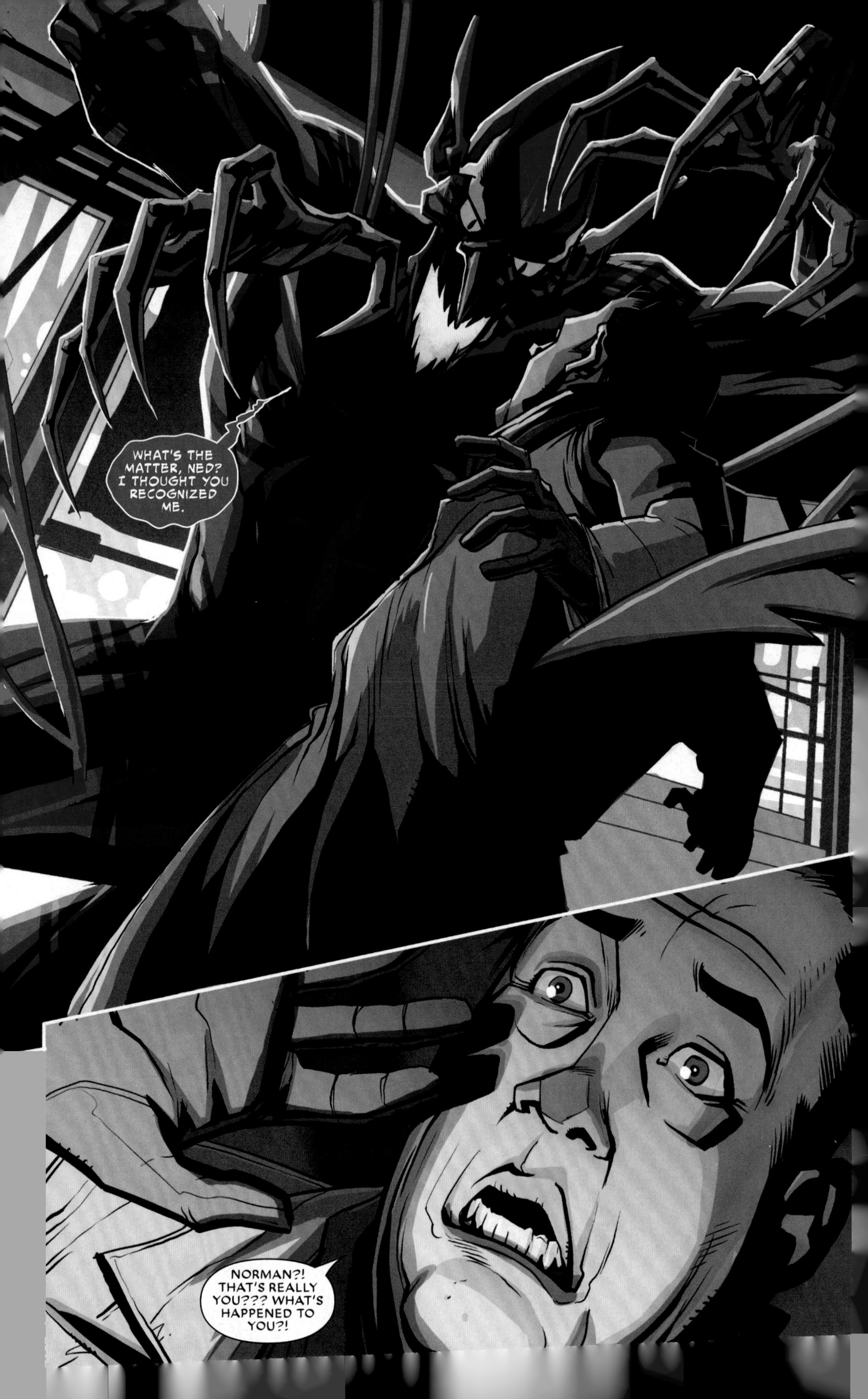
WHAT'S THE MATTER, NED? I THOUGHT YOU RECOGNIZED ME.
NORMAN?! THAT'S REALLY YOU??? WHAT'S HAPPENED TO YOU?!

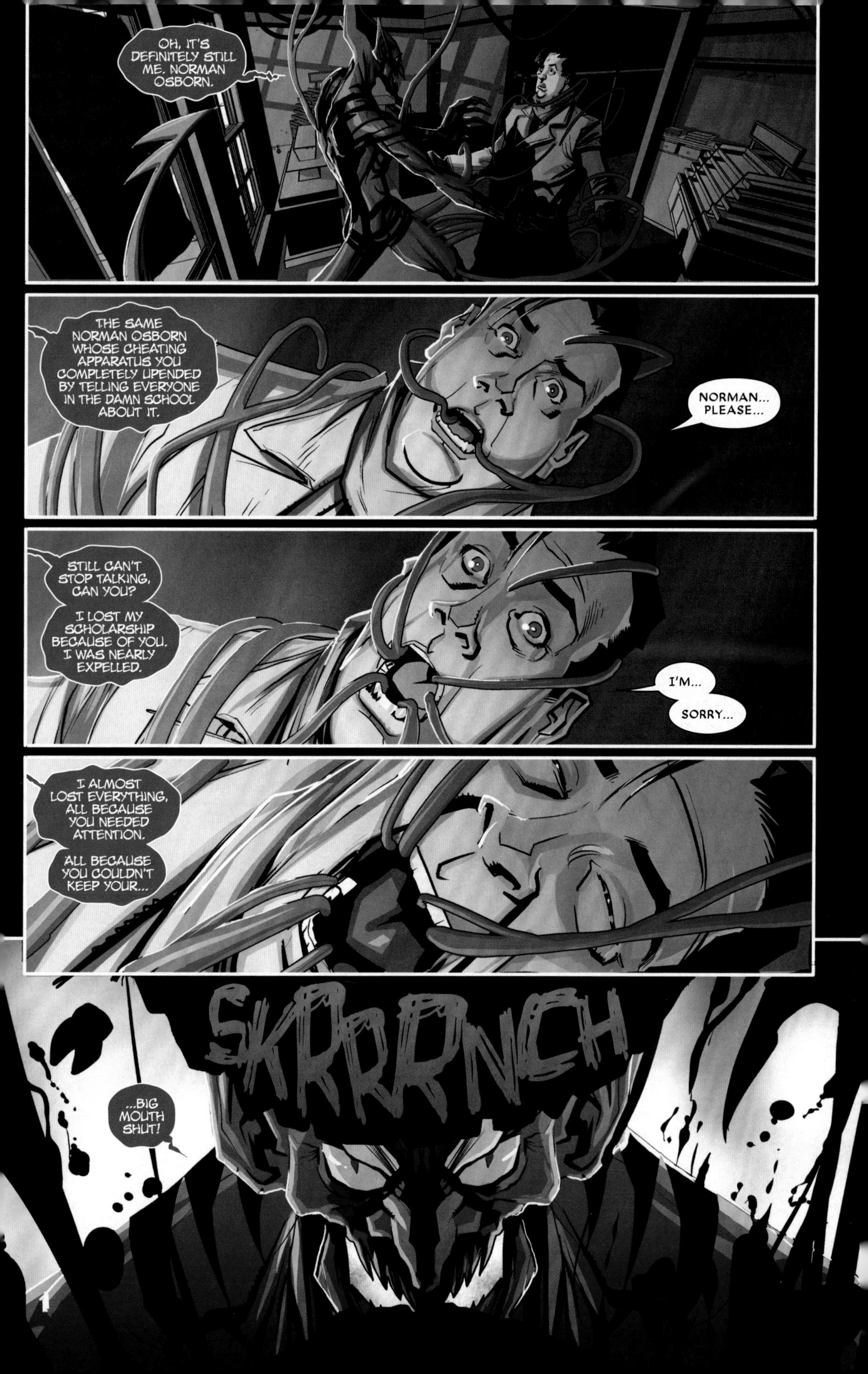
OH, IT'S DEFINITELY STILL ME. NORMAN OSBORN.
THE SAME NORMAN OSBORN WHOSE CHEATING APPARATUS YOU COMPLETELY UPENDED BY TELLING EVERYONE IN THE DAMN SCHOOL ABOUT IT.
NORMAN... PLEASE...
STILL CAN'T STOP TALKING, CAN YOU?
I LOST MY SCHOLARSHIP BECAUSE OF YOU. I WAS NEARLY EXPELLED.
I'M...
SORRY...
I ALMOST LOST EVERYTHING, ALL BECAUSE YOU NEEDED ATTENTION.
ALL BECAUSE YOU COULDN'T KEEP YOUR...
SKRRRNCH
...BIG MOUTH SHUT!

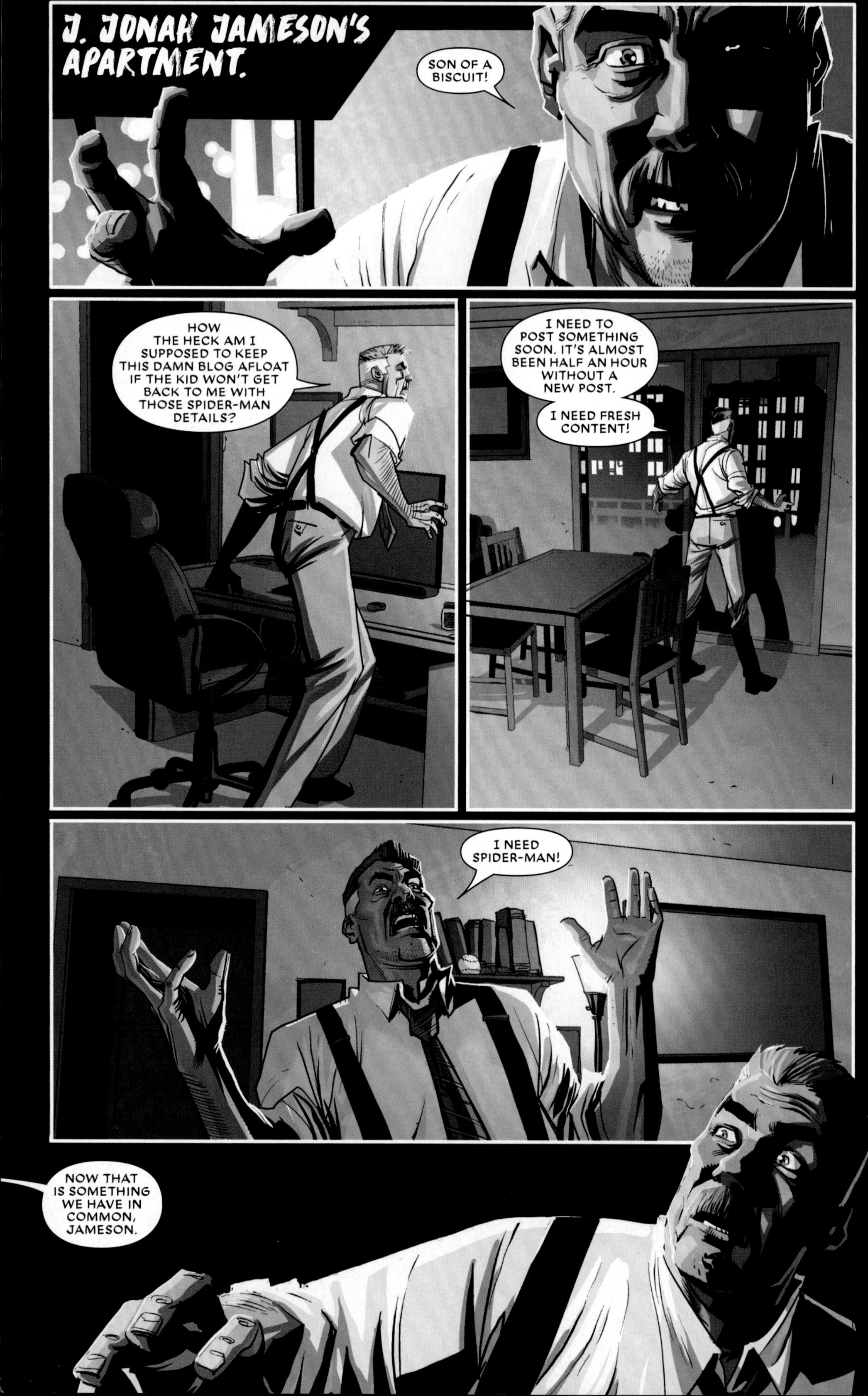
J. JONAH JAMESON'S APARTMENT.
SON OF A BISCUIT!
HOW THE HECK AM I SUPPOSED TO KEEP THIS DAMN BLOG AFLOAT IF THE KID WON'T GET BACK TO ME WITH THOSE SPIDER-MAN DETAILS?
I NEED TO POST SOMETHING SOON. IT'S ALMOST BEEN HALF AN HOUR WITHOUT A NEW POST.
I NEED FRESH CONTENT!
I NEED SPIDER-MAN!
NOW THAT IS SOMETHING WE HAVE IN COMMON, JAMESON.

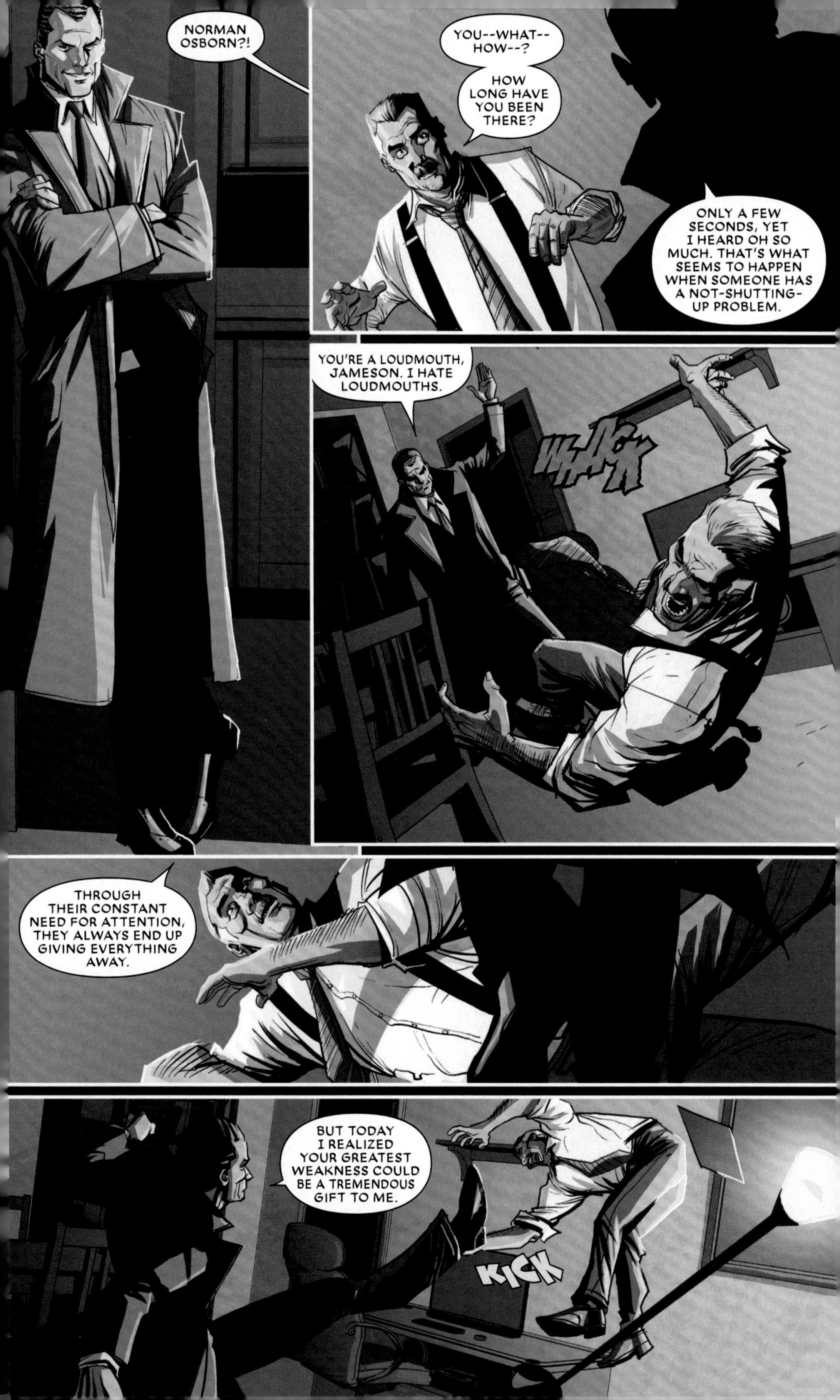
NORMAN OSBORN?!
YOU--WHAT--HOW--?
HOW LONG HAVE YOU BEEN THERE?
ONLY A FEW SECONDS, YET I HEARD OH SO MUCH. THAT'S WHAT SEEMS TO HAPPEN WHEN SOMEONE HAS A NOT-SHUTTING-UP PROBLEM.
YOU'RE A LOUDMOUTH, JAMESON. I HATE LOUDMOUTHS.
WHACK
THROUGH THEIR CONSTANT NEED FOR ATTENTION, THEY ALWAYS END UP GIVING EVERYTHING AWAY.
BUT TODAY I REALIZED YOUR GREATEST WEAKNESS COULD BE A TREMENDOUS GIFT TO ME.
KICK

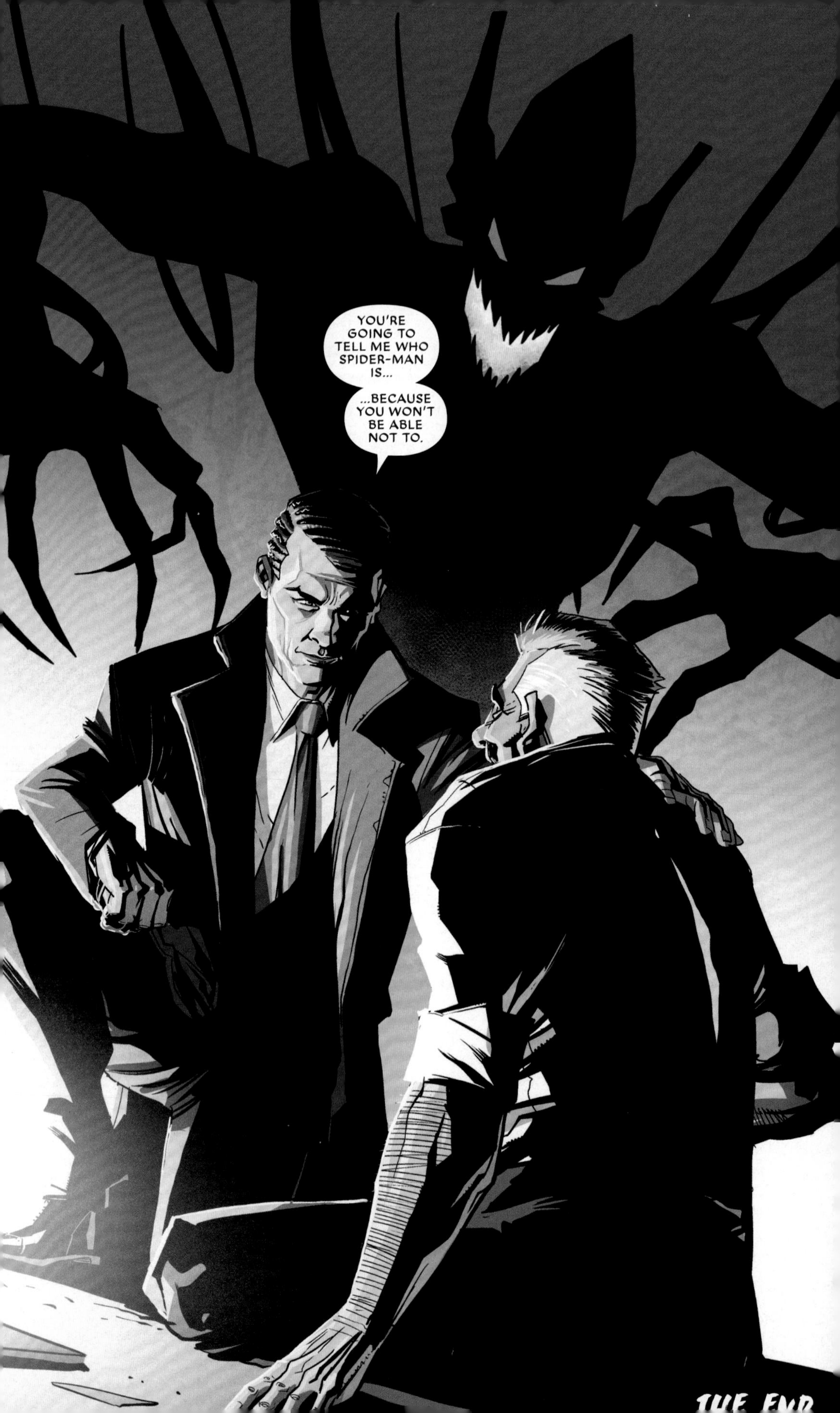
YOU'RE GOING TO TELL ME WHO SPIDER-MAN IS...
...BECAUSE YOU WON'T BE ABLE NOT TO.
THE END

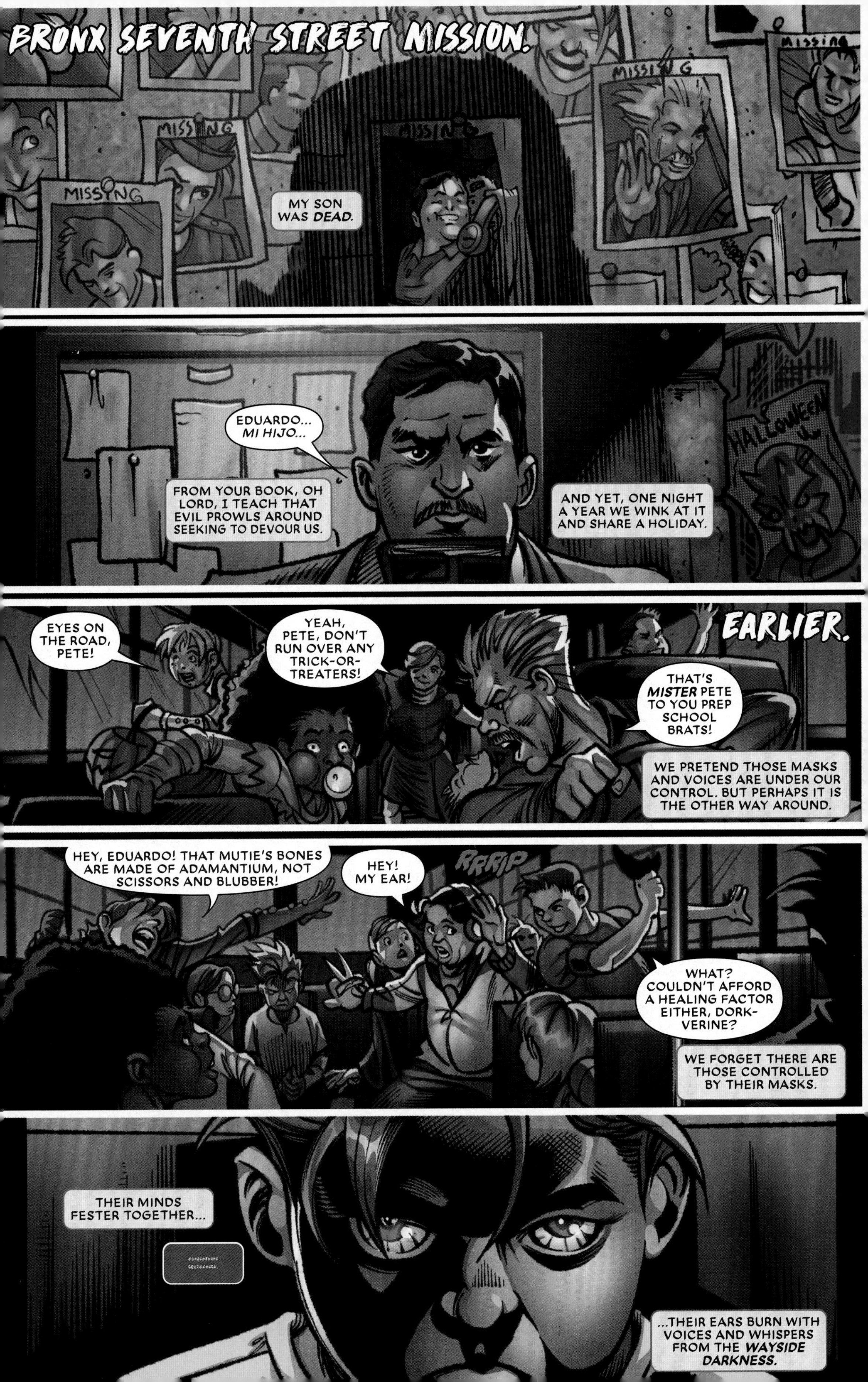
BRONX SEVENTH STREET MISSION.
MISSING
MISSING
MISSING
MISSING
MISSING
MY SON WAS *DEAD*.
EDUARDO... *MI HIJO*...
FROM YOUR BOOK, OH LORD, I TEACH THAT EVIL PROWLS AROUND SEEKING TO DEVOUR US.
AND YET, ONE NIGHT A YEAR WE WINK AT IT AND SHARE A HOLIDAY.
HALLOWEEN
EARLIER.
EYES ON THE ROAD, PETE!
YEAH, PETE, DON'T RUN OVER ANY TRICK-OR-TREATERS!
THAT'S *MISTER* PETE TO YOU PREP SCHOOL BRATS!
WE PRETEND THOSE MASKS AND VOICES ARE UNDER OUR CONTROL. BUT PERHAPS IT IS THE OTHER WAY AROUND.
HEY, EDUARDO! THAT MUTIE'S BONES ARE MADE OF ADAMANTIUM, NOT SCISSORS AND BLUBBER!
HEY! MY EAR!
RRRIP
WHAT? COULDN'T AFFORD A HEALING FACTOR EITHER, DORK-VERINE?
WE FORGET THERE ARE THOSE CONTROLLED BY THEIR MASKS.
THEIR MINDS FESTER TOGETHER...
...THEIR EARS BURN WITH VOICES AND WHISPERS FROM THE *WAYSIDE DARKNESS*.

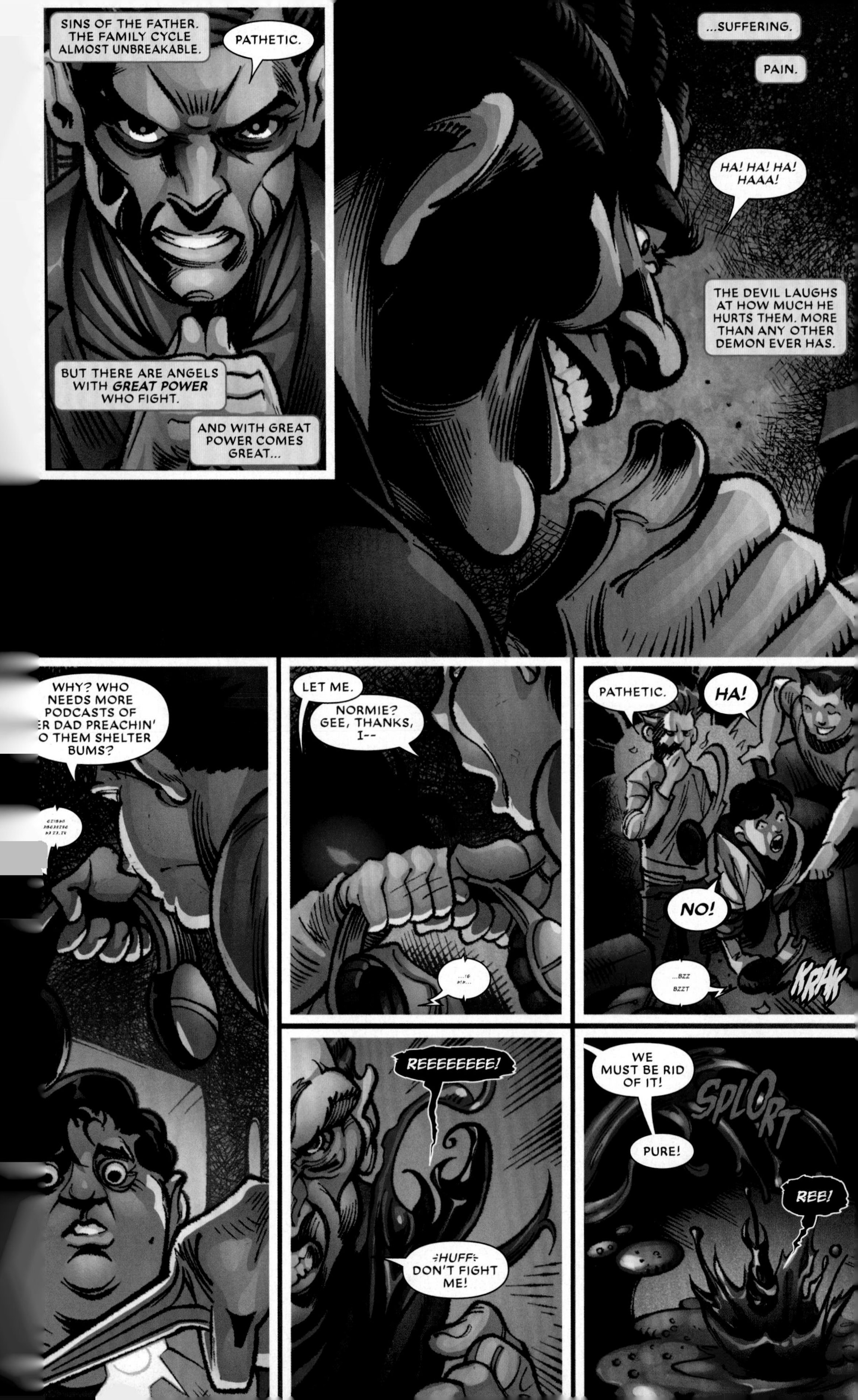
SINS OF THE FATHER. THE FAMILY CYCLE ALMOST UNBREAKABLE.
PATHETIC.
BUT THERE ARE ANGELS WITH GREAT POWER WHO FIGHT.
AND WITH GREAT POWER COMES GREAT...
...SUFFERING.
PAIN.
HA! HA! HA! HAAA!
THE DEVIL LAUGHS AT HOW MUCH HE HURTS THEM. MORE THAN ANY OTHER DEMON EVER HAS.
WHY? WHO NEEDS MORE PODCASTS OF
ER DAD PREACHIN'
O THEM SHELTER BUMS?
LET ME.
NORMIE? GEE, THANKS, I--
PATHETIC.
HA!
NO!
...BZZ
BZZT
KRAK
REEEEEEEE!
HUFF DON'T FIGHT ME!
WE MUST BE RID OF IT!
SPLORT
PURE!
REE!

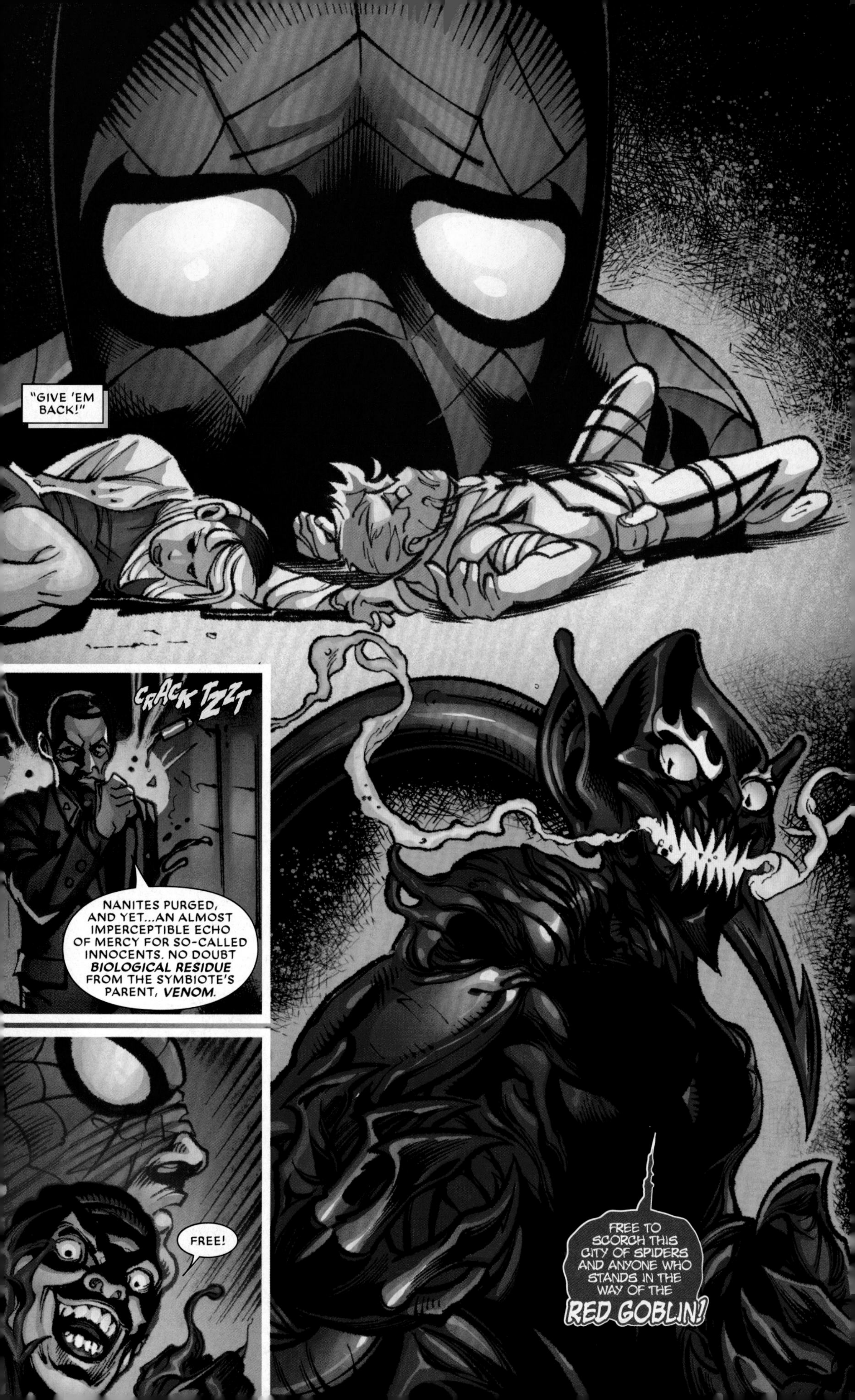
"GIVE 'EM BACK!"
CRACK TZZT
NANITES PURGED, AND YET...AN ALMOST IMPERCEPTIBLE ECHO OF MERCY FOR SO-CALLED INNOCENTS. NO DOUBT *BIOLOGICAL RESIDUE* FROM THE SYMBIOTE'S PARENT, *VENOM*.
FREE!
FREE TO SCORCH THIS CITY OF SPIDERS AND ANYONE WHO STANDS IN THE WAY OF THE RED GOBLIN!

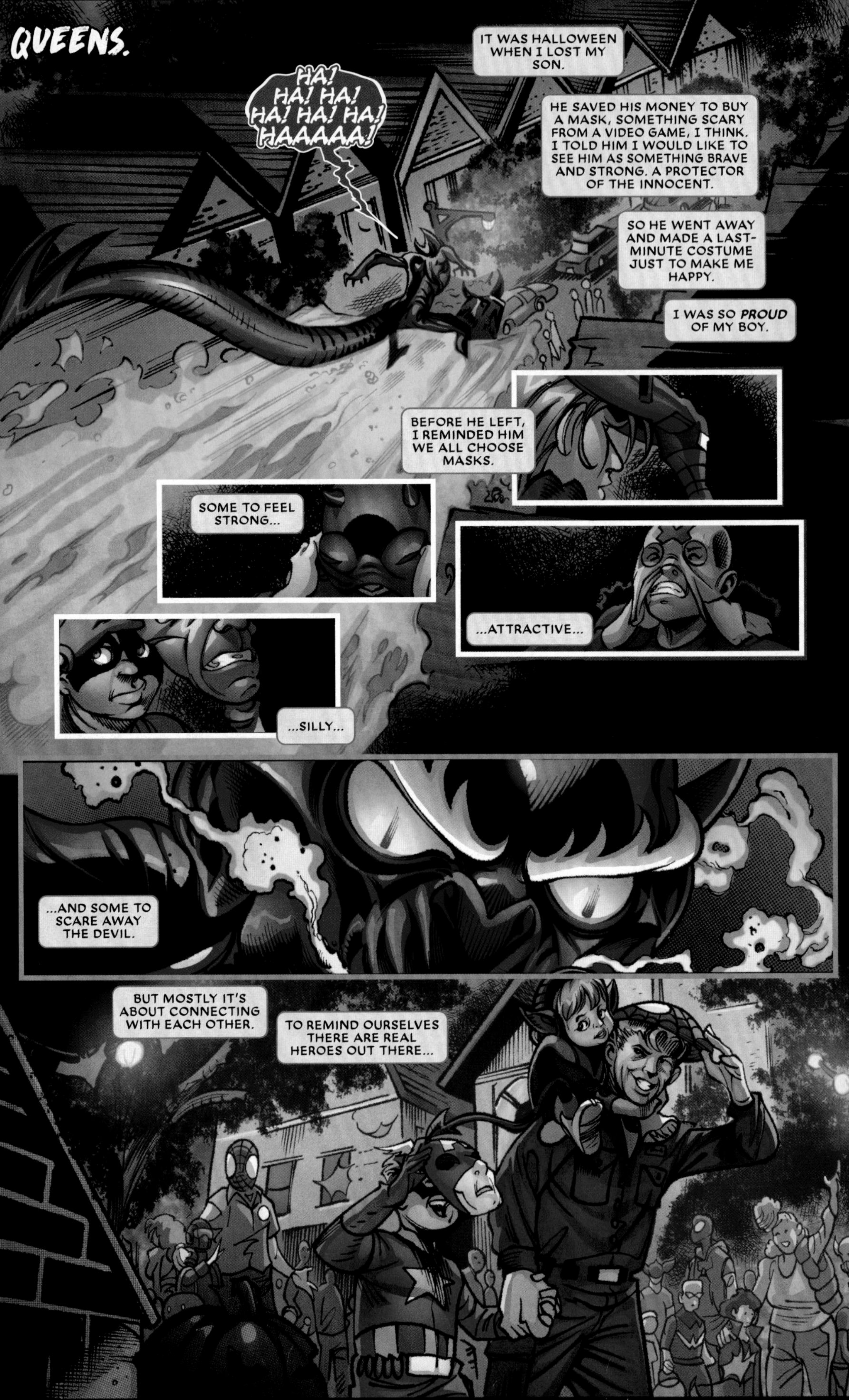
QUEENS.
IT WAS HALLOWEEN WHEN I LOST MY SON.
HA! HA! HA! HA! HA! HA! HAAAAA!
HE SAVED HIS MONEY TO BUY A MASK, SOMETHING SCARY FROM A VIDEO GAME, I THINK. I TOLD HIM I WOULD LIKE TO SEE HIM AS SOMETHING BRAVE AND STRONG. A PROTECTOR OF THE INNOCENT.
SO HE WENT AWAY AND MADE A LAST-MINUTE COSTUME JUST TO MAKE ME HAPPY.
I WAS SO *PROUD* OF MY BOY.
BEFORE HE LEFT, I REMINDED HIM WE ALL CHOOSE MASKS.
SOME TO FEEL STRONG...
...ATTRACTIVE...
...SILLY...
...AND SOME TO SCARE AWAY THE DEVIL.
BUT MOSTLY IT'S ABOUT CONNECTING WITH EACH OTHER.
TO REMIND OURSELVES THERE ARE REAL HEROES OUT THERE...

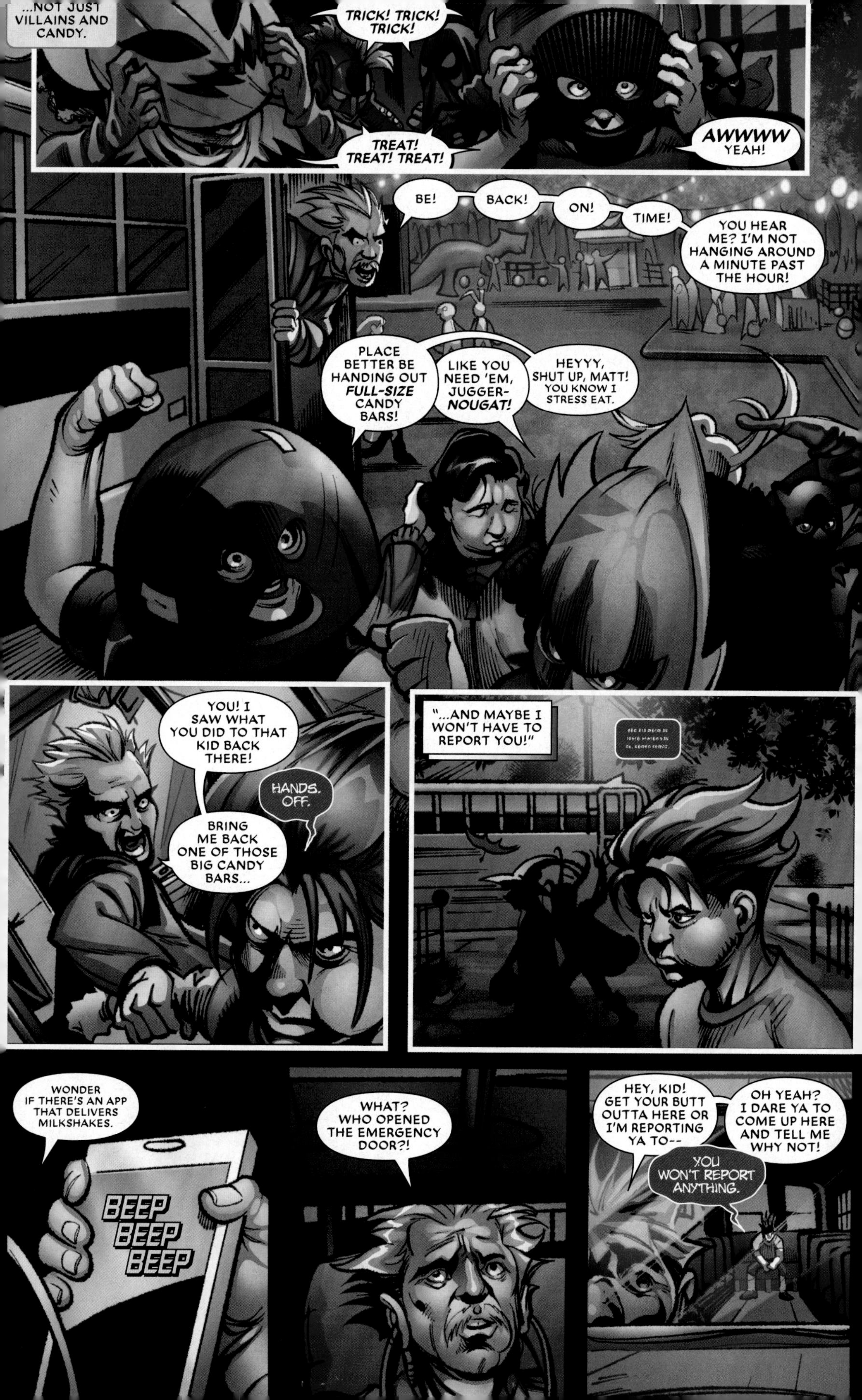
...NOT JUST VILLAINS AND CANDY.
TRICK! TRICK! TRICK!
TREAT! TREAT! TREAT!
AWWWW YEAH!
BE!
BACK!
ON!
TIME!
YOU HEAR ME? I'M NOT HANGING AROUND A MINUTE PAST THE HOUR!
PLACE BETTER BE HANDING OUT FULL-SIZE CANDY BARS!
LIKE YOU NEED 'EM, JUGGER-NOUGAT!
HEYYY, SHUT UP, MATT! YOU KNOW I STRESS EAT.
YOU! I SAW WHAT YOU DID TO THAT KID BACK THERE!
BRING ME BACK ONE OF THOSE BIG CANDY BARS...
HANDS. OFF.
"...AND MAYBE I WON'T HAVE TO REPORT YOU!"
WONDER IF THERE'S AN APP THAT DELIVERS MILKSHAKES.
BEEP BEEP BEEP
WHAT? WHO OPENED THE EMERGENCY DOOR?!
HEY, KID! GET YOUR BUTT OUTTA HERE OR I'M REPORTING YA TO--
OH YEAH? I DARE YA TO COME UP HERE AND TELL ME WHY NOT!
YOU WON'T REPORT ANYTHING.

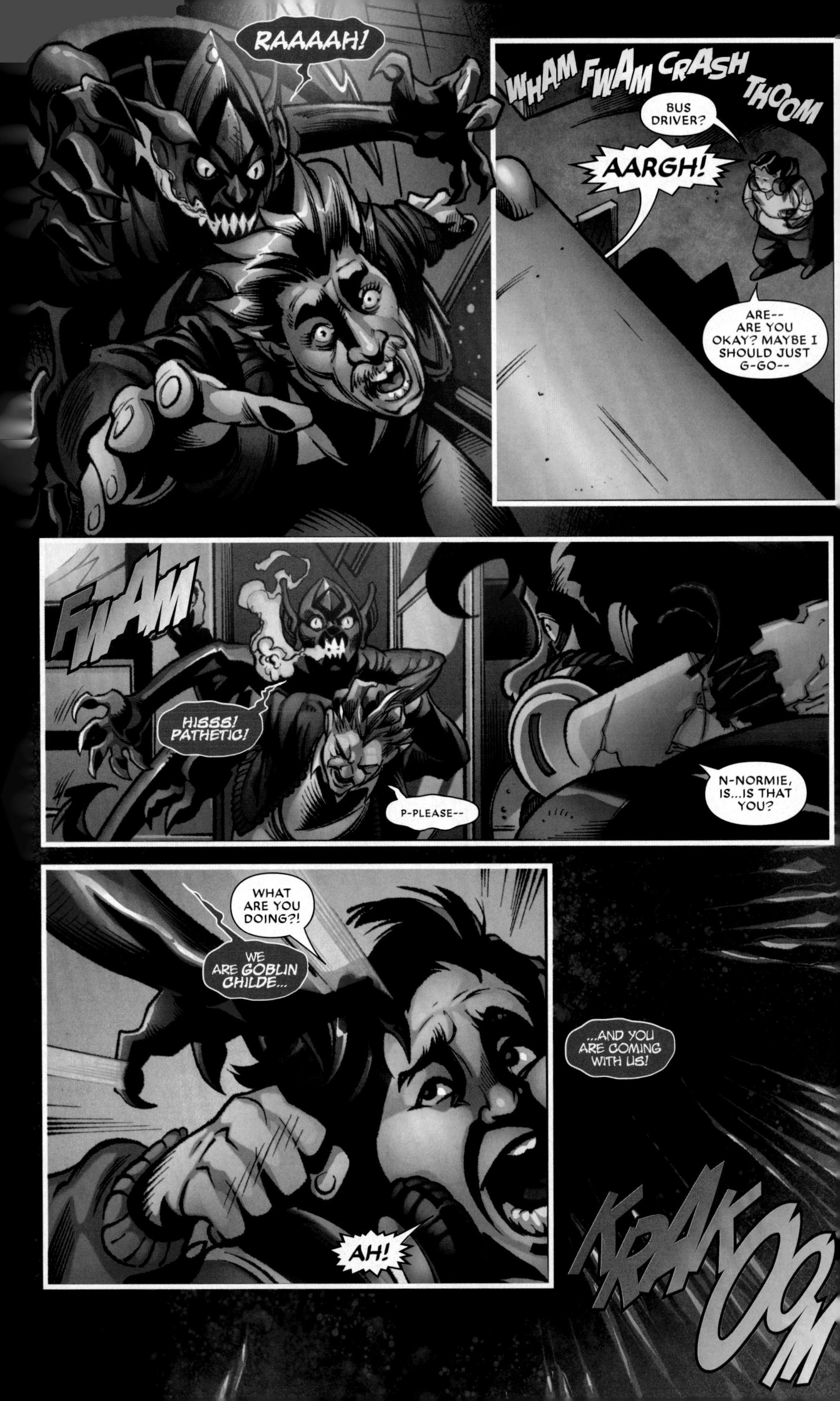
RAAAAH!
WHAM FWAM CRASH THOOM
BUS DRIVER?
AARGH!
ARE-- ARE YOU OKAY? MAYBE I SHOULD JUST G-GO--
FWAM
HISSS! PATHETIC!
P-PLEASE--
N-NORMIE, IS...IS THAT YOU?
WHAT ARE YOU DOING?!
WE ARE GOBLIN CHILDE...
...AND YOU ARE COMING WITH US!
AH!
KRAKOOM

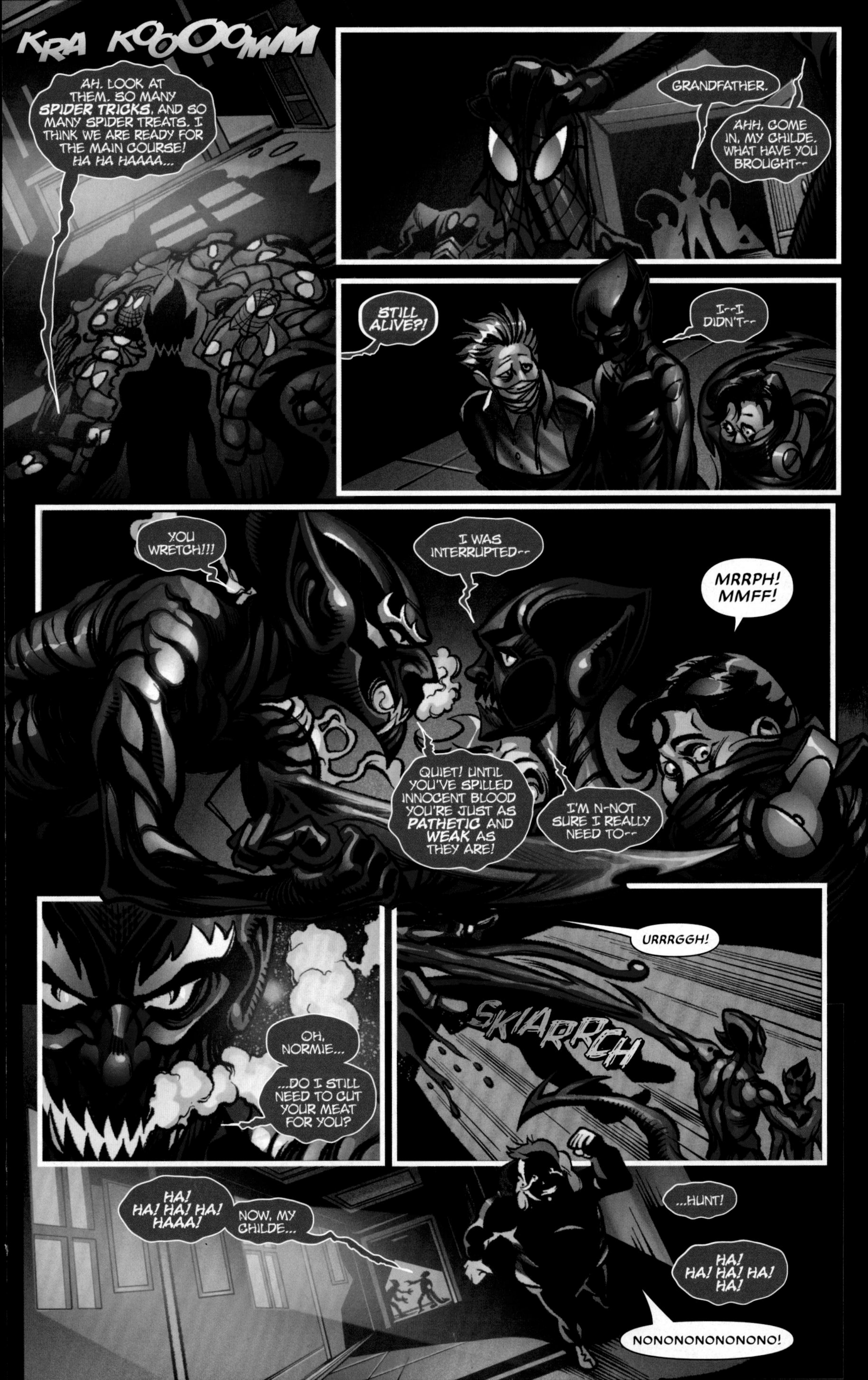
KRA KOOOOOMM
AH. LOOK AT THEM. SO MANY SPIDER TRICKS, AND SO MANY SPIDER TREATS. I THINK WE ARE READY FOR THE MAIN COURSE! HA HA HAAAA...
GRANDFATHER.
AHH, COME IN, MY CHILDE. WHAT HAVE YOU BROUGHT--
STILL ALIVE?!
I--I DIDN'T--
YOU WRETCH!!!
I WAS INTERRUPTED--
MRRPH! MMFF!
QUIET! UNTIL YOU'VE SPILLED INNOCENT BLOOD YOU'RE JUST AS PATHETIC AND WEAK AS THEY ARE!
I'M N-NOT SURE I REALLY NEED TO--
OH, NORMIE...
...DO I STILL NEED TO CUT YOUR MEAT FOR YOU?
URRRGGH!
SKIARRCH
HA! HA! HA! HA! HAAA!
NOW, MY CHILDE...
...HUNT!
HA! HA! HA! HA! HA!
NONONONONONONO!

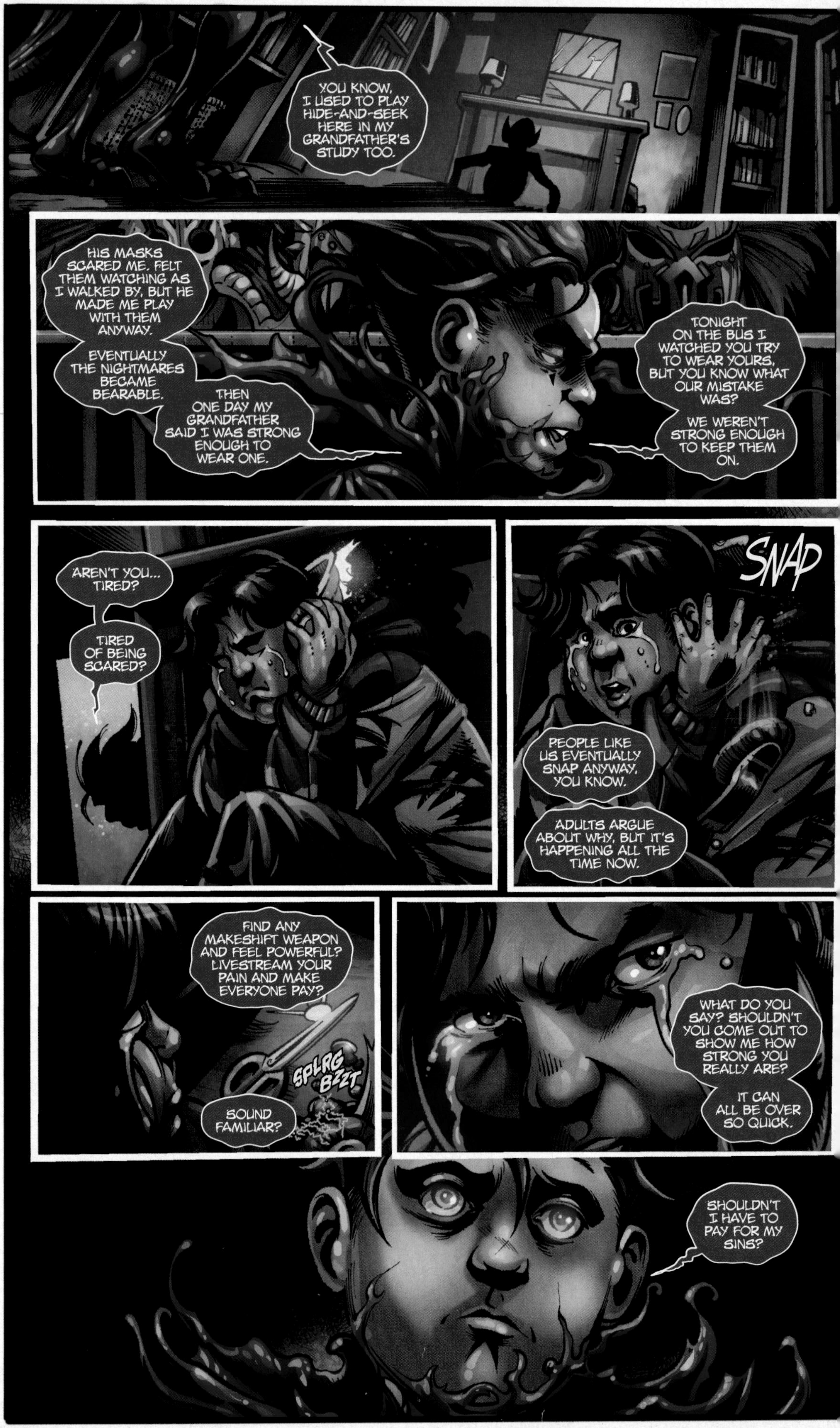
YOU KNOW, I USED TO PLAY HIDE-AND-SEEK HERE IN MY GRANDFATHER'S STUDY TOO.
HIS MASKS SCARED ME. FELT THEM WATCHING AS I WALKED BY, BUT HE MADE ME PLAY WITH THEM ANYWAY.
EVENTUALLY THE NIGHTMARES BECAME BEARABLE.
THEN ONE DAY MY GRANDFATHER SAID I WAS STRONG ENOUGH TO WEAR ONE.
TONIGHT ON THE BUS I WATCHED YOU TRY TO WEAR YOURS, BUT YOU KNOW WHAT OUR MISTAKE WAS?
WE WEREN'T STRONG ENOUGH TO KEEP THEM ON.
AREN'T YOU... TIRED?
TIRED OF BEING SCARED?
SNAP
PEOPLE LIKE US EVENTUALLY SNAP ANYWAY, YOU KNOW.
ADULTS ARGUE ABOUT WHY, BUT IT'S HAPPENING ALL THE TIME NOW.
FIND ANY MAKESHIFT WEAPON AND FEEL POWERFUL? LIVESTREAM YOUR PAIN AND MAKE EVERYONE PAY?
SPLRG BZZT
SOUND FAMILIAR?
WHAT DO YOU SAY? SHOULDN'T YOU COME OUT TO SHOW ME HOW STRONG YOU REALLY ARE?
IT CAN ALL BE OVER SO QUICK.
SHOULDN'T I HAVE TO PAY FOR MY SINS?

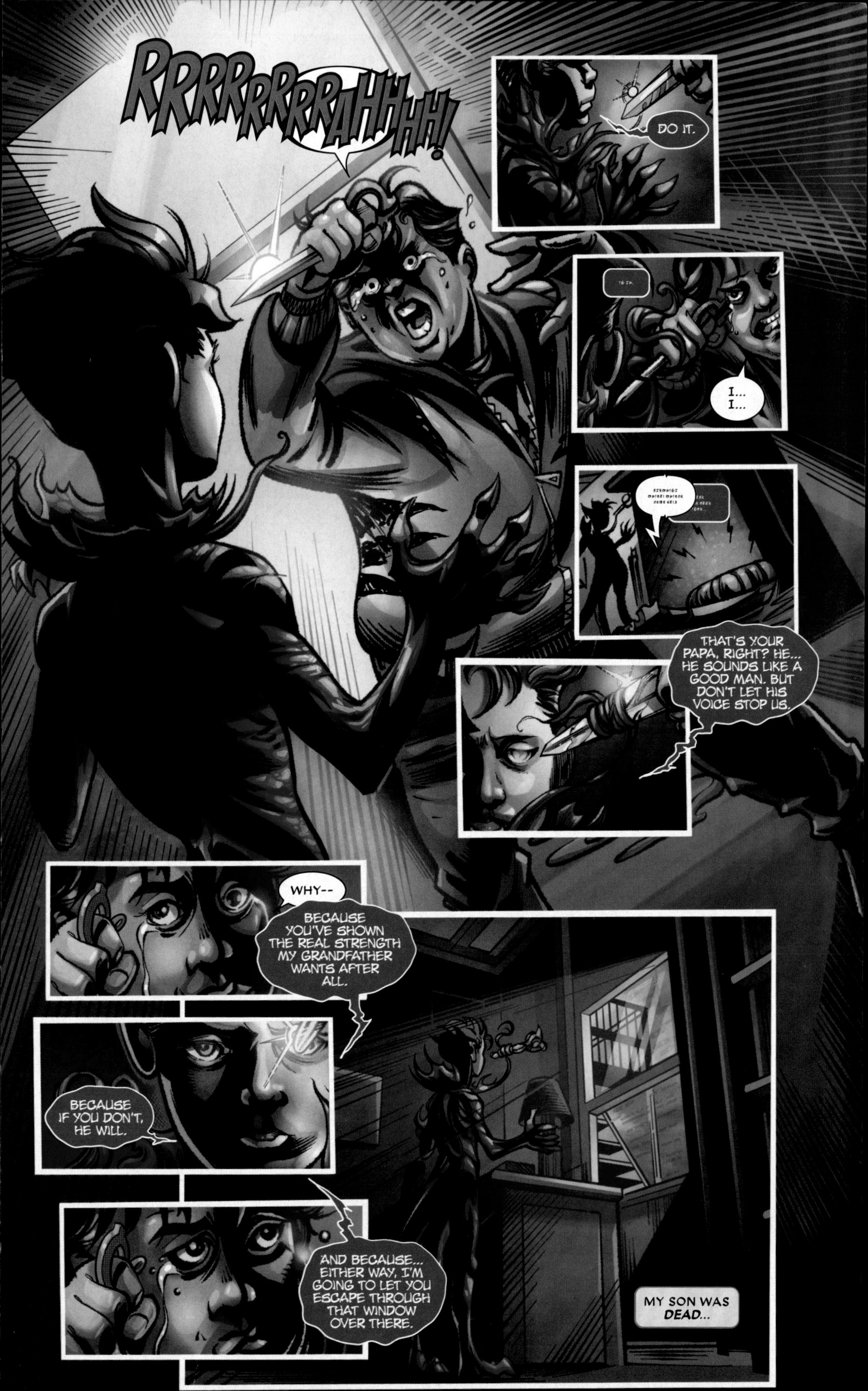
RRRRRRRRAHHHHH!
DO IT.
I... I...
THAT'S YOUR PAPA, RIGHT? HE... HE SOUNDS LIKE A GOOD MAN. BUT DON'T LET HIS VOICE STOP US.
WHY--
BECAUSE YOU'VE SHOWN THE REAL STRENGTH MY GRANDFATHER WANTS AFTER ALL.
BECAUSE IF YOU DON'T, HE WILL.
AND BECAUSE... EITHER WAY, I'M GOING TO LET YOU ESCAPE THROUGH THAT WINDOW OVER THERE.
MY SON WAS *DEAD*...

EDUARDO... MI HIJO...

...BUT NOW HE IS ALIVE.

HE WAS LOST...

...BUT NOW IS FOUND.

EDUARDO, MI HIJO... YA ESTAS EN CASA.

DIDN'T YOU SAY SOME BULLIES BROKE YOUR HEADPHONES?

THEY FELL IN SOME SORT OF SMART GOO AND SOMEHOW FUSED BACK TOGETHER OR SOMETHING. I DON'T KNOW.

YOU STILL CAN'T REMEMBER ANYTHING ABOUT WHAT HAPPENED?

UM...NOT MUCH ELSE RIGHT NOW. MAYBE IN THE MORNING AFTER WE GET SOME HALF-PRICED CANDY FROM THE MARKET?

HA HA, ALLLLLL RIGHT. DON'T FORGET YOUR PRAYERS.

OKAY.

GOOD NIGHT, MI HIJO.

GOOD NIGHT, PAPA.

I'LL LEAVE THE DOOR OPEN A CRACK SO YOU DON'T GET SCARED.

PAPA? YOU DON'T HAVE TO DO THAT ANYMORE.

OH?

CLICK

WE'RE NOT GOING TO BE SCARED OF ANYTHING FROM NOW ON.

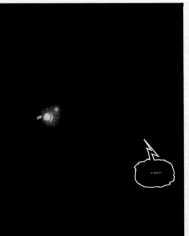

THE END???

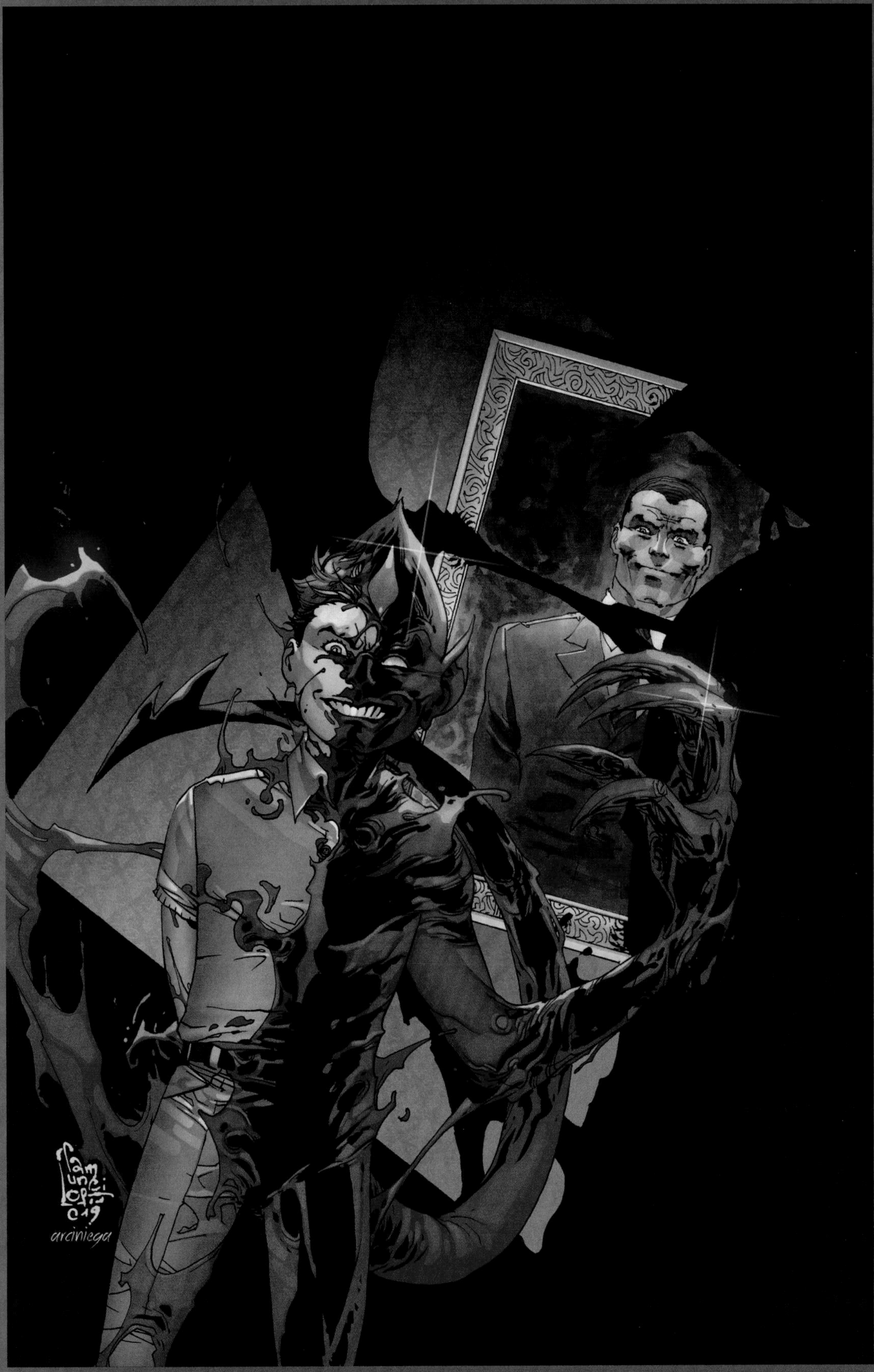
arciniega

#30 CODEX VARIANT BY GIUSEPPE CAMUNCOLI & ERICK ARCINIEGA

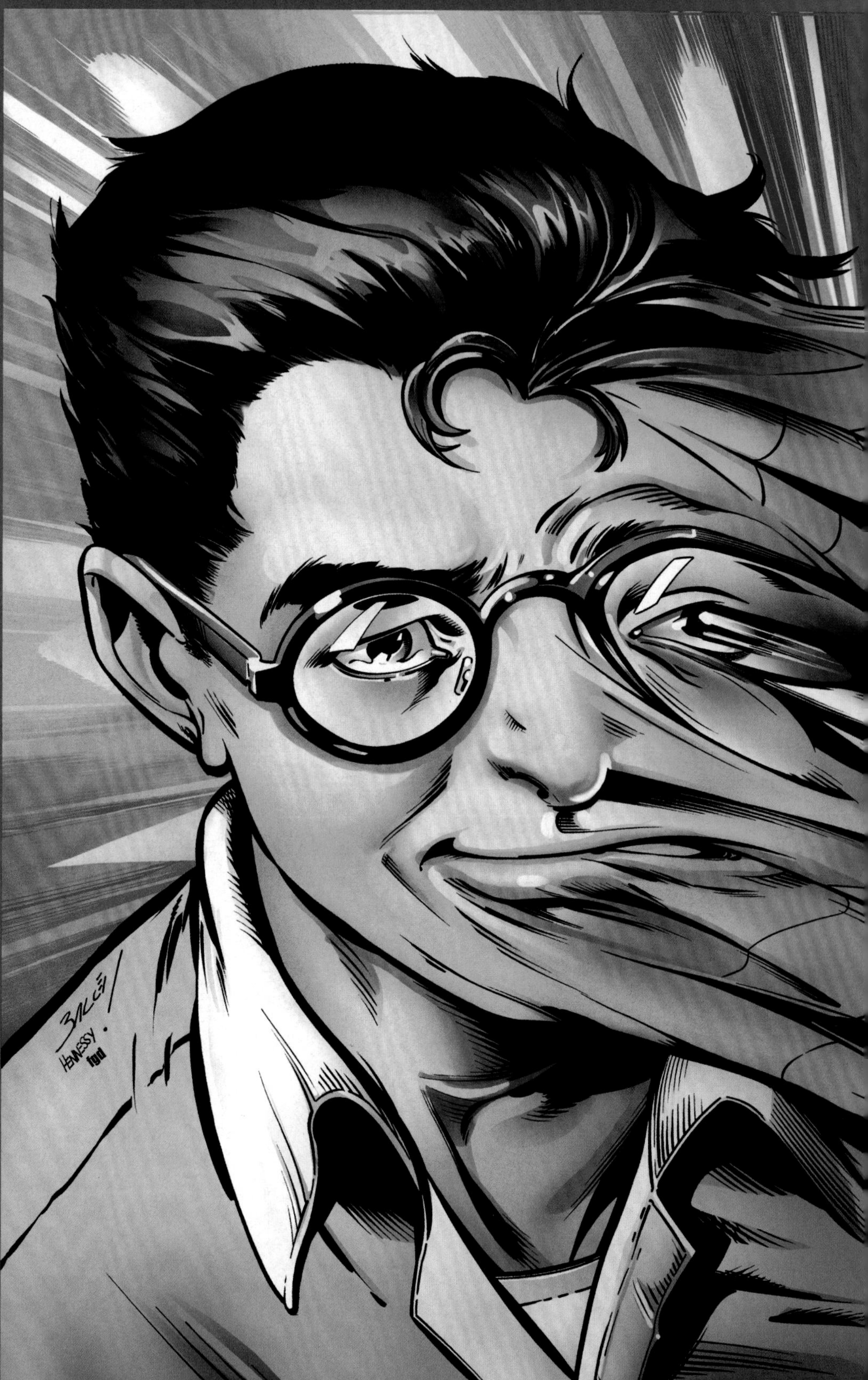

#29 IMMORTAL WRAPAROUND VARIANT BY MARK BAGLEY, ANDREW HENNESSY & FRANK D'ARMATA

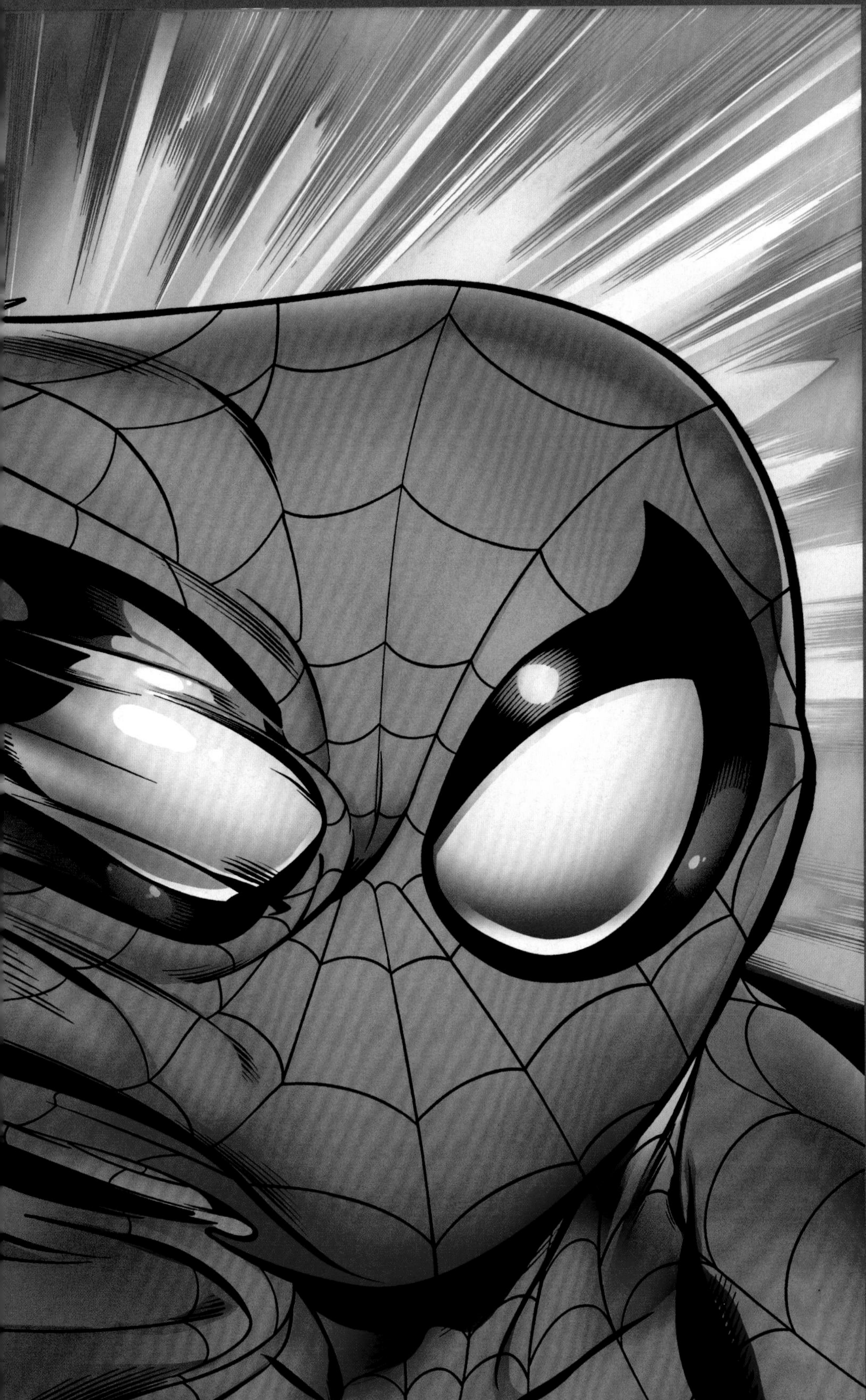

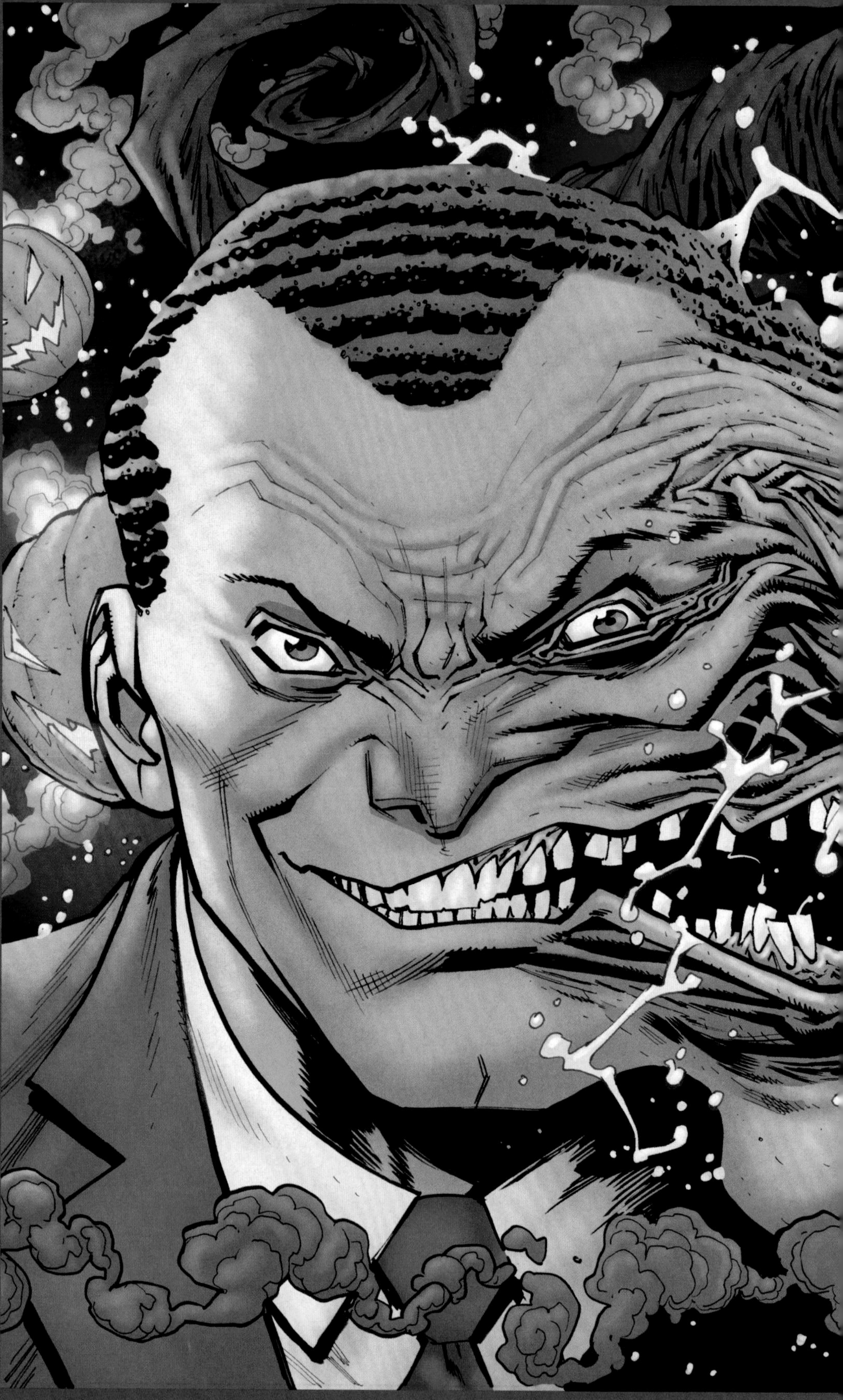

#30 IMMORTAL WRAPAROUND VARIANT BY RYAN OTTLEY & NATHAN FAIRBAIRN

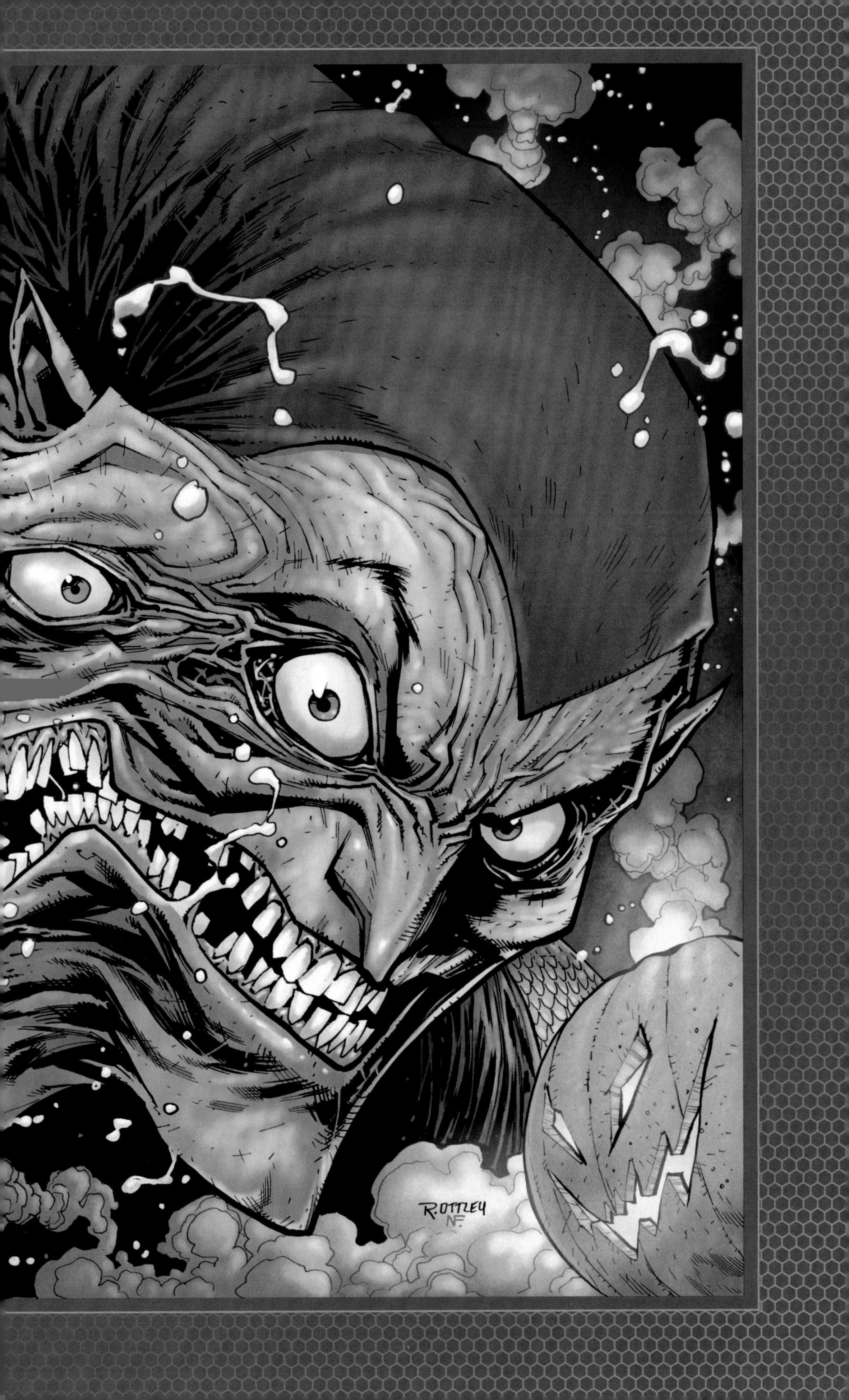
R.OTTLEY
NF.

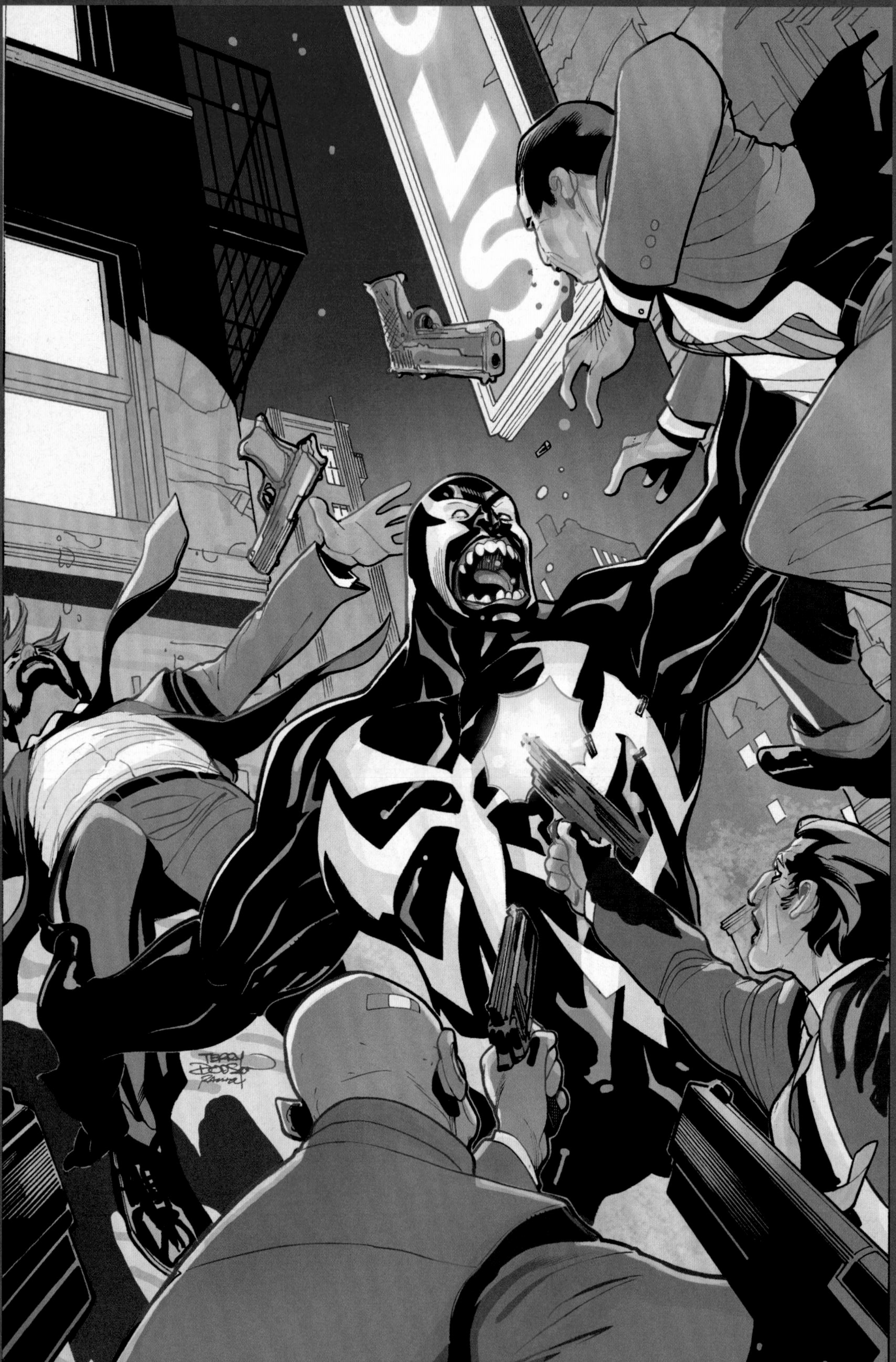

#31 CODEX VARIANT BY TERRY DODSON & RACHEL DODSON

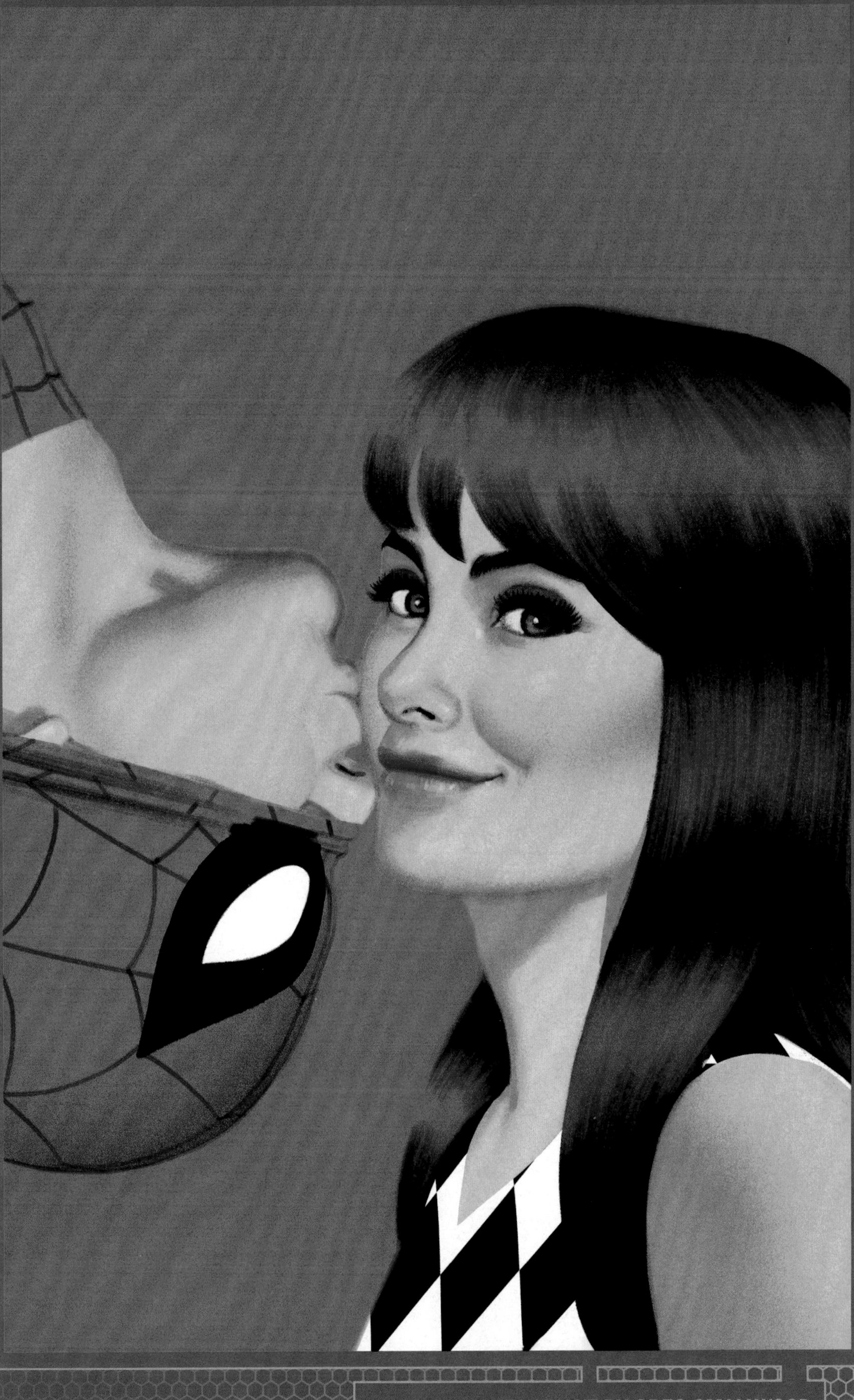

#31 MARY JANE VARIANT BY GREG SMALLWOOD

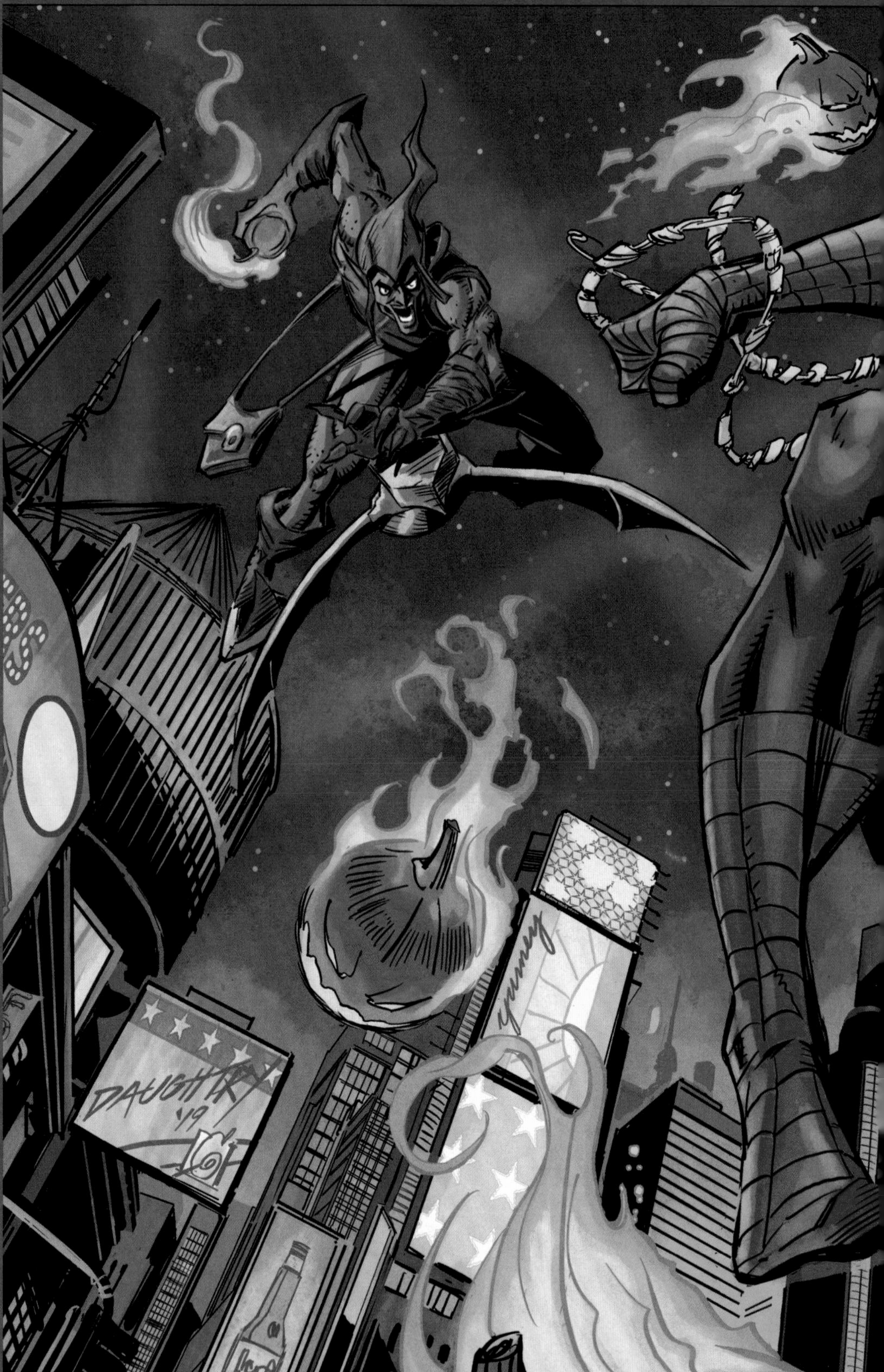
DAUGHTRY
'19
GARNEY

RED GOBLIN: RED DEATH #1 VARIANT BY CHRIS DAUGHTRY, RON GARNEY & DAVE STEWART

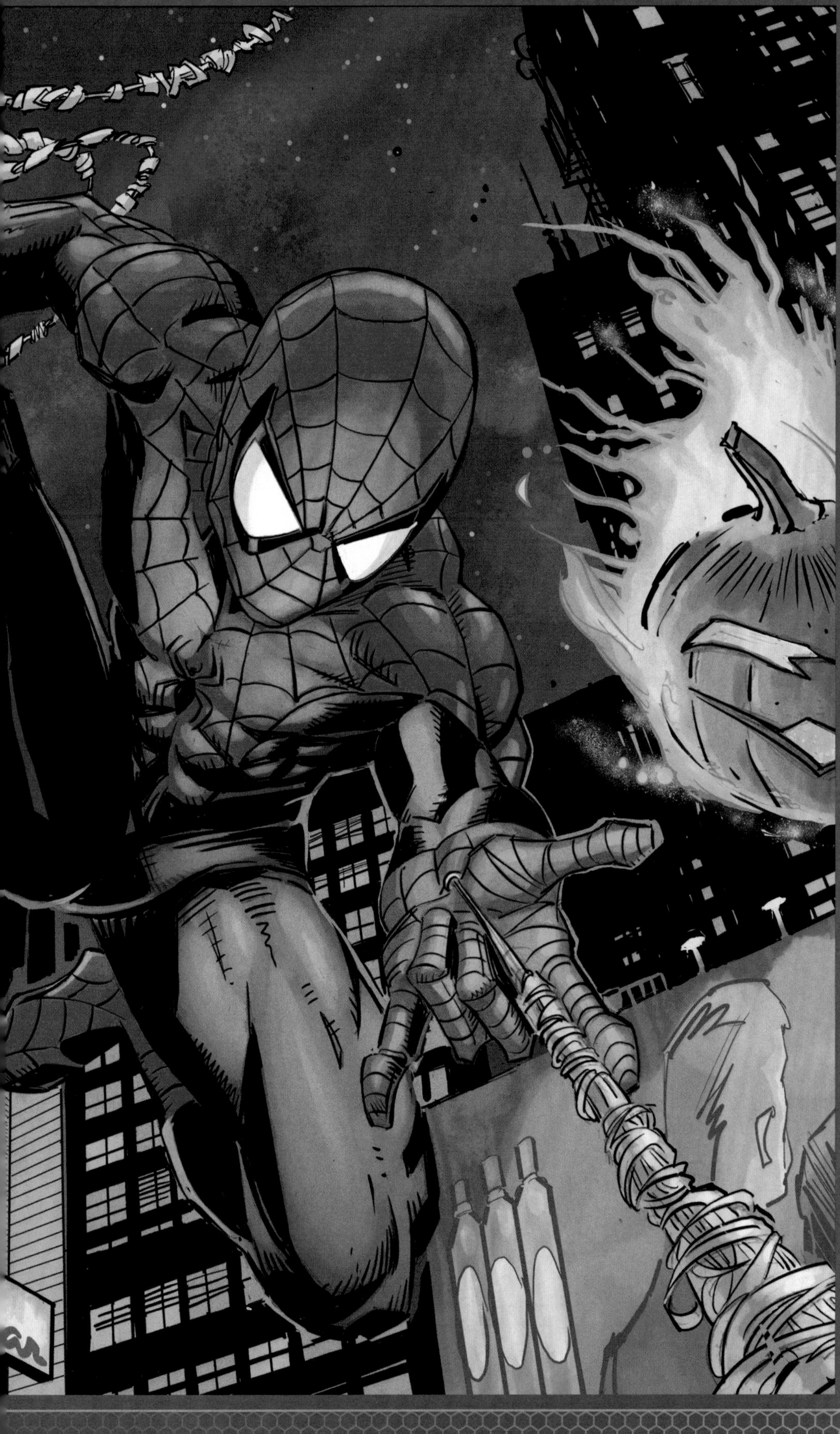

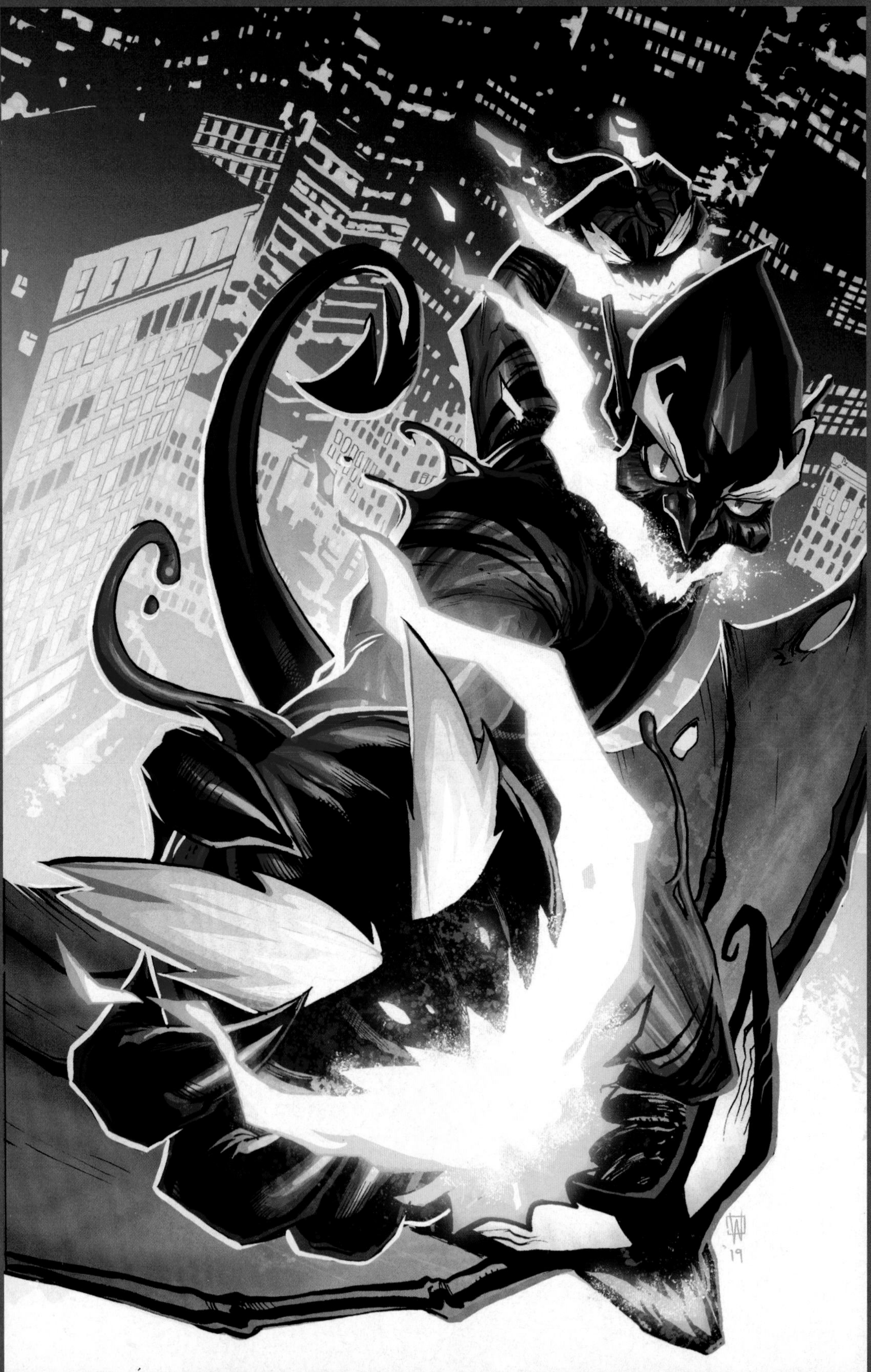

RED GOBLIN: RED DEATH #1 VARIANT BY PETE WOODS

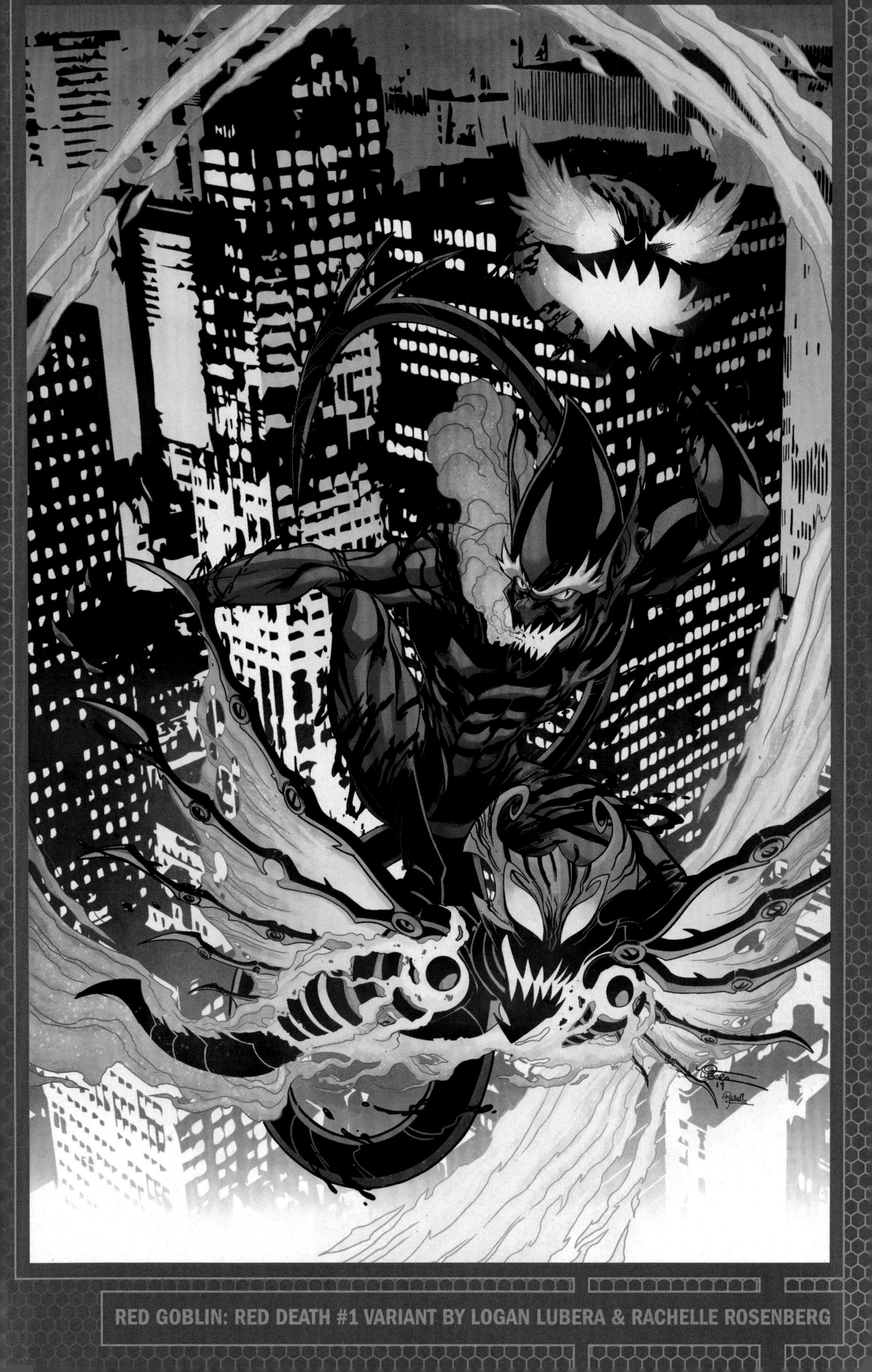

RED GOBLIN: RED DEATH #1 VARIANT BY LOGAN LUBERA & RACHELLE ROSENBERG

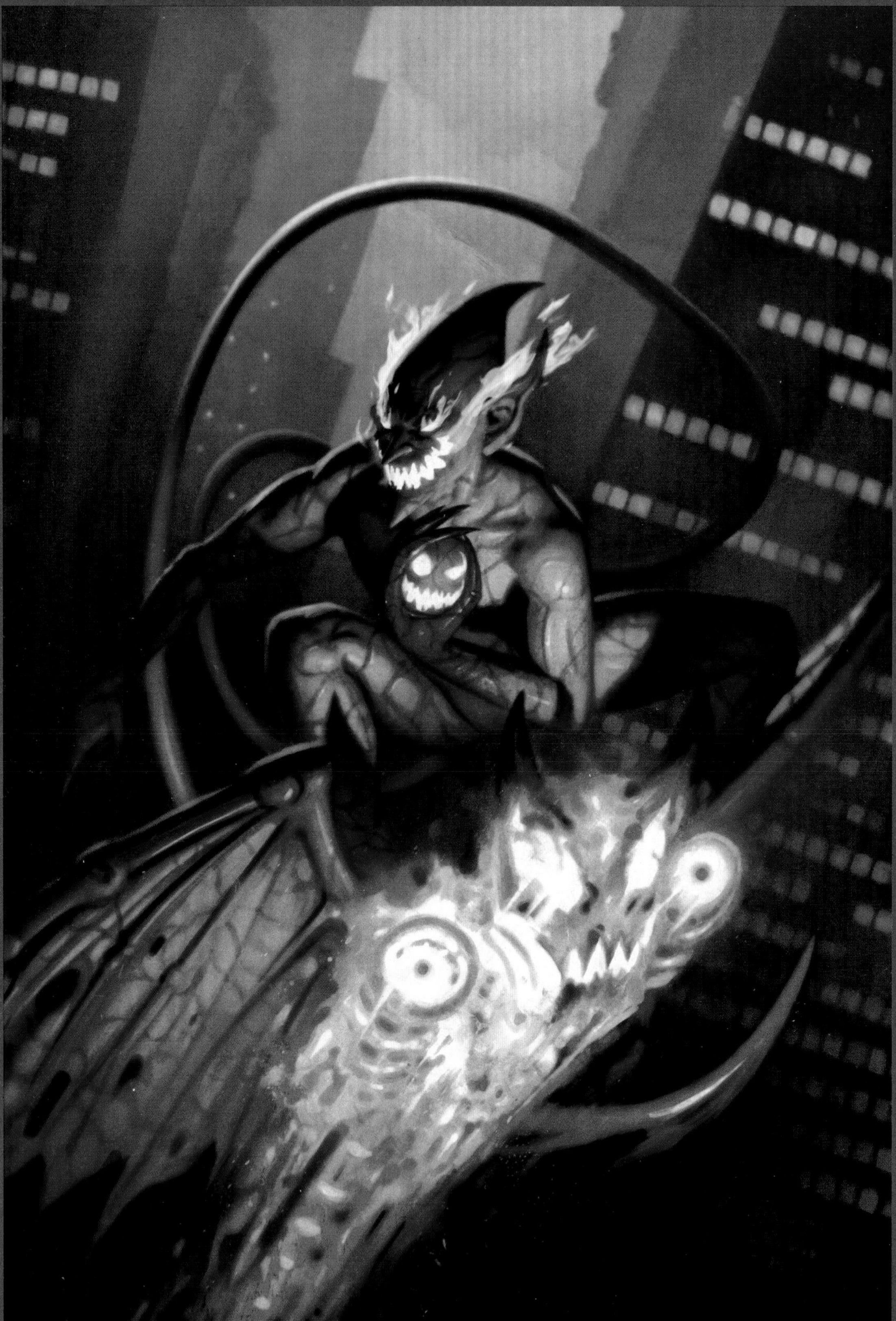

RED GOBLIN: RED DEATH #1 VARIANT BY RYAN BROWN